READING HISTORY

General Editor: Michael Biddiss
Professor of History, University of Reading

D0169687

THE INDUSTRIAL REVOLUTION

PAT HUDSON
Professor of Economic and Social History
University of Liverpool

A member of the Hodder Headline Group
LONDON • NEW YORK • SYDNEY • AUCKLAND

First published in Great Britain in 1992 by Edward Arnold
Sixth impression 1996 by Arnold,
a member of the Hodder Headline Group
338 Euston Road, London NW1 3BH
175 Fifth Avenue, New York, NY 10010

Distributed exclusively in the USA by
St Martin's Press Inc.
175 Fifth Avenue,
New York, NY 10010, USA

British Library Cataloguing in Publication Data
Hudson, Pat
The Industrial Revolution. – (Reading history)
I. Title   II. Series
330.941

Library of Congress Cataloging-in-Publication Data
A catalog record for this book is available from the Library of Congress

ISBN 0 7131 6531 6

Typeset in Times Roman by Saxon Printing Ltd, Derby
Printed and bound in Great Britain by J W Arrowsmith Ltd, Bristol

CONTENTS

Figures

Tables

GENERAL EDITOR'S PREFACE

The aim of this series is to provide for students, especially at undergraduate level, a number of volumes devoted to major historical issues. Each of the selected topics is of such importance and complexity as to have produced the kind of scholarly controversy which not only sharpens our understanding of the particular problem in hand but also illuminates more generally the nature of history as a developing discipline. The authors have certainly been asked to examine the present state of knowledge and debate in their chosen fields, and to outline and justify their own current interpretations. But they have also been set two other important objectives. One has been that of quite explicitly alerting readers to the nature, range, and variety of the primary sources most germane to their topics, and to the kind of difficulties (about, say, the completeness, authenticity, or reliability of such materials) which the scholar then faces in using them as evidence. The second task has been to indicate how and why, even before our own time, the course of the particular scholarly controversy at issue actually developed in the way that it did – through, for example, enlargements in the scale of the available primary sources, or changes in historical philosophy or technique, or alterations in the social and political environment within which the debaters have been structuring their questions and devising their answers. Each author in the series has been left to determine the specific framework by means of which such aims might best be fulfilled within any single volume. However, all of us involved in 'Reading History' are united in our hope that the resulting books will be widely welcomed as up-to-date accounts worthy of recommendation to students who need not only reliable introductory guides to the subjects chosen but also texts that will help to enhance their more general appreciation of the contribution which historical scholarship and debate can make towards the strengthening of a critical and sceptical habit of mind.

MICHAEL BIDDISS

Professor of History
University of Reading

PREFACE AND ACKNOWLEDGEMENTS

The social and economic history of Britain in the late eighteenth and early nineteenth centuries has had considerable attention from historians and continues to be a focus of research. Rather than attempting to discuss the full range of relevant historiography this book considers recent literature covering key aspects of the period against the backcloth of earlier interpretations. It thus aims to fulfil the purpose of the Reading History series which calls for an examination of the ways in which research interests and the use of sources have changed over time to reveal different perspectives and interpretations.

After an introduction which discusses the specification and measurement of 'industrial revolution', Part One is devoted to shifts in interpretation which have occurred in the last century and a half followed by a discussion of recent work on macroeconomic indicators, the role of the state, and the place of agriculture in industrialisation. Part Two concentrates upon topics of central importance to our understanding of the period as one of radical socio-economic and political change which justifies the notion of industrial revolution.

The subject of the book is the industrial revolution in Britain, but discussion is frequently narrowed to England because of the availability of comparable data and research for the rest of Britain. There is, for example, no counterpart for Wales, Scotland or Northern Ireland to Wrigley and Schofield's work on the population history of England, and most of the macroeconomic series are available only for England. It is necessary to mention a further point about the Anglo-centric nature of this study (and others). Space has not allowed a chapter on comparative industrialisation but to understand fully the nature of change in Britain and its component countries it is essential to read about how patterns of industrialisation differ, over time and space, socially, politically and economically.[1] Finally, although the

---

[1] T. Kemp, *Historical Patterns of Industrialisation* (London, 1978); Kemp, *Industrialisation in Nineteenth-Century Europe* (London, 1969); E. L. Jones, *The European Miracle: Environments, Economies and Geopolitics in the History of Europe and Asia* (Cambridge, 1981); S. Pollard, *Peaceful Conquest: the Industrialisation of Europe 1760–1970* (Oxford, 1981); B. Moore, *Social Origins of Dictatorship and Democracy* (London, 1967); I. Wallerstein, *The Modern World System* (New York, 1974) and *The Capitalist World Economy* (New York, 1979); P. K. O'Brien. 'Do We Have a Typology for the Study of European Industrialisation in the Nineteenth Century?' *Journal of European Economic History* 15 (1986).

book includes some discussion of the nature and impact of international trade, militarism and colonialism it cannot be overemphasised that British economic and social history of the period was a part of global development with British interests playing a reactive as well as a proactive role.

This book owes a great deal to the assistance and inspiration of many friends and colleagues over the years. Readers will be left in little doubt about those historians of the industrial revolution (past and present) whose writings I most admire. The classic works of Paul Mantoux, T. S. Ashton, Herbert Heaton, John Clapham, and A. P. Wadsworth and Julia Le Mann are, like others of their vintage, a renewable source of ideas and empirical evidence. Of more recent works, I have depended particularly on those of E. A. Wrigley, E. J. Hobsbawm, E. P. Thompson, Joel Mokyr, N. F. R. Crafts, Peter Mathias, François Crouzet, David Landes, Patrick O'Brien, Sidney Pollard and E. L. Jones. Individual chapters rely heavily on the current research of other historians to all of whom I owe a significant debt. They include John Brewer, R. C. Allen, Jan de Vries, David Levine, Jack Langton, F. F. Mendels, Adrian Randall, Patrick Joyce, Mark Overton, Maxine Berg, Julian Hoppit, and Jeffrey Williamson. I am particularly grateful to Maxine Berg for her friendship, support and specifically for those elements of our joint work included in chapters 2 and 5, which appeared in 'Rehabilitating the Industrial Revolution', *Economic History Review* xlv (1992). Mark Overton kindly read an early draft of chapter 3, Gerry Kearns and Steve King did the same with chapter 5, and Rory Miller, Mike Tadman and John Styles read drafts of chapter 6. Eric Taplin and Andy Davies provided helpful comments on chapter 7 whilst Mike Power valiantly read early drafts of no less than four of the chapters and kept me going through some difficult stages. Tony Lane provided me with time to write by taking the kids on exciting expeditions and by cooking meals. My year as a Simon Senior Research Fellow at the University of Manchester (1989–90) was also vital in freeing me from teaching and providing me with a new and helpful group of colleagues.

Finally, I must thank a long succession of my students at Liverpool who have endured my lectures on the eighteenth century and on the industrial revolution, showing me which issues most interested them, keeping my hyperboles in check, smiling at my enthusiasms and eccentricities, and giving me a great deal of guidance on the sort of text to write. I hope that the result will please them and be of use to their successors at Liverpool and elsewhere.

Pat Hudson
Liverpool, April 1991

INTRODUCTION

Current interpretations of the British industrial revolution are dominated by the view that 'less happened, less dramatically than was once thought'.[1] It may thus seem a strange time to be writing a text about a period which never before has appeared to stand out so little from the broad sweep of evolutionary change. But the current gradualist perspective does suggest a need to step back and examine the origins and foundations of the consensus view, and to reassess those elements of radical change and historical discontinuity recognised in the writings of earlier historians and contemporary commentators but increasingly ignored today.

Much of our opinion of the extent to which the period from the late eighteenth to the early nineteenth centuries was one of industrial revolution will depend on two things: how we specify 'industrial revolution' and how we attempt to measure it. The fact that definitions and measurements have varied over the last century largely accounts for radical shifts in interpretation. Our understanding of the timing of change has also been affected by whether analysis is focused upon technological change, economic growth, organisational innovation, the development of markets, demography, urban growth, class formation, or whatever. It is the ordering hand of the historian that creates continuities and discontinuities and establishes their timing.

Measurement

Where it is possible to quantify, such as with output growth, capital investment or the movement of wages, there is a tendency to regard the results of research as a more reliable yardstick of change than where one is forced to rely on contemporary commentary and clues from non-numerical sources. But this attitude is seldom justified for a period in which the quantitative evidence is sparse, and always in need of adjustments to allow for errors and omissions in recording. The cure for excess in metaphor is not always counting as McCloskey was rash enough once to suggest.[2] Quantitative estimates for the period are valuable but have to be examined carefully with respect to their sources and the elements of 'guesstimation' which they include. It is always wise to consider quantitative estimates of output, productivity

[1] D. Cannadine, 'British History: Past, Present, and Future?' *Past and Present* 116 (1987), p.183.
[2] D. McCloskey, 'The Industrial Revolution 1780–1860: A Survey', in R. C. Floud and D. McCloskey, eds., *The Economic History of Britain since 1700* (Cambridge, 1981) I, p.105.

growth, real wages and the like, alongside the qualitative evidence available. The current methodological fashion in economic history and in much social history demands more statistics, more rigour and more proof, less speculation or even imagination. But our understanding of the industrial revolution would indeed be impoverished if historians were not willing to be detectives as well as scientists.

Problems involved in the selection and evaluation of evidence concerning the industrial revolution open the door to considerable variation in interpretation even where historians share the same conceptualisation of their topic. This is as true of current macroeconomic interpretations and measures as of past debates about the progress of technology or the standard of living where both descriptive and quantitative assessments have been employed. Problems concerning measurement, the use of sources and the evaluation of evidence crop up in all the chapters of this book.

Specifying the industrial revolution

Should historians confine their analysis to changes in industry, should they include the economy more generally or should they consider the wider notion of a changing mode of production which embodies social, political and cultural transformation?

Most recent writing which has played down the extent of revolutionary change in the late eighteenth and early nineteenth centuries has implied that 'industrial revolution' must involve, and be reflected in, a simultaneous radical discontinuity in macroeconomic indicators such as national income, industrial output, capital formation, GDP per head and productivity. But an economy experiencing widespread and rapid innovation across many sectors may not show a significant shift in output growth or productivity. Fundamental restructuring of an economy may indeed be inimical to the achievement of rapid economic growth in the short term, particularly in a pioneering industrial nation which had no example to follow. Thus, recent estimates of macroeconomic variables may have highlighted the rashness of Hobsbawm's claim made in 1962 that 'it was then [the 1780s]... that all the relevant statistical indices took that sudden sharp, almost vertical turn upwards which marks the take-off',[3] but they have not proved the absence of fundamental change in the economy and in society.

Perhaps it is more important, in defining the industrial revolution, to stress the sustained nature of the economic growth which the period initiated rather than its speed. Of course economic change and productivity growth were not new in the late eighteenth century. But unlike earlier periods, such as the innovative century after 1540, growth was thereafter sustained and periods of unprecedented acceleration were made possible. In Hartwell's words of 1967:

[3] E. J. Hobsbawm, *The Age of Revolution 1789-1848* (London, 1962), p.28.

On any historical accounting the industrial revolution of England began one of the great discontinuities of history marking 'the great divide' between a world of slow economic growth, in which population and real incomes were increasing slowly or not at all, and a world of much faster economic growth, in which population has increased at an almost frightening rate and in which there have been sustained increases in real income per head.[4]

For the first time with the industrial revolution substantial growth in income per head occurred despite a sharp increase in population. Since then it has become normal for per capita real income to double every half century. Thus the economic changes of the period may be seen as revolutionary irrespective of their reflection in macroeconomic indicators because no previous society had been able to escape the barriers which preindustrial technology and culture placed on production.

Innovation is central to most concepts of industrial revolution. This is often associated with the advent of capital intensive plant and equipment, steam power and factories. It is this sort of innovation which has most potential impact upon macroeconomic indicators and productivity estimates. Although unprecedented in its nature and in its possibilities for the future, innovation of this kind has been shown to have been patchy and restricted to certain processes in a limited number of sectors and regions of Britain before 1850. However, new products, changes in the quality of outputs and inputs, changes in the organisation of production, in marketing, in finance, in the commercial infrastructure, in consumer manipulation, and in handicraft skills are increasingly seen as central to a fuller understanding of change in the period. These innovations take one beyond the narrow confines of manufacturing industry and include changes in the economy across the board from agriculture to finance and international trade. The functioning of the industrial sector is impossible to evaluate in isolation from innovation in other sectors of the economy. These innovations may not have had immediate or large-scale impact on productivity but their implications for work, for leisure and consumption, for workers, the family economy, gender relations, and entrepreneurship were substantial.

Changing attitudes and practices with respect to the market and to competition are also involved in many conceptualisations of the industrial revolution. The continued expansion of industry and trade outside guild and corporate controls, the repeal of restrictive economic legislation, cycles of innovative activity and of cost cutting impelled by competition, and the new primacy and moral legitimacy given to market forces feature prominently in various accounts of the period.

[4] R. M. Hartwell, 'Introduction' in Hartwell, ed., *The Causes of the Industrial Revolution in England* (London, 1967), p.1.

The industrial revolution saw the growing efficiency of factor and commodity markets and, more importantly, a gradual acceptance by the bulk of the population that markets and competition were immutable facts of life.[5]

Behind the sustained nature of growth lay another aspect of change which must be included in any evaluation of the industrial revolution: a radical shift in the structure of the economy – in the composition of total output, in raw material and energy inputs and in the distribution of employment. Many historians believe it is this which gives concrete meaning to the idea of an industrial revolution.[6] The shift from agrarian and rural-based occupations to predominantly urban-based industrial and service employments accelerated markedly. It was achieved by a combination of agrarian change, population growth and urbanisation which involved a radical transformation in the way of life of a large proportion of the population both rural and urban. This transformation, marked by social and political unrest (rioting, local insurrections, machine wrecking, anti-Poor Law and factory reform campaigns, and Chartism), makes the decades of the industrial revolution really stand out.

Flinn argued some years ago that

> in the enthusiasm for quantification, the non-measurable factors get pushed into the background or are forgotten completely...The last two decades of the eighteenth century may, in a purely statistical sense, be merely an extrapolation of a curve... but...the...developments...were accompanied by such a plethora of...revolutionary changes concerned with methods of production, social institutions, and the growth of towns that, in the broadest historical perspective, the relatively slight upward shifts in output and trade (earlier)...were dwarfed by the overwhelming transformation of society initiated (in the last two decades of the eighteenth century)...[7]

In Mokyr's eloquence:

> More changed in Britain than just the way in which goods and services were produced. The nature of the family and household, the status of women and children, the role of the church, how

---

[5] K. Polanyi, *The Great Transformation* (New York, 1944); W. Reddy, *The Rise of Market Culture: The Textile Trade and French Society 1750–1900* (Cambridge, 1984).
[6] See for example the two most important texts of recent years on the subject: N. F. R. Crafts, *British Economic Growth During the Industrial Revolution* (Oxford, 1985), and E. A. Wrigley, *Continuity, Chance and Change: The Character of the Industrial Revolution in England* (Cambridge 1988). Both stress the redeployment of the population although Wrigley also places emphasis on the shift from organic to inorganic sources of raw materials and to new forms of energy.
[7] M. W. Flinn, *Origins of the Industrial Revolution* (London, 1966), p.14.

people chose their rulers and supported their poor, what they knew about the world and what they wanted to know – all of these were transformed.[8]

Too often, particularly in recent economic history, an artificial separation has been created between the economy on the one hand and urbanisation, class formation, popular politics, government, the arts and religion of the other, implying that these were effects of the industrial revolution and not integral parts of it. This volume adopts the broader concept of industrial revolution and recognises the period as one of fundamental and, in many respects, unique changes. These changes should be seen as part of a process rather than events in themselves, a process which gathered a particular momentum in the late eighteenth and early nineteenth centuries. We thus concentrate on the period from the 1760s to the 1830s. Discussion rarely strays beyond the second quarter of the nineteenth century but considerable attention is paid to the eighteenth century as a whole because this is necessary to our analysis of the dynamics of change in later decades.

The causes of the industrial revolution
The causes of the industrial revolution became a focus of interest with the expansion of development economics and policies in the 1950s. Most textbooks of the 1950s and 60s drew up lists of factors or preconditions for industrialisation in Britain, elevating one or another to the status of prime cause. Hartwell suggested:

an increase in the rate of capital formation (either because of low interest rates encouraging investment, or because of profit inflation); an increase in world trade (the natural result of an expanding geographical frontier), in which England gained disproportionately (thus stimulating export industries and, finally, general growth); a technological revolution (the result of an autonomous increase in knoweldge, the application of which transformed the machinery and organisation of industry making it much more productive); and growth of laissez faire and of a rational ethic towards wealth (the result of changes both in philosophic and religious convictions) which liberalised the context and possibilities of enterprise.[9]

One could add: agricultural change (which enabled the economy to support an increasing non-agricultural workforce); population growth (which increased the demand for goods and services and the supply of

[8] J. Mokyr, 'The Industrial Revolution and the New Economic History', in Mokyr, ed., *The Economics of the Industrial Revolution* (London, 1985), p.1. This is an excellent essay on approaches to interpreting the industrial revolution.
[9] Hartwell, Introduction, p.10.

cheap labour); and shifts in internal consumption which were not just an extension of traditional demands but represented an increased desire to buy and to possess material goods together with new forms of salesmanship aimed to create and intensify demands.

The array of causal analyses, produced in the 1950s and 1960s, of both favourable long-term conditions and immediate precipitators resulted in a series of rather unproductive confrontations. One major meeting in 1960, attended by a large, representative group of British economic historians, apparently 'did nothing to further understanding of the causes of the industrial revolution'.[10] In the 1970s and 1980s research confirmed the difficulty of isolating any single factor although the implications of England's agrarian class relations provided the focus of a major debate.[11] The resulting foray into the idea of random or accidental causation[12] confirmed that the future lay in integrated study of social and economic conditions internally and of shifts in political power both internally and internationally which were part cause and part effect of the process of change. This is the approach adopted in the present volume. Thus the analysis of causes appears in each chapter with particular attention being paid to the interplay of internal and external stimuli.

[10] R. M. Hartwell, 'The Industrial Revolution: An Essay in Methodology', in Hartwell, ed., *Causes*, p.57.
[11] For references to this see chapter 3.
[12] N.F. R. Crafts, 'Industrial Revolution in England and France: Some Thoughts on the Question "Why was England first?"', *Economic History Review* xxx (1977). Wrigley also suggested accidental cause, largely as a protest against the teleological interpretation of why the industrial revolution happened in England first: E. A. Wrigley, 'The Process of Modernisation and the Industrial Revolution in England', *Journal of Interdisciplinary History* iii (1972–3), p.259.

I

Writing and Rewriting History

1 PERSPECTIVES ON THE INDUSTRIAL REVOLUTION

The failure of growth, particularly industrial growth since the 1960s, has prompted a search for the origins of the British malaise. In this light the industrial revolution has come to be seen as unspectacular, incomplete and largely responsible for the poor competitive potential of the British economy ever since.[1] In addition, the new Conservatism in Britain, the emphasis on private ownership, free markets, enterprise culture and Victorian values has had its effect on perceptions of industrialisation, on the role of the state, the structure of business and the formation of class consciousness.[2] To understand current interpretations of the industrial revolution we must be aware of the impact of contemporary economic and political circumstances. But these are not the only influences acting upon historians either today or in the past. The preoccupations of individual writers, the development of particular academic disciplines, fashions in research methods and the changing acceptability and use of sources are also important, as well as the evolution of computer technology which has enabled historians to pose both old and new questions in entirely new ways. Anyone wishing to examine the industrial revolution must consider the influences acting upon historians, past and present. In doing so, it becomes easier to evaluate interpretations and to suggest new ones.

Early interpretations

The view that the late eighteenth and early nineteenth centuries represented a significant watershed in historical development had its origins in a mass of commentary written at the time.

In 1814 Patrick Colquhoun wrote:

It is impossible to contemplate the progress of manufactures in Great Britain within the last thirty years without wonder and

---

[1] See for example, N. F. R. Crafts, *British Economic Growth During the Industrial Revolution* (Oxford, 1985); M. J. Weiner, *English Culture and the Decline of the Industrial Spirit 1850–1980* (Cambridge, 1981). For a survey of the emergence of such interpretations against the backcloth of earlier historiography see D. Cannadine, 'The Present and the Past in the English Industrial Revolution 1880–1980', *Past and Present* 103 (1984) on which this chapter relies heavily.
[2] See more detailed discussion later in this chapter and in chapters 4 and 7. For a thought-provoking account of these influences see J. Raven, 'British History and the Enterprise Culture', *Past and Present* 123 (1989).

astonishment. Its rapidity, particularly since the French revolutionary war, exceeds all credibility. The improvement of the steam engines, but above all the facilities afforded to the great branches of the woollen and cotton manufactories by ingenious machinery, invigorated by capital and skill, are beyond all calculation...these machines are rendered applicable to silk, linen, hosiery and various other branches...[3]

Thomas Carlyle commented in 1826 'how wealth has more and more increased, and at the same time gathered itself more and more into masses, strangely altering the old relations, and increasing the distance between rich and poor'.[4] And Peter Gaskell wrote to Lord Melbourne in 1834 of a dual society desperately divided;

Since the steam engine has concentrated men into particular localities – has drawn together the population into dense masses – and since an imperfect education has enlarged and to some degree distorted their views, union is become easy and from being so closely packed, simultaneous action is readily excited. The organisation of these working class societies is now so complete that they form an empire within an empire of the most obnoxious description. Labour and capital are coming into collision – the operative and the master are at issue, and the peace and well being of the kingdom are at stake.[5]

In the same year, E. C. Tufnell argued:

Where combinations have been most frequent and powerful, a complete separation of feeling seems to have taken place between masters and men. Each party looks upon the other as an enemy, and suspicion and distrust have driven out the mutual sentiments of kindness and goodwill by which their intercourse was previously marked.[6]

Contemporary commentaries such as these express no doubt about the radical nature of the changes which were taking place. And until the 1930s, historians of the British industrial revolution were similarly

[3] P. Colquhoun, *A Treatise on the Wealth, Power and Resources of the British Empire* (London, 1814, Second edn., 1815, p.68).
[4] T. Carlyle, 'Signs of the Times', 1829, quoted in A. H. R. Ball, *Selections from Carlyle* (Cambridge, 1929), p.107.
[5] Quoted by A. Briggs in 'The Language of Class in Early Nineteenth-Century England', in A. Briggs and J. Saville, eds., *Essays in Labour History* (London, 1960), p.63. This article remains a fascinating introduction to changing perceptions of social difference and social conflict in the period.
[6] E.C. Tufnell, *The Character, Objects and Effects of Trades Unions* (London, 1834), p.97.

agreed that the period witnessed a uniquely important conjunction of technological innovation, industrial development, overseas expansion, population growth, urbanisation and proletarianisation which involved marked changes in living standards and in social and political relationships.

The term industrial revolution was widely used in England by the 1840s. It appears to have originated amongst French commentators at the turn of the century who suggested that nations were experiencing a profound economic and social transformation. Used as a direct analogy to the French revolution the term implied that radical change would occur in a definable time period and when Engels wrote his chronicle in 1844 of the effects of the new industrialism on the living conditions of the masses, the term industrial revolution was employed in dramatic manner.[7] It was fixed in the language of historians with respect to Britain by Arnold Toynbee in his famous Oxford lectures published in 1884. Toynbee saw a sharp break in the development process occurring around 1760 followed by a period of intensive industrialisation to 1850 when the process was essentially complete. For him the old order 'was suddenly broken in pieces by the mighty blows of the steam engine and the power loom'.[8]

Toynbee stressed the rise of competitive market society, the rapid growth of population, and the relative (and later absolute) decline of the agricultural population made possible by increased productivity. He saw the substitution of the factory for the domestic system arising directly from mechanical innovation. He stressed the improvement of communications, the expansion of trade and the redistribution of wealth into the hands of capitalists and farmers at the expense of workers. A central element in the chronology of Toynbee's revolution, and in the eyes of most of his contemporaries, was invention. He identified major landmarks of mechanical invention clustered in the 1760s and 1770s and coinciding with a major upturn in parliamentary enclosure. The starting point of the industrial revolution was thus fixed around 1760 with the invention of the rotary steam engine, and new spinning and metallurgical technologies. The dominant view in Toynbee's time was that 'the change...was sudden and violent....In little more than twenty years all the great inventions of Watt, Arkwright and Bolton had been completed...and the modern factory system had fairly begun'.[9]

Toynbee was part of a generation of historians and social commentators, including the Webbs, the Hammonds and Charles Beard, who had witnessed the poverty and insecurity, the urban squalor and the

[7] F. Engels, *The Condition of the Working Class in England* (London, 1844).
[8] A. Toynbee, *Lectures on the Industrial Revolution in England* (London, 1884), p.31.
[9] H. de B. Gibbons, *Industry in England* (London, 1897), p.341.

disease which abounded alongside the accumulation of wealth by a minority and the achievement of Britain's position as the major industrial and trading power in the world. They wrote in a period, between the 1880s and the 1920s, characterised by growing foreign competition and industrial unrest. They stressed the rapidity of change and the terrible effects of industrial transformation upon the living standards of the masses. They focused their attacks on the principles of the free market, *laissez-faire* economy and advocated more humane government intervention to mould economic change and to modify its social impact. This humanitarian and collectivist stance was influenced by the surveys of poverty undertaken by Booth and Rowntree and by the intensive use of parliamentary papers and Blue Books as major sources of evidence.[10]

The view that industrial change and socio-political developments were closely linked and that the magnitude of the former could not be assessed in isolation from the latter was a strong element in nineteenth-century writing. Marx, for example, saw the industrial revolution as marking a major transformation of the way in which goods and services were produced and distributed (the mode of production). The hallmarks of this transformation were a decisive shift in the production of goods for commercial markets rather than for immediate or localised use: the divorce of labour from the land and the rise of proletarianised wage labour; the division of labour and its greater control by employers (both of which alienated labour from the satisfaction of producing a finite product); mechanisation and centralisation of work; the increasing use of industrial or fixed capital in place of merchant or circulating capital, resulting in a new type of profit generation. Although these changes also resulted in unemployment, deskilling and intensified exploitation of labour, at the same time growing centralisation and homogenisation of work increased the potential for collective consciousness and action on the part of workers to defend their position.

For Marx the new mode of production was intimately connected with a radically changing society. Relations of production were increasingly based purely on a cash nexus between capitalist employers and wage-dependent employees. This replaced the relations between masters and journeymen or between members of village communities where reciprocity and custom were as important as the market. The rise of a new bourgeoisie of industrial employers wrought a major

---

[10] See J. T. Thorold Rogers, *Six Centuries of Work and Wages* (London, 1884); C. Beard, *The Industrial Revolution* (London, 1901); W. Cunningham, *The Growth of English Industry and Commerce in Modern Times* (Cambridge, 1907); J. L. and B. Hammond, *The Rise of Modern Industry* (London, 1925); S. and B. Webb, *English Local Government from the Revolution to the Decay of the Municipal Corporations Act* (London, 8 vols., 1906–29).

change in government, in the social heirarchy, in class perceptions and in political alignments and actions.[11]

For Mantoux, whose classic study of the eighteenth century was published in 1906, the industrial revolution was a culmination of movements long underway, but both he and his contemporary Ashley had a strong sense of the unique and radical nature of the change and of the legitimacy of assigning a precise period to it.[12] The process, argued Mantoux, was virtually at an end by 1802 with the passing of the law which inaugurated factory legislation:

> By then the great technical inventions... had all become practical realities. Many factories were already at work which, apart from certain details as to tools were identical with those of today. Great centres of industry had begun to grow up, a factory proletariat made its appearance, the old trade regulations, already more than half destroyed, made way for the system of laissez faire...the stage was already set; there was nothing left but to follow the working out of the drama.[13]

Thus the earliest interpretations of the industrial revolution were of revolutionary technological change in industry and of innovation in the rest of the economy accompanied by radical shifts in society and in social relations.

The revolution challenged

The 1920s and 1930s saw the publication of a number of major studies of industrial sectors and industrial regions as well as more research on the early modern period. These studies used a wide range of documentary primary sources such as business records, estate papers, parish accounts, newspapers and the papers of central and local governments. The outcome was to shift the dominant interpretation of the industrial revolution to one which doubted the validity of confining radical economic change uniquely to the period. 'A revolution which continued for 150 years and had been in preparation for at least another 150 years may well seem to need a new label', argued Heaton in 1932.[14]

---

[11] K. Marx, *Capital* I (London, 1867).
[12] P. Mantoux, *The Industrial Revolution in the Eighteenth Century* (London, 1928; French edn. 1906); W. J. Ashley, *The Economic Organisation of England: An Outline History* (London, 1914).
[13] Mantoux, *Industrial Revolution*, p.43.
[14] H. Heaton, 'Industrial Revolution', in *Encyclopaedia of the Social Sciences* VIII (London, 1933), p.5. Major studies of the 1920s and 1930s include: H. Heaton, *The*

The change to a more gradualist interpretation came most notably with the publication of J. H. Clapham's three-volume *Economic History of Modern Britain* between 1926 and 1938. He attacked the established view on two fronts. First, he showed how gradual, localised and incomplete the industrial revolution was by examining the non-mechanised industries which predominated in the second quarter of the nineteenth century: 'no single British industry had passed through a complete technical revolution before 1830. The country abounded with ancient types of industrial organisation and transitional types of every variety'.[15] Even in cotton the machine operative was not the most representative worker in 1850, the steam engine had not been generally introduced until well after 1830, and typical firm size even in the cotton and iron sectors was small. Secondly, Clapham attacked the notion that living standards were generally declining for the masses as Marx, Engels and then Toynbee and the Webbs and others had portrayed. With the exceptions of the dying trades like handloom weaving, Clapham argued that, by contemporary standards, living conditions were improving. He, along with several of his contemporaries like Heaton and Redford, consciously avoided using the term industrial revolution.[16]

Clapham's work ushered in a period when a more gradual interpretation of the industrial revolution became orthodox. Lipson stressed the long continuity of economic development and of conflict between capital and labour.[17] Other empirical work uncovered further evidence of considerable industrial expansion, organisational developments in both manufacturing and trade, and change in technology before the mid eighteenth century. Carus-Wilson talked of a revolution in the thirteenth century with the introduction of the fulling mill; Wadsworth and Mann's detailed study showed that innovation in

---

Yorkshire Woollen and Worsted Industries (Oxford, 1920); T.S. Ashton, *Iron and Steel in the Industrial Revolution* (Manchester, 1924); T. S. Ashton and J. Sykes, *The Coal Industry of the Eighteenth Century* (Manchester, 1929); G. C. Allen, *The Industrial Development of Birmingham and the Black Country 1860–1927* (London, 1929); A. H. Dodd, *The Industrial Revolution in North Wales* (Cardiff, 1933); W.H.B. Court, *The Rise of the Midland Industries* (Oxford, 1938); G. H. Tupling, *The Economic History of Rossendale* (London, 1927); A. P. Wadsworth and J. de L. Mann, *The Cotton Trade and Industrial Lancashire 1600–1780* (Manchester, 1931); A. Redford, *The Economic History of England 1760–1860* (London, 1931). H.L. Beales swam very much against the tide of historiographical opinion in these years by stating that 'the industrial revolution replaced one social system, one civilisation by another': *The Industrial Revolution 1750–1850* (London, 1928).
15 J. H. Clapham, *An Economic History of Modern Britain* (Cambridge, 3 vols., 1926–38), I, pp.143–5.
16 *Ibid.*
17 E. Lipson, *The Economic History of England* (London, 1934).

Lancashire textile manufacture had a long history; Tawney stressed the importance of earlier attitudinal changes and Nef made a strong case that the most revolutionary turning point in the development of industry and large-scale technology in Britain occurred between 1540 and 1640.[18] That period saw marked expansion in coal mining, major technological advances and the multiplication of large, privately controlled enterprises. And Unwin's earlier work had stressed the fundamental shift occurring in the institutional structure of business in the sixteenth and seventeenth centuries with the decline of guilds and regulated companies.[19] Thus for a time much less prominence was given to the view of the industrial revolution as a unique or important watershed in economic or social life.

Economic cycles and the industrial revolution

In the interwar years economists like Beveridge and Schumpeter looked back to the late eighteenth century for evidence to support their analyses of the nature of cycles in the twentieth century. Schumpeter was interested in long waves of development (of 30–50 years) in which the upturns were a function of the clustering of innovations sparked by groups of dynamic risk-taking entrepreneurs, whom he saw as the prime movers in growth and change. One major clustering centred around Watt's engine but there was another wave in the 1830s–1840s associated with railways and a third in the 1870s–1880s associated with steel-making innovations. Schumpeter thus rejected the view that the industrial revolution was a unique event or series of events that created a new economic order; it was on a par with similar periods which preceded it and at least two more which followed.[20]

Schumpeter's arguments were in line with earlier work by Kondratieff who isolated a cycle of around 50 years duration marked by waves of basic technological innovation. Kondratieff argued that major scientific breakthroughs generated new technologies across a broad front stimulating trade and investment for several decades before the system settled down to await the next wave. In this scheme the industrial revolution was one of the most significant periods of innovation marking the up-phase of a Kondratieff wave. The Kondratieff perspective denied the industrial revolution its *unique*

---

[18] E. M. Carus-Wilson, 'The Industrial Revolution Reconsidered', *Journal of Economic History* III (1943); Wadsworth and Mann, *Cotton Trade*; R. H. Tawney, *Religion and the Rise of Capitalism* (London, 1938); J. U. Nef, 'The Progress of Technology and the Growth of Large-Scale Industry in Great Britain 1540–1640', *Economic History Review* v (1934).

[19] G. Unwin, *Industrial Organisation in the Sixteenth and Seventeenth Centuries* (London, 1904).

[20] J. A. Schumpeter, *Business Cycles* (Cambridge, Mass., 2 vols., 1939); Schumpeter, *The Theory of Economic Development* (Cambridge, Mass., 1934); W. Beveridge, 'The Trade Cycle in Britain before 1850', *Oxford Economic Papers* III (1940).

historical discontinuity but did recognise and stress the wider repercussions of breakthroughs in technology on social and cultural life.[21]

Other work of the interwar period was concerned with short-term fluctuations in the level of effective demand and investment and was influenced by the contemporary theories of Keynes. Gilboy suggested that the role of demand had been underplayed in discussing the causes of the industrial revolution.[22] And Beveridge argued that a particular type of cycle emerged from the later eighteenth century as an integral part of the industrial market economy. The work of Rostow and others confirmed this analysis. The post industrial revolution cycle reflected deep-seated movements in investment and the multiplier. These were linked closely to cycles of trans-Atlantic trade and, by the third quarter of the nineteenth century, were also linked to shifts between trans-Atlantic and domestic investment. Thus the industrial revolution was seen to mark a transition to an economy in which the sporadic effects of harvest failures or wars were replaced by more regular cycles with a determinant periodicity. The Juglar cycle (the standard business cycle, lasting between seven and eleven years) was identified as present and seemingly inherent in all advanced economies from the start of the industrialisation process until major changes in the international economy upset the pattern after the second world war.[23]

Economic growth models

After 1945 attempts were made to renconcile evolutionary, revolutionary and cyclical accounts of the industrial revolution and new textbooks were produced which emphasised the discontinuities as well as the continuities of the period. Ashton's classic work of 1948 analysed not only developments in industry, agriculture and transport but also the nature of entrepreneurship, the role of science and inventive activity, variations in the level of public debt, changes in the age structure of the population, the role of religious Dissent (particularly in education and entrepreneurship), and the importance of

[21] N. D. Kondratieff, 'The Long Waves in Economic Life', *Review of Economics and Statistics* xvii (1935). For a recent discussion of the Kondratieff cycle and its applicability to the industrial revolution see R. Lloyd-Jones, 'The First Kondratieff: the Long Wave and the British Industrial Revolution', *Journal of Interdisciplinary History* xx (1990).

[22] E. Gilboy, 'Demand as a Factor in the Industrial Revolution', in A. H. Cole, ed., *Facts and Factors in Economic History* (Cambridge, Mass., 1932), repr. in R. M. Hartwell, ed., *The Causes of the Industrial Revolution in England* (London, 1967).

[23] Beveridge, 'Trade Cycle'; W. W. Rostow, *British Economy of the Nineteenth Century* (Oxford, 1948); T. S. Ashton, *Economic Fluctuations in England 1700–1800* (Oxford, 1959); A. K. Cairncross, *Home and Foreign Investment, 1870–1913* (Cambridge, 1953); B. Thomas, *Migration and Economic Growth: A Study of Great Britain and the Atlantic Economy* (Cambridge, 1954); E. W. Cooney, 'Long Waves in Building in the British Economy in the Nineteenth Century', *Economic History Review* xiii (1960); A. D. Gayer. W. W. Rostow and A. J. Schwartz, *The Growth and Fluctuation of the British Economy 1790–1850* (Oxford, 2 vols., 1953). For a useful introduction to the literature on cycles in the period see D. H. Aldcroft and P. Fearon, eds., *British Economic Fluctuations 1790–1939* (London, 1972).

the rate of interest and the supply of capital in stimulating cycles of economic expansion. He stressed what had been a nineteenth-century assumption: that the changes were not merely industrial but social and intellectual. This return to the earlier broader specification of the industrial revolution made the notion of revolutionary change much more seductive.[24]

The notion of a fundamental and once-only economic transition was sustained even more strongly by work of the 1950s and early 1960s on economic development. Against the backcloth of increasing Western prosperity the literature of this period was marked by a preoccupation with growth models which might assist development policies for the Third World. Inequalities of wealth and power between different areas of the world were largely explained by the idea that the speed and timing of industrialisation varied: England was first, others followed, and the less developed laggards would eventually catch up. The dominant idea was that any economy could achieve growth with the right policies and that industrialisation was a successful path down which all must follow.

Gerschenkron argued that the speed of industrialisation within Europe was affected by the extent to which a country lagged behind Britain and that Britain's industrial revolution was inevitably slow because it was first. The process was mirrored more rapidly by others because they benefited from importing advanced technology and know-how and were, in many cases, propelled by state intervention in a conscious drive to compete and industrialise.[25]

The most notable work which linked analysis of the nature of the British industrial revolution with prescriptions for industrialisation elsewhere was Rostow's *Stages of Economic Growth*, published in 1960. Rostow systematised the process of economic growth into a model embodying five stages based on the British experience. These stages were 'primitive society', 'the preconditions of take-off', 'the take-off into self-sustained growth', 'the drive to maturity' and 'the age of high mass consumption'. It was the 'take-off' which resurrected the notion of the industrial revolution as a fundamental discontinuity. After the British 'take-off', which Rostow pinned down to the years 1783–1802, growth became the economy's normal condition. Furthermore, for Rostow the 'take-off' had very specific characteristics: a rise in the investment ratio to over 10% of national income, the emergence of a succession of high growth sectors of the economy whose impact

[24] T. S. Ashton, *The Industrial Revolution 1760–1830* (Oxford, 1948).
[25] A. Gerschenkron, *Economic Backwardness in Historical Perspective* (Cambridge, Mass., 1966). Other theories of the 1950s and 1960s about the conditions for economic development and industrialisation include: A. N. Agarawala and S. P. Singh, eds., *The Economics of Development* (Oxford, 1958); P. Bauer and B. S. Yamey, *The Economics of Underdeveloped Countries* (London, 1957); W. A. Lewis, *The Theory of Economic Growth* (London, 1955); S. Kuznets, *Economic Growth and Structure* (London, 1965).

was substantial, and the existence of a favourable political, social and institutional framework. Rostow argued that in the British case the succession of high growth sectors (canal construction followed by cotton then railway development) acted via their multiplier effects to create sustained industrialisation with cotton playing the key role in the take-off in Britain. He was heavily criticised for being over precise in his specifications and chronology of stages, for failing to identify the mechanism linking one stage with the next, and for exaggerating the impact of the cotton sector in Britain. But his ideas were important in highlighting aspects of the mechanism of economic growth. Since Rostow, historians of the industrial revolution have focused attention upon changes in rates of growth and investment and on the multiplier effects of the development of particular sectors in a way not seen previously.[26]

Rostow's *Stages* was explicitly a non-communist manifesto designed to explain how the West could bring growth to the third world. His volume was addressed to 'the men in Djakarta, Rangoon, New Dehli, and Karachi...in Tehran, Bagdad and Cairo' and elsewhere.[27] He believed that the process of development in Asia, the Middle East, Africa and Latin America was analogous to the stages of preconditions and take-off of Western societies in the late eighteenth and nineteenth centuries. In the ensuing literature on development economics, debate focused on the need for massive injections of capital in developing countries alongside the raising of the savings ratio and on whether growth should be balanced or uneven.[28] But, in the 1960s, it was increasingly suggested that the differences between the predicament of underdeveloped countries and the historical circumstances of pre-industrial Western Europe were so significant that comparison and prescription was difficult. Development economists came to see the British experience as unique and unrepeatable because it was first. It came about in a country which already dominated a large part of the world market and did not have to compete for resources and markets with other industrialised power blocks. By the 1960s it was becoming obvious that the gap between rich and poor nations of the world was in most cases widening and that many underdeveloped countries were

---

[26] W. W. Rostow, *The Stages of Economic Growth: A Non-Communist Manifesto* (Cambridge, 1960). See also Rostow, *The Process of Economic Growth* (Oxford, 1953).
[27] Rostow, *Stages*, p.166. See also Rostow, *View from the Seventh Floor* (London, 1964).
[28] See for example the contributions in W. W. Rostow, ed., *The Economics of Take-off into Sustained Growth* (London, 1963); S. Kuznets, *Modern Economic Growth: Rate Structure and Speed* (New Haven, 1966); R. Nurkse, *Problems of Capital Formation in Underdeveloped Countries* (Oxford, 1953); Lewis, *Theory*; Lewis, 'Economic

failing to develop any of the 'classic' signs of industrialisation despite injections of capital and international aid. Clearly it was ceasing to be possible to explain international inequalities solely by reference to factors internal to the individual countries. Third World development economists led the way in emphasising exogenous factors which affected a country's potential for growth. In particular, they stressed the deleterious effects of imperialism, both direct colonisation and its legacies (formal imperialism), and economic domination (informal imperialism) which distorted development in weaker trading partners.[29]

Dependency theories
Acknowledging and exploring the nature and impact of forms of political and economic subordination resulted in the emergence of a variety of dependency theories of economic development which were used by nationalist movements in the Third World. An early model in this mould, by Frank, divided nations into those which constituted the metropolis of trade and those which were satellites. He argued that the metropolis drew the surplus and profits of production from the satellite countries and distorted their production to suit its needs for raw materials and mass markets. Trade, manufacturing and finance in satellite areas were organised and controlled by metropolitan capital and by enclaves of foreign businessmen whose activities would have no positive effect on the broad development of the host economy.[30] Wallerstein evolved a more sophisticated version of dependency theory by dividing the 'capitalist world system' of trading into three hierarchical groups: core, periphery and semi-periphery. His model is of particular interest for historians because he extended the analysis back in time arguing that the world system which gave rise to this trading hierarchy began in the fifteenth century with the establishment of integrated world trade. The hierarchy was firmly endorsed in Western Europe from the mid eighteenth century: industrialisation, indeed, magnified the economic and political inequalities in world

Development with Unlimited Supplies of Labour', *The Manchester School* xxii (1954). For a survey of these discussions with particular reference to industrialisation in Britain see F. Crouzet, ed., *Capital Formation in the Industrial Revolution* (London, 1972), 'Introduction'.
[29] For an account of this shift in interpretation see I. Roxburgh, *Theories of Underdevelopment* (London, 1979).
[30] A. G. Frank, *Capitalism and Underdevelopment in Latin America* (New York, 1967); Frank, *Dependent Accumulation and Underdevelopment* (London, 1979). See also S. Amin, *Unequal Development* (Brighton, 1976).

trade that had emerged from the integrated world trading system and from the general crises of the seventeenth century.[31]

Thus, according to dependency theory, one country's industrial revolution is another country's underdevelopment and these are two sides of the same coin of world capitalist development. Industrialising countries need cheap food, raw materials and markets, and their involvement in world trade (often using forms of political or military domination as well as economic coercion) distorts the economies of less developed countries to secure the needs of the core. These theories have brought the constraints imposed on industrialisation by the location of economic and political power to the centre stage. It is no longer possible to discuss the industrialisation of any country or region without reference to its position in international economic and political relations. In addition, these theories have highlighted the very different sorts of problems facing today's newly industrialising and non-industrialised countries compared with those facing Britain and other countries of Western Europe which industrialised much earlier.

The transition debate

During the 1950s and 1960s debate about the nature of the industrial revolution also flourished within the framework of Marxist scholarship and by the 1970s this had developed a significant overlap with the historiography of dependency.

Following the publication of Dobb's *Studies in the Development of Capitalism* in 1948, a series of major articles discussed important aspects of the transition from feudalism through the pre-industrial period of 'merchant capitalism' and 'primary accumulation' to the era of the new industrial capitalist order. In this debate the fact of transition or of the applicability of the term industrial revolution was never questioned. What was at issue was the source of the dynamic impelling development from one mode of production and associated social formation to another. Whilst some writers stressed the role of trade and the growth of towns others gave primacy to class struggle.[32] Sweezy and later Wallerstein stressed the importance of trade in the British case: the influence of market extension on both production and proletarianisation and the importance for national development of

[31] I. Wallerstein, *The Modern World System* (New York, 1974); Wallerstein, *The Capitalist World Economy* (New York, 1979). Though much criticised for its historical inaccuracies, the theoretical structure of this analysis remains interesting. For further reading on the European crisis of the seventeenth century and its significance in understanding European industrialisation see Wallerstein, 'Crisis of the Seventeenth Century', *New Left Review* 110 (1978); E. J. Hobsbawm, 'The General Crisis of the European Economy in the Seventeenth Century', *Past and Present* 5 (1954), and T. H. Aston, ed. *Crisis in Europe 1560–1660* (London, 1965), in which the Hobsbawm article is reprinted.

[32] M. Dobb, *Studies in the Development of Capitalism* (London, 1948). Major articles of the transition debate of the 1950s and 1960s are contained in R. Hilton, *The Transition from Feudalism to Capitalism* (London, 1976).

achieving international economic power through trade.[33] Brenner, on the other hand, following in the tradition of Dobb suggested that trade could only be a dynamic influence once social and class relations had been changed by social conflict to allow the extension of the market and proletarianisation.[34]

Alongside this debate Macpherson developed an analysis of the evolution of English political theory in Hobbes and Locke which saw these writers endorsing possessive individualism, private property and market relationships.[35] Marxist writings thus contributed to a view of the industrial revolution as one of unprecedented change both economic and social.

Heroic accounts

Rehabilitation of a sense of the dramatic nature of the age was also endorsed in the 1950s and 1960s by a boom in business history. Histories of major firms were commissioned and other studies appeared that were overwhelmingly related to large successful companies whose records had survived and were accessible: Marshalls of Leeds (flax spinners), Fosters of Black Dyke Mills (worsted manufacturers), Courtaulds, Unilever, the large brewers, Wedgwood.[36] Some historians took a strong lead from Schumpeter's view of the entrepreneur as the prime mover in innovation and hence the initiator of economic growth.[37] It was argued that Britain's relative retardation in the late nineteenth century owed much to a decline in the quality of entrepreneurship from the high point reached during the industrial revolution.[38]

The role of risk-taking, innovative businessmen of a specific sociological and psychological type was greatly extolled. They were

[33] See Sweezy's critique of Dobb in Hilton, *Transition;* Wallerstein, *Capitalist World Economy.*
[34] Contributions by Brenner to this debate, and critiques of the Brenner thesis are collected in T. H. Aston and C. H. Philbin, eds., *The Brenner Debate: Agrarian Class Structure and Economic Development in Pre-industrial Europe* (Cambridge, 1985). See also R. Brenner, 'The Origins of Capitalist Development: A Critique of Neo-Smithian Marxism', *New Left Review* 108 (1978).
[35] C. B. Macpherson, *The Political Theory of Possessive Individualism* (Oxford, 1962).
[36] W. Rimmer, *Marshall's of Leeds: Flaxspinners 1786–1886* (Cambridge, 1960); E. M. Sigsworth, *Black Dyke Mills: A History with Introductory Chapters on the Development of the Worsted Industry in the Nineteenth Century* Liverpool, 1958; C. Wilson, *The History of Unilever* (2 vols., London 1954); P. Mathias, *The Brewing Industry in England 1700–1830* (Cambridge, 1959); M. W. Flinn, *Men of Iron: The Crowleys in the Early Iron Industry* (London, 1962); N. McKendrick, 'Josiah Wedgwood: An Eighteenth-century Entrepreneur in Salesmanship and Marketing Techniques', *Economic History Review* XII (1959–60); D. C. Coleman, *Courtaulds: An Economic and Social History* (London, 2 vols., 1969).
[37] Schumpeter, *Theory.* For example see C. Wilson, 'The Entrepreneur in the Industrial Revolution in Britain', *Explorations in Entrepreneurial History* VII (1955).
[38] See for example D. Aldcroft, 'The Entrepreneur and the British Economy 1870–1914', *Economic History Review* XVII (1964).

often seen as energetic, self-sacrificing heroes: 'Their origins were often humble, and they were as hard on themselves as they were on others; business was their consuming interest and they continued to lead the simple lives to which they had early been accustomed, practising a stringent personal economy and a rigid austerity, which maximised their savings.'[39]

Despite the accumulating evidence of rather more luxurious lifestyles among businessmen of the period and their tendency to invest as much in French wine, fine art and south American railway shares as in their own firms, the nature and quality of the entrepreneur during the industrial revolution was little questioned before the mid 1970s. The ability to accept responsibility, to make decisions and to be thrifty and diligent was sometimes related to the strength and toleration of religious nonconformity in Britain. The ideas of Weber and Tawney about religion, the protestant ethic and the rise of capitalism were given new prominence.[40] Hagen and McClelland, for example, developed major theories of the formation of the successful businessman, McClelland stressing the importance of child-rearing practices which encouraged independence and effort.[41] Most studies however doubted that dissenting beliefs had a major effect, in themselves, on the formation of the entrepreneurial character. The disproportionate number of nonconformists amongst the entrepreneurial group was probably more a result of their exclusion from parliament and from the universities. They did not therefore dissipate their wealth in costly political careers and were forced to seek upward social mobility and social status through other channels. Ashton placed particular stress on the role of nonconformist schools and academies which were not tied to traditional classical syllabuses and which included practical and theoretical training in science.[42]

By the late 1960s and 1970s much more balanced views of entrepreneurship during the industrial revolution were appearing. Stress was placed on the uniquely favourable environment in which businessmen of the period worked. There was internal political stability and a framework of law and institutions which encouraged commerce and manufacturing and left businessmen lightly taxed compared with the mass of the population. The market environment was favourable with considerable expansion of both home and foreign markets, the latter enjoying military support and monopolistic advantages. The ubiquity of credit eased the entry of firms into industry and, finally, the expanding economy multiplied the opportunities for

[39] Crouzet, *Capital Formation*, p.188.
[40] M. Weber, *The Protestant Ethic and the Spirit of Capitalism* (London, 1930); R. H. Tawney, *Religion and the Rise of Capitalism* (London, 1926).
[41] D. C. McClelland, *The Achieving Society* (Princeton, 1961); E. E. Hagen, *On the Theory of Social Change* (London, 1964).
[42] Ashton, *Industrial Revolution*, p.19.

business success and encouraged favourable social attitudes to upward mobility because it was not obviously occurring at the expense of others. Thus, although bankruptcy rates were high in the period, poor accounting practices and ill-judged investment decisions often went unpunished because of the favourable conditions of the time.[43] As Samuel Smiles suggested: 'Anybody who devotes himself to making money body and soul can scarcely fail to make himself rich. Very little brains will do.'[44] But heroic and revisionist accounts recognised in common that the industrial revolution period was one of widespread and successful entrepreneurial activity.

Technology

The 1960s also saw heroic accounts of technological change, epitomised in Landes' *Unbound Prometheus* which conveyed a real sense of the excitement and dynamism of the age:

> In the eighteenth century, a series of inventions transformed the manufacture of cotton in England and gave rise to a new mode of production – the factory system. During these years, other branches of industry effected comparable advances, and all these together mutually reinforcing one another, made possible further gains on an ever widening front...they may be subsumed under three principles: the substitution of machines – rapid, regular, precise, tireless – for human skill and effort; the substitution of inanimate for animate sources of power...thereby opening to man a new and almost unlimited supply of energy; the use of new and far more abundant raw materials, in particular, the substitution of mineral for vegetable or animal substances.[45]

Von Tunzelmann's later account of the diffusion of the steam engine was more tempered but he still estimated that the Watt engine may have saved £185,000 of fuel in 1800 and that the jenny in the woollen industry saved about 2% of national income that year not counting its contribution in the cotton sector.[46]

Renewed discussion of technological change was orientated around certain questions, in particular the relationship between industrial inventions and scientific advance. Most historians argued that there

[43] See for example S. Pollard, *The Genesis of Modern Management: a Study of the Industrial Revolution in Great Britain* (London, 1965); P. Payne, *British Entrepreneurship in the Nineteenth Century* (London, 1974).
[44] Quoted in Payne, *British Entrepreneurship*, p.35.
[45] D. S. Landes, *The Unbound Prometheus: Technological Change and Industrial Development in Western Europe. 1750 to the present* (Cambridge, 1969), p.41; G. N. von Tunzelmann, *Steam Power and British Industrialisation to 1860* (Oxford, 1978); von Tunzelmann 'Technical Progress During the Industrial Revolution', in R. C. Floud and D. McCloskey, eds., *The Economic History of Britain since 1700* (Cambridge, 1981) I pp.143–63.
[46] von Tunzelmann, *Steam Power*, ch. 2.

was almost no exchange of ideas between scientists and industrial innovators. Scientific advance at the time lay mainly in fields such as astronomy, analytical mechanics, and crystalography – far removed from the sphere of major industrial advances. Science was further developed on the Continent, but in Britain generalised knowledge was increasingly widespread, practical tinkering and on-the-spot adjustments to machinery and processes, themselves insignificant were cumulatively as important as major inventions. The productivity of the steam engine in Cornwall was for example increased almost four times in the first half of the nineteenth century by higher pressure operation, the lagging of pipes, and other adjustments. By contrast James Watt had increased the productivity of the engine by about two and a half times at most.[47] The importance assigned to such anonymous technological change suggested that innovativeness was widespread.

Further work was also done on the relationship and delays between invention and innovation and on the determinants of the latter. The introduction of a new process or improved technology requires a particular environment of competition and demand, often also of capital and labour supply. Habakkuk argued that cheap labour supplies slowed down the rate of labour-saving innovation in Britain in the nineteenth century compared with the United States. Britain's older industrial heritage may also have been a disadvantage in some sectors because wherever existing fixed capital was significant there was likely to be a bias towards retaining the older process. Some historians concentrated on the determinants of the clustering of innovations. They claimed that booms encouraged risk taking and innovation although others showed that booms encouraged complacency and that slumps were needed to stimulate advances. Von Tunzelmann argued that the response to boom or slump depends on how much capital the innovation requires. Thus improvements in steam engines and the introduction of machinery would be diffused in a period of slump whilst the high-cost cylinder and boilers themselves would be more favoured by the easier credit conditions and higher profit expectations of the upswing. This fits with Matthews' suggestion that entrepreneurs in cotton invested excessively in power-driven factories in booms and filled them up with machinery in the ensuing slumps. The mainsprings of innovation may also have changed over time. In the iron industry in the eighteenth century, for example, innovation was used to create windfall profits. By the nineteenth century entrepreneurs were *forced* to adopt new methods in order to maintain profits threatened by falling price levels and by increased

---

[47] von Tunzelmann, 'Technical Progress', p.151; Landes, *Unbound Prometheus*. For the links between science and industry see A. E. Musson and E. Robinson, *Science and Technology in the Industrial Revolution* (Manchester, 1969).

competition.[48] Far from being dynamic risk-taking individuals most businessmen of the later period at least were forced to innovate on pain of elimination. They were enmeshed in a competitive dynamic which was not of their own choosing.[49] The industrial revolution was clearly not only a period of pervasive innovation but was marked also by change in the competitive climate and in business behaviour.

Capital formation

The sudden upward leap of capital formation suggested by Lewis and Rostow in the 1950s as a hallmark of the industrial revolution was questioned empirically by Deane and Habakkuk but it was somewhat rehabilitated by Kuznets, Pollard and Feinstein in the 1960s and 1970s.[50] They used gross figures (allowing for maintenance and for rapid obsolescence) and showed that domestic fixed capital as a proportion of GDP had already risen to 10% by 1800 but then it stabilised around 10–11% until after the 1850s, despite a threefold rise in annual GDP at factor cost between the 1810s and 1850s. The build up of fixed capital in the industrial revolution decades was slow because early machinery was cheap and factory premises were often rented or converted from other uses. Room and power in a mill were often shared by several concerns and steam engines and other equipment could be bought on hire purchase. There was also a flourishing second-hand market in machinery. Clearly, slow growth of capital intensity was compatible with considerable technological and organisational advances.[51]

Much debate in the 1970s and 1980s concerned the sources as well as the magnitude of industrial investment outlays. Historians differentiated between the funds required to start businesses and those needed for expansion. Attention was also paid to the very different sources of finance for fixed outlays (on plant and equipment) compared with circulating needs (for wage payments, stockholding, purchasing and marketing). Before 1850 most manufacturing concerns continued to require more circulating capital than fixed although the ratio was

[48] H. J. Habakkuk, *American and British Technology in the Nineteenth Century: The Search for Labour-saving Inventions* (Cambridge, 1962); C. K. Hyde, *Technological Change and the British Iron Industry* (Princeton, 1977), pp.199–200; Matthews, 'Trade-Cycle History', p.131, quoted in von Tunzelmann, 'Technical Progress', p.153.
[49] P. Sweezy, 'Schumpeter's Theory of Innovation' in Sweezy, ed., *The Present as History* (New York, 1953).
[50] Rostow, *Stages*; Lewis *Theory*; P. Deane and H. J. Habakkuk, 'The Take-off in Britain', in Rostow, ed., *Economics of Take-off*; Kuznets, *Modern Economic Growth*; J.P.P. Higgins and S. Pollard, eds., *Aspects of Capital Investment in Great Britain 1750–1850* (London, 1971), pp.6–7, 27, 150, 186–7; C. Feinstein, 'Capital Formation in Great Britain', in P. Mathias and M. M. Postan, eds., *Cambridge Economic History of Europe* (Cambridge, 1978) vii, pt 1, pp.28–96.
[51] For examples of this see P. Hudson, *The Genesis of Industrial Capital: A Study of the West Riding Wool Textile Industry c.1750–1850* (Cambridge, 1986); M. Berg, *The Age of Manufactures* (London, 1985).

gradually altering. More investment in fixed capital helped to liberate circulating capital by speeding up the turnover time of production and eliminating the delays involved in many putting-out structures which tied up large amounts of capital in stock and work in progress. The shifting needs for fixed and circulating capital necessarily involved changes in the sources of finance away from trade credit and plough-back in favour of larger partnerships, joint stock arrangements and the institutions of the formal capital and mortgage markets.[52]

The ubiquity of credit dealings in the eighteenth century, especially in the supply of raw materials, helped to ease the path from small to larger scale operations whilst capital from the family or personal and social contacts was frequently the major initial outlay in establishing a business. Landholdings were commonly used as collateral to raise loans, and the raising of finance on a local and regional level was expedited by the role of attorneys and later banks active in industrial areas in putting lenders in touch with borrowers and arranging the transfer of funds.

Ploughed back profits used to be seen as the major source of industrial investment. Ashton, for example, wrote that 'industrial capital has been its own chief progenitor'. However, recent work has shown that by the 1830s and 1840s, bank loans were more important than reinvestment during periods of expansion of capacity in the wool textile industry. Profits accumulated gradually whilst investment was lumpy and often required a mix of internal and external sources. Profit levels were also suffering under the impact of overproduction and competition in the second quarter of the nineteenth century and profitability often rested on the ability to squeeze wages (the most flexible and usually the largest production cost) by delays in wage payments and by the use of the truck system. Finally, reinvestment appears to have been more closely related to the lifecycles of individuals and of businesses than to the asceticism of entrepreneurs.[53]

[52] Feinstein, 'Capital Formation'. The results of various sectoral studies of the magnitude of capital formation are collected in C. H. Feinstein and S. Pollard, eds., *Studies in Capital Formation in the United Kingdom 1750–1920* (Oxford, 1988). See also S. Shapiro, *Capital and the Cotton Industry in the Industrial Revolution* (Ithaca, 1967). On sources see Hudson, *Genesis*, which includes a survey of the earlier literature, and cf. P. Richardson, 'The Structure of Capital During the Industrial Revolution Revisited', *Economic History Review* XLII (1990), which reaches different conclusions about fixed and circulating ratios but is based on a very limited sample of unrepresentative firms.

[53] Ashton, *Industrial Revolution*, p.97. On attorneys see: B. L. Anderson, 'The Attorney and the Early Capital Market in Lancashire', in J. R. Harris, ed., *Liverpool and Merseyside: Essays in the Economic and Social History of the Port and its Hinterland* (Liverpool, 1969), and M. Miles, 'The Money Market in the Early Industrial Revolution: The Evidence from West Riding Attorneys 1750–1800', *Business History* XXIII (1981). On banks see L. S. Presnell, *Country Banking in the Industrial Revolution* (Oxford, 1956); R. Cameron, ed., *Banking in the Early Stages of Industrialisation: A Study in Comparative Economic History* (New York, 1967), ch.2; Hudson, *Genesis*, ch.9.

Thus recent capital formation studies have indicated that the industrial revolution, although marked by moderate capital deepening, did involve major shifts in the magnitude, the nature and the sources of finance required to maintain a competitive footing in many manufacturing sectors.

The factory system and its alternatives

The industrial revolution is most often associated with the coming of centralised, factory production and with powered mechanised processes. Before the 1970s most accounts stressed this as a major feature of the period.[54] Even historians like Clapham who wrote of the incomplete nature of the transition nevertheless maintained the idea that inherently less efficient dispersed and small-scale handicraft technologies were being gradually replaced with their centralised and mechanised counterparts.[55] And this linear perspective was repeated in the bulk of the literature on proto-industrialisation which emerged in the 1970s. According to Mendels, industrialisation was a two-stage process. The first stage was characterised by the spread of rural domestic manufacturing for distant markets (proto-industrialisation). This created a dynamic build up of capital, entrepreneurial and manufacturing skills, mercantile contacts and markets, and a growing wage-labour force. Thus successful proto-industry would develop into stage two or industrialisation proper based on the factory and capital-intensive mechanisation. The proto-industrial system had inherent limits within a competitive environment. As businesses increased in size, activities were spread over a wider geographical area and marginal costs tended to rise. Also lack of control over the often unspecialised work-force made production deadlines and uniform quality difficult to achieve, and embezzlement of materials became an increasing problem. Centralised production was seen to result because it solved these difficulties.[56]

Classic accounts of the rise of the factory argued that the factory became necessary once machinery became too large and complex to be accommodated in smaller premises:

> The industrial revolution...required machines which not only replaced hand labour but compelled the concentration of production in factories – in other words machines whose appetite for energy was too large for domestic sources of power and whose mechanical superiority was sufficient to break down the resistance of the older forms of hand production.[57]

---

[54] A classic account is H. D. Fong, *The Triumph of the Factory System* (Tientsin, 1930).
[55] Clapham, *Economic History of Britain*.
[56] F. F. Mendels, 'Proto-industrialisation: The First Phase of the Industrialisation Process', *Journal of Economic History* xxxii (1972).
[57] Landes, *Unbound Prometheus*, p.81.

But proto-industrialisation theory placed greater stress on the need to supervise and discipline labour (the key production cost). This had earlier been argued by Marx and the debate about the mainsprings of factory development was revived in the 1980s principally by Marglin and Landes.[58] Marglin argued that the inspiration for the factory system was the substitution of capitalists' for workers' control of the production process and that in most industries centralisation occurred before mechanisation and this then provided a market for the new powered processes. Gott's Mill in Leeds, the biggest in Yorkshire in the 1800s, worked for 25 years without the mechanisation of spinning, relying on the gains of centralisation and labour discipline. Likewise Peter Stubs gathered filemakers under one roof in Warrington without in the first instance technical change.[59] The industrial revolution was therefore as much about the shift from task to time discipline as it was about the rise of entirely new productive methods.[60] Landes, however, contends that the gains from increased supervision and division of labour were not sufficient to determine factory innovation: 'What made the factory successful...was not the wish but the muscle: the machines and the engines; nothing less would have overcome the cost advantage of dispersed production'. He argues that the 'forced' and disciplined labour of women, children and paupers in the early factories was important in the transition but 'had they not been available the mills would have found what they needed, paid the price and still made money because (they) were so efficient by comparison with hand labour'.[61] Clearly the two processes of innovation – greater intensity of labour and technological change – went hand in hand.

Writings on proto-industry and the Marglin/Landes debate draw evidence mainly from developments in the textile industry. Thus the continuing role of muscle power and dispersed manufacturing during the industrial revolution and well after tends to be downplayed. Even in textiles there are many examples of the viability and longevity of dispersed and handicraft forms of manufacture existing alongside and in competition with factory production long after 1830, but in other

[58] S. Marglin. 'What Do Bosses Do?', in A. Gorz, ed., *The Division of Labour: The Labour Process and Class Struggle in Modern Capitalism* (Brighton, 1976); Marglin, 'Knowledge and Power', in F. H. Stephen, ed., *Firms, Organisation and Labour: Approaches to the Economics of Work Organisation* (London, 1984); D. S. Landes, 'What Do Bosses Really Do?', *Journal of Economic History* XLVI (1986).
[59] W. B. Crump, *The Leeds Woollen Industry 1780–1820* (Leeds, 1931), pp.24–5, 31; T. S. Ashton, *An Eighteenth-Century Industrialist: Peter Stubs of Warrington* (Manchester, 1939).
[60] See E. P. Thompson, 'Time, Work-discipline and Industrial Capitalism', *Past and Present* 38 (1967).
[61] Landes, 'Bosses', pp.606–7.

sectors too concentrations of workers under one roof and the application of steam were in fact unusual in most processes. But there was much innovation embodied in the multiplication of units using mainly hand labour and muscle power which went on alongside capital-intensive technological changes. These units remained viable and flourished partly because of the unevenness of technological and market development between sectors, and the unsuitability of certain jobs for mechanisation. The cheap and ready supply of female and child labour also discouraged the substitution of capital for labour because large gains in productivity could be achieved from the increasing intensity of handwork. In addition, the centralised, powered, high-productivity sectors brought into being a host of very differently organised subcontractors, input suppliers and other off-shoots. And the nature of the market for many consumer goods, where fashion changes and the desire for individuality encouraged short production runs, ensured the viability of firms outside of mass production. Enduring and innovative alternatives to the factory are clearly just as much a part of the story of the industrial revolution as the rise of centralised production. Interpretations which cite the restricted nature of factory development as evidence of incomplete industrialisation need to consider the dynamic nature of the non-factory manufacturing sector.[62]

The standard of living

Between the interwar period and the early 1960s discussion of the social impact of the industrial revolution was dominated by the controversy over standards of living. This resurrected a debate which had started in the mid nineteenth century. Optimists like Porter had challenged the pessimistic accounts of Engels and Marx.[63] From the 1930s discussion was renewed by Clapham and Ashton who concentrated largely on the movement of working-class real incomes and came to optimistic conclusions.[64] By the 1960s the standard of living debate had become one of the most vitriolic to hit the pages of

[62] For an interesting survey of the range and innovativeness of the non-factory and non-mechanised sectors see R. Samuel. 'The Workshop of the World', *History Workshop, Journal* 3 (1977). See also C. Sabel and J. Zeitlin, 'Historical Alternatives to Mass-production', *Past and Present* 108 (1985). For further discussion see chapter 2.
[63] G. R. Porter, *The Progress of the Nation* (London, 1851).
[64] Clapham, *Economic History of Britain* II; T. S. Ashton, 'The Standard of Life of the Workers in England 1790–1830', *Journal of Economic History* suppl. IX (1949).

academic journals.[65] Scope for intense disagreement arose partly from the difficulties of defining living standards and from the problems of measurement. Hartwell's optimistic assertions stuck to quantitative aspects using real wage movements, mortality figures and consumption statistics. Hobsbawm attacked the reliability of these and also argued that the question of whether the working class received marginally greater or smaller real incomes is not of itself of great importance compared with the impact of change in the whole nature of society under capitalist conditions.[66] Hobsbawm together with Thompson and others stressed the need to consider new working and urban conditions, the political suppression of discontent, unemployment and the harshness of the new Poor Law.[67]

Even with the narrow real wage conception of living standards, amassing reliable indices of the movements of money wages and the prices of the changing mix of food, rents and other living costs is extremely difficult. And because all of these fluctuated widely, assessment of trends depends a great deal on the choice of starting and finishing dates. The task is further aggravated by the gulfs of experience between skilled and unskilled workers, factory and outworkers, artisans and labourers, males and females, indigenous workers and immigrants; to say nothing of the marked differences in the development and labour demands (hence both family earnings and price movements) of different industrial sectors and regions of the country. Allowing for the changing incidence of unemployment over seasons and cycles, for the movement of family rather than individual incomes and for the role of perquisites in remuneration are near impossible tasks when pushed beyond the boundaries of a localised study.[68]

[65] See for example E. J. Hobsbawm, 'The British Standard of Living 1790–1850', *Economic History Review* x (1957); R. M. Hartwell, 'The Rising Standard of Living in England 1800–1850', *Economic History Review* xiii (1961). These and other contributions are collected in A. J. Taylor, ed., *The Standard of Living in Britain in the Industrial Revolution* (London, 1975). Also D. Woodruff, 'Capitalism and the Historians', *Journal of Economic History* xvi (1956) and W. H. Chaloner and W. O. Henderson, 'Introduction' to F. Engels, *Condition of the Working Class in England* (London, 1958). Chaloner and Henderson stressed the feckless spending of the working classes and the harsh reality of pre-industrial manufacturing wages and conditions. But exploited domestic handworkers were not a class supplanted by the industrial revolution; their numbers multiplied in the early nineteenth century as part of the industrialisation process. See E. J. Hobsbawm, 'History and "The dark satanic mills"' in Hobsbawm, ed., *Labouring Men* (London, 1964).
[66] Hobsbawm, ibid., and in his *Industry and Empire* (London, 1968), ch.4.
[67] E. P. Thompson, *The Making of the English Working Class* (London, 1963), esp.ch.10.
[68] For localised studies see R. S. Neale, 'The Standard of Living 1780–1844: A Regional and Class Study', *Economic History Review* xix (1966); T. R. Gourvish, 'The Cost of Living in Glasgow in the Early Nineteenth Century', *Economic History Review*, xxv (1972); R. Cage, 'The Standard of Living Debate: Glasgow 1800–1850', *Journal of Economic History* xliii (1983).

In surveying the state of the debate in 1975, Taylor emphasised that there is no doubt that the incomes of the working class lagged increasingly behind the nation at large. Had working-class incomes kept pace with the growth of national income the average worker would have been 50% better off in real terms in 1840 than in 1810, but even the most sanguine of optimists were not claiming this. The working class lost out in income terms because of unrestricted employment before the Factory Acts, weak trade unions, the force of population pressure which created an oversupply especially of unskilled labour, and regressive taxation and inflation during the Napoleonic wars.[69]

Subsequently, various quantitative studies have failed to prove the existence of any major increase in real incomes for the mass of the population before the 1820s. Even the calculations of Lindert and Williamson, which suggest a doubling of real wages between 1820 and 1850, can be criticised for relying on adult male wage indices, for poor evidence on rents, misleading evidence on white collar wages, and for being out of line with regional experiences especially in the case of London.[70] Quantitative work has however now moved on by providing new cost of living series with a broad remit to include such elements as the disutility of urban living (a quantitative indicator of the health, social and cultural costs of migration from country to town). According to one author urban disutility in the north-west before 1840 was probably sufficient to cancel any real gains from income changes.[71]

The qualitative aspects of living standards have also been firmly placed back at the centre stage: the common experience of many workers in factories, workshops and cottage industries in losing control over the pace and nature of work, becoming more dependent on larger industrialists or merchants for credit and employment, and being more at the mercy of unemployment without landholdings to cushion families against hard times. Thompson and others have pointed to the unprecedented agitations of the period most of which turned on issues other than wages: Luddism, the arming and drilling of the war years, the Ten Hours Movement, factory reform, strikes against the truck system, and Chartism. The social and cultural upheavals and deprivations of rapid urbanisation, the partiality of the

---

[69] Taylor, ed., *Standard of Living*, 'Introduction'.
[70] P. Lindert and J. G. Williamson, 'English Workers' Living Standards During the Industrial Revolution: A New Look', *Economic History Review* xxxvi (1983). See also M. W. Flinn, 'Trends in Real Wages 1750–1850', *Economic History Review* xxvii (1974); G. N. von Tunzelmann, 'Trends in Real Wages 1750–1850: Revisited', *Economic History Review* xxxii (1979); L. D. Schwarz, 'Income Distribution and Social Structure in London', *Economic History Review* xxxii (1979).
[71] J. C. Brown, 'The Condition of England and the Standard of Living: Cotton Textiles in the North-West 1806–1850', *Journal of Economic History* L (1990); cf. J. G. Williamson, *Coping with City Growth During the British Industrial Revolution* (Cambridge, 1990), ch. 9.

law, the suspension of Habeas Corpus, the Combination Acts and the infiltration of government spies and *agents provocateurs* into working-class organisations as well as the overt use of military repression have all been stressed. More troops were deployed internally during the Napoleonic Wars than were sent to fight in the Peninsula: 'the working class were forced into political and social apartheid' during the wars in which they also had to fight and all of this was coincident with growing political consciousness and wider aspirations encouraged by the French Revolution and the libertarian philosophies of writers like Tom Paine.[72]

The literature on the standard of living does little to dispel the idea that the industrial revolution stands out as a particularly harsh time for the mass of the population. Income distribution shifted massively in favour of the middle and upper classes, and consumption (for the vast majority of people) was squeezed in favour of state and private investment.[73] These points add further weight to the notion that the industrial revolution was a period of marked economic and social transition.

Class and class conflict

In the 1960s and early 1970s, alongside the more dramatic interpretations of the economic history of the period, came a shift in social history in favour of broader social and cultural concerns. One element of this was 'history from below'. This involved the use of new sources, and a different use of older evidence to tease out the lives, thoughts and attitudes of ordinary people in the process of historical change: to rescue the working class and the poor from a history which until then hardly recognised their existence let alone their agency in economic change. This new emphasis was epitomised in the work of E. P. Thompson whose *Making of the English Working Class* remains a major landmark in the historiography. He emphasised that the industrial revolution period saw class formation, class consciousness and radical oppositional politics.

The flowering of social history since the mid 1960s, and the new conceptualisations of social relationships and social consciousness, structure and agency which this has involved, must be seen against the background of major expansion of universities and especially of the social sciences which encouraged the growth of interdisciplinary concerns among historians. Historians borrowed ideas from sociology and anthropology. The student revolution, CND, the anti-Vietnam war campaign, the changing political face of Europe all had their effects on orientations in the social sciences. In a period of social

[72] The classic account of all this remains Thompson, *Making of the English Working Class*.
[73] S. Pollard, 'Investment, Consumption and the Industrial Revolution', *Economic History Review* XI (1958); J. Brewer, *The Sinews of Power* (London, 1989), esp.ch. 4.

revolution of various kinds more excitement was required from history and more was demanded about the roots and methods of mass protest in particular.

Much of the work on the industrial revolution which emerged hinged on a set of questions. Did the working class increasingly exhibit a common consciousness during the industrial revolution and a recognition that its interests were incompatible with those of employers and landowners? Did they set about forming associations with the express purpose of attempting to change the political and economic system to their benefit? Did the working class become a class 'for itself' in this sense? Did it even exhibit a revolutionary class consciousness (the overt and avowed desire to overthrow the economic and political status quo)? Or were working-class agitations largely attempts to gain concessions and to improve the lot of workers within the changing economic system?[74]

According to Perkin whose popular text appeared in 1969, the industrial revolution saw the emergence of three broad and mutually antagonistic classes: the landed aristocracy, the bourgeoisie, and the mass of the working population who were wage dependent. Antagonism was sparked by the catalyst of opposing ideals. Against the entrepreneurial ideal of *laissez-faire* and competition was posed that of the working class: an ideal of the productive independent worker (an indictment of the uproductive landowner and rentier) and of co-operation.[75] Organised resistance around opposing ideologies was also central to Thompson's thesis that the period from the 1790s to the 1830s saw the making of the English working class. He documents a growing identity of interests between diverse groups of the working population (as against the interests of other classes) which manifested itself in the emergence of strongly based and self-conscious working-class institutions and movements.[76]

In the 1960s and 1970s more research appeared on specific radical movements of the early nineteenth century, seeing them as unprecedented in their numerical influence and in the degree of popular opposition to the political status quo. Thompson argued that trade unions were forced underground by the prohibitions of the Napoleonic War period where they merged with mass insurrectionary activity and with machine wrecking and other agitations. Historians considered the revolutionary fervour of the 'Black Lamp' in mass arming and drilling on the Pennine moors in the 1800s and the overlaps between Chartism,

[74] For a survey of this literature and of the origins of these concepts see R. J. Morris, *Class and Class Consciousness in the Industrial Revolution 1780-1850* (London, 1979).
[75] H. Perkin, *Origins of Modern English Society 1780–1880* (London, 1969).
[76] Thompson, *Making of the English Working Class*.

Owenite socialism, factory reform and anti-Poor Law movements.[77] At least one writer argued that the 1830s and 1840s saw the emergence of revolutionary class consciousness in the textile areas.[78]

There was also active debate about the degree of acquiesence of the working masses to change in the third quarter of the nineteenth century. The increased respectability of nationally organised trade unions, with the accent on self-help friendly society functions and using the strike weapon only as a last resort, were characteristics emphasised by the Webbs. Lenin had also stressed the growth of working-class reformism which accompanied the prosperity and economic stability of a power enjoying the fruits of imperial expansion.[79] Cole had taken up this debate in a classic article of the 1930s but the discussion was resurrected more fully in the 1970s.[80] A large body of research and theorising appeared on the role of a labour aristocracy, of social control, state policy and economic conditions (including imperial expansion) in securing the mid and late nineteenth-century political calm and greater adherence to the ideals of self-help, respectability and nationalism.[81] There was some disagreement about the extent to which the third quarter of the century was accompanied by a fundamental shift in working-class ideology or politics. Some historians highlighted continued attacks on the status quo by the rank

[77] For these debates see Thompson, *Making of the English Working Class*; Perkin, *Origins*; R. A. Church and S. D. Chapman, 'Gravenor Henson and the Making of the English Working Class', in E. L. Jones and G. E. Mingay, eds., *Land, Labour and Population in the Industrial Revolution* (London, 1967); M. I. Thomis, *The Luddites: Machine Breaking in Regency England* (Newton Abbot, 1970); A. E. Musson, *British Trade Unions 1800–1875* (London, 1972); R. S. Neale, *Class and Ideology in the Nineteenth Century* (London, 1972); F. K. Donelly, 'Ideology and Early English Working Class History: Edward Thompson and his Critics', *Social History* 1 (1976).
[78] J. Foster, *Class Struggle and the Industrial Revolution: Early Industrial Capitalism in Three English Towns* (London, 1974). For critical reviews of this see A. E. Musson in *Social History* 1 (1976); J. Saville in *Socialist Register* (1974); and G. Stedman Jones in *New Left Review* 90 (1975).
[79] S. and B. Webb, *The History of Trades Unionism 1666–1920* (London, 1919). For a critique of the Webbs' periodisation see V. L. Allen, 'A Methodological Criticism of the Webbs as Trade Union Historians', *Labour History Society Bulletin* 4 (1962). See also V. I. Lenin, *Imperialism the Highest Stage of Capitalism* (Moscow, 1916; English trans. London, 1969).
[80] G. D. H. Cole, 'Some Notes on British Trade Unions in the Third Quarter of the Nineteenth Century', *International Review of Social History* 2 (1937), repr. in E. M. Carus-Wilson, ed., *Essays in Economic History* iii (London, 1965).
[81] E. J. Hobsbawm, 'The Labour Aristocracy in Nineteenth-Century Britain', in Hobsbawm, ed., *Labouring Men*; Foster, *Class Struggle*; R. Q. Gray, *The Aristocracy of Labour in Nineteenth-Century Britain c.1850–1900* (London, 1981); H. F. Moorehouse, 'The Marxist Theory of the Labour Aristocracy', *Social History* 3 (1978); A. Reid, 'Politics and Economics in the Formation of the British Working Class: A Reponse to H.F. Moorehouse', *Social History* 3 (1987); H. F. Moorehouse, 'History, Sociology and the Quiescence of the British Working Class: A Reply to Reid', *Social History* 4 (1979); A. P. Donajgrodzki, *Social Control in Nineteenth-Century Britain* (London, 1977); F.M.L. Thompson, 'Social Control in Victorian England', *Economic History Review* xxxiv (1981); N. Kirk, *The Growth of Working Class Reformism* (London, 1985), ch. 1.

and file of the working class and the widespread rejection of orthodox political economy. Musson on the other hand insisted that, even in the early nineteenth century, trade unionism was mainly an activity of skilled workers with respectable mutual insurance aims. But the dominant view until very recently implied that the industrial revolution was marked by a peak of political upheaval and instability.[82]

Current perspectives

Interpretations of the industrial revolution as a period of radical economic and technological discontinuity and political turbulence have declined since the later 1970s in the face of new research projects and methods. As British industry has suffered more than most Western countries in the last two decades and there has been a revolution in government policy, it is not surprising that many current interpretations of the industrial revolution seek to explain the roots of Britain's contemporary decline as well as her contemporary politics. This has led historians to consider how the structure of the economy and society differs from that of other industrialised nations. In economic history, promoted by a renewed emphasis on quantitative research and economic modelling (and aided by developments in computer technology), the 1980s were dominated by macroeconomic analyses which stressed the very slow growth of the economy and particularly of industry in the industrial revolution period and beyond. Crafts, for example, has argued that in Britain's 'idiosyncratic' industrialisation, labour transferred from agriculture to industry on a significant scale but technological change was very slow and patchy; hence productivity growth was limited and this was aggravated by insufficient investment. Britain neglected education and concentrated on producing low-wage factory fodder rather than high-wage technicians. This set a pattern repeated in the twentieth century of low home investment, slow productivity growth, and limited comparative advantage deriving from technological advance.[83]

In social and cultural history feminist approaches have done much to sophisticate our understanding of working-class politics, domestic ideals and the role of gender ideology in the period. Recently, too, class conflict has been played down and the fragmentation as well as the loyalism, royalism and the basic constitutionalism of the masses emphasised. This makes the late twentieth-century fragmentation of

[82] Musson, *British Trade Unions*; R. V. Clements, 'British Trade Unions and Popular Political Economy 1850–75', *Economic History Review* xiv (1961); E. I. Biagini, 'British Trade Unions and Popular Political Economy 1860–1880', *Historical Journal* 30 (1987); S. Pollard, ed., *The Sheffield Outrages*, esp. Introduction; R. Price, *Masters, Unions and Men: Work Control in Building and the Rise of Labour 1830–1914* (Oxford, 1981); Price, 'The Other Face of Respectability: Violence in the Manchester Brick-Making Trade 1859–1870', *Past and Present* 66 (1975).
[83] Crafts, *British Economic Growth*. For further discussion of these recent interpretations see chapter 2.

workers' politics and the divided Labour party easier to explain as an extension of long-term factors affecting the ideology of the working class. Attention has also shifted from study of the working classes to the nature and ideology of the capitalist class.[84] A dominant interpretation now is that the triumph of the bourgeoisie in economic and political life, traditionally regarded as a hallmark of the industrial revolution, is a myth. Variously expressed by writers such as Weiner and Anderson, it is suggested that England's present lack of commitment to a growth mentality can be traced back to the industrial revolution when the patrician land-based society never gave way to the new industrialism. The power and influence of industrialists, though increasing, failed to gain the ascendancy over the landed élite and its offshoots in metropolitan and international finance. Thus Britain has always had the disease of a slow-growing economy because industry has always been sacrificed to the needs of international finance and the rentier interest. In this perspective the whole period from the industrial revolution to the decline of British economic supremacy can be seen as an ephemeral episode between one rural-based/rentier society and another: between the old and a new feudalism, according to Bellini. Britain had a flirtation with industrialisation and factory culture but the industrial revolution was a 'flash in the pan'.[85] Thus in the late 1980s the logical extension of the 'limits to growth school' replaced the notion of 'take-off in to self-sustained growth':

> Instead of being depicted as the paradigmatic case, the first and most famous instance of economic growth, the British industrial revolution is now depicted in a more negative light, as a limited, restricted, piecemeal phenomenon in which various things did not happen or where they did, they had far less effect than was previously supposed.[86]

The remaining chapters examine current interpretations in greater depth and suggest ways in which our understanding can be improved by drawing upon older historiographical traditions and by starting some new ones.

---

[84] For discussion of this very broad span of the literature see chapter 7.
[85] Weiner, *English Culture;* P. Anderson, 'The Figures of Descent', *New Left Review* 161 (1987); J. Bellini, *Rule Britannia: A Progress Report for Domesday 1986* (London, 1981), pp.5, 6, 63.
[86] Cannadine, 'Present and the Past', p.162.

2 THE ECONOMY AND THE STATE

This chapter discusses macroeconomic accounts of the English industrial revolution which dominate recent economic history of the period. We ask: what are the major problems associated with this approach? What does it leave out and to what extent may economic change be underplayed by such analyses? We conclude that the current preoccupation with economic growth as the major indicator of radical change is misleading and that the time is ripe for a reconsideration and rehabilitation of those aspects of transformation which had only limited impact on the macroeconomic indicators. The second part of the chapter considers the influence on economic growth of the central state, traditionally seen as having a minimal role. If the full economic, social and political impact of state revenue raising and expenditure is considered, the door opens to a more radical interpretation of the contribution of the state to commercial and industrial advance.

The macroeconomic perspective

The last decade or so has produced new estimates of occupational structure, living standards, industrial output, GDP growth and productivity change. Together these indicate a more minimal picture of economic change in the industrial revolution than has ever emerged before. Productivity and industrial output were slow to grow, fixed capital proportions, saving and investment changed only gradually, workers' living standards and personal consumption remained largely unaffected before 1830 and were certainly not squeezed. The macroeconomic indicators of economic transformation were not present, apart from the marked shift of the working population out of agrarian occupations. The existence of any sort of industrial revolution is therefore placed in doubt.[1]

Macro estimates and macro interpretations

Hoffman in the 1950s and Deane and Cole in the 1960s were the first historians to attempt to measure the output of the British economy in the eighteenth and early nineteenth centuries. Hoffman's index of industrial output showed considerable growth in the classic industrial

[1] N. F. R. Crafts, *British Economic Growth During the Industrial Revolution* (Oxford, 1985); P. H. Lindert and J. G. Williamson, 'English Workers' Living Standards During the Industrial Revolution: A New Look', *Economic History Review* XXXVI (1983).

revolution period as did Deane and Cole although their figures showed that more rapid growth began as far back as the 1740s and that change was a gradual and cumulative process.[2] An early contribution to the current orthodoxy which minimises industrial output and productivity growth in the industrial revolution came from Harley in 1982.

He argued that Hoffman and Deane and Cole had overestimated growth in the period 1770–1815 and that Deane and Cole had relied too heavily on export figures and retained imports to calculate industrial output. His own more direct indicators, derived from growth in the use of industrial raw materials and from excise figures, suggested that the size of the early eighteenth-century industrial sector was bigger than Deane and Cole had thought and that subsequent growth was thus much less dramatic. At about the same time Wrigley and Schofield's demographic estimates, based on the analysis of more than 400 parish registers, indicated that the growth of population started earlier than Deane and Cole had supposed. This was important because population estimates are vital in assessing some sectoral outputs where direct information is unavailable.[3]

The next important step in the rewriting of England's industrial revolution came in Lindert and Williamson's revision of the structure of occupations and incomes in the eighteenth century. Previously Deane and Cole and others had relied on the contemporary social structure estimates of Gregory King (1688), Joseph Massie (1759) and Patrick Colquhoun (1801–3). Lindert and Williamson used burial records and wage data which suggested that King's estimates had been biased in favour of agriculture. This had important implications for the existing macro analyses by indicating that the extent of per capita growth of production in both manufacture and services had been overplayed.[4] Crafts has made the single biggest contribution to the macroeconomic revisionism by bringing together some of the new estimates, employing Lindert and Williamson's occupational distribution and adding his own estimates and 'guesstimates' of per capita and aggregate growth by sector. He suggests that per capita income growth was significantly lower throughout the century to 1830 than previously thought and he attributes this to very slow productivity growth especially in manufacturing. Total factor productivity growth (TFP) amounted only to 0.2% per annum for the period 1760–1801 and 0.4% for 1801–31. Even TFP for the entire economy, inflated in Craft's opinion by the performance of agriculture, grew very slowly: 0.2%

[2] W. G. Hoffman, *British Industry 1700–1950* (Oxford, 1955); P. Deane and W. A. Cole, *British Economic Growth 1688–1959* (Cambridge, 1969).

[3] C. K. Harley, 'British Industrialisation Before 1841: Evidence of Slower Growth During the Industrial Revolution', *Journal of Economic History* 42 (1982); E. A. Wrigley and R. S. Schofield, *The Population History of England 1541–1871* (London, 1981).

[4] P. H. Lindert and J. G. Williamson, 'Revising England's Social Tables', *Explorations in Economic History* 19 (1982).

1760–1801, 0.7% 1801–31, reaching 1.0% only in 1831–60. Growth
rates of real output in the economy as a whole did not reach 2% per
annum until the 1820s and a 3% rate was delayed until after 1830 (a
rate which Deane and Cole had supposed achieved as early as the
1780s). Seeing the industrial economy as remaining dominated by
traditional sectors and backward production methods, Crafts argued
that one small atypical sector – cotton – probably accounted for half of
all productivity change in manufacturing. It was a modern sector
floating in a sea of tradition: 'not only was the triumph of ingenuity
slow to come to fruition but it does not seem appropriate to regard
innovativeness as pervasive'.[5]

Table 2.1: Crafts' estimates of national product growth compared with
those of Deane and Cole (% per year)

	Present Estimates		Deane and Cole's Estimates	
	National Product	National Product per Head	National Product	National Product per Head
1700–60	0.69	0.31	0.66	0.45
1760–80	0.70	0.01	0.65	−0.04
1780–1801	1.32	0.35	2.06	1.08
1801–31	1.97	0.52	3.06	1.61

Source: N.F.R. Crafts, *British Economic Growth during the Industrial
Revolution* (Oxford, 1985), p.45.

Because Crafts finds no evidence of marked discontinuity in growth
indicators he draws the conclusion that innovative activity was limited.
The major constraint on the growth of the economy came from the
supply-side problem that Britain lacked sufficient high-return investment opportunities. This made productivity advance too uneven and
the unmodernised sector remained a drag on the economy. Floud
reviewed Craft's argument thus:

> Britain underwent the pain of structural change but without the
> reward of rapid income growth... Technical change came slowly
> and patchily, with spectacular changes in textiles disguising the
> backwardness of many other sectors. Thus although an extra-
> ordinary proportion of workers entered industry, Britain did not
> get as much from them as it should have done... Britain therefore
> emerged from the Industrial Revolution only half heartedly
> transformed. Once set on this path and committed to the staple
> industries of cotton, coal, iron and steel, it found either an
> increase in speed or a change in direction difficult to achieve.

[5] Crafts, *British Economic Growth*, pp.31, 81, 84, 85, 87.

Britain sensibly pursued its comparative advantage in these industries and in foreign investment, but became locked into them, unable to adapt to the new demands of the world economy after the First World War.[6]

Looking back from the perspective of the economic problems of the 1970s and 1980s it is clear that Crafts' analysis is partly a search for the roots of current difficulties. It yields interesting arguments about the relative retardation of the British economy in the late nineteenth century and the unemployment of the interwar period. But it is difficult to sustain that idea that the economy got so little out of its early generations of industrial workers or that it contained such a dead-weight backward sector at that time. We return to these points on pp.45–51.

Williamson has also contributed to the revisionist view of the industrial revolution by reanalysing the new macro estimates. He employs a neo-classical equilibrium model to assess sector shares, the nature of factor markets and the obstacles to growth. He argues that the high level of growth and productivity assigned to agriculture by Crafts would have caused deindustrialisation. More importantly, his model suggests that it was a failure of the labour and capital markets in the industrial revolution period which really slowed down British industrialisation. To demonstrate the absence of integrated labour markets he uses evidence of urban/rural wage differences. The real wage gaps between regions which Williamson computes are relatively small but the impact of labour market imperfection was magnified by associated employment, distribution and accumulation effects which when introduced to his equation suggest that labour market failure may have lost the economy 3% of GNP particularly in the 1830s and 1840s.[7]

The failure of the capital market was even more pronounced, according to Williamson, especially during the Napoleonic Wars. His major thesis is that wartime investment both in the 1770s and between 1790 and 1815 crowded out civilian accumulation, inhibited growth and contributed to poor working-class living standards. The mobilisation of the war period and the impact of distorted prices also played an important part, but when these are eliminated from the general equilibrium model the overriding influence of crowding out is exposed. In the early decades of the nineteenth century Williamson estimates that the crowding out effect was enough to lose more that 8% of GNP. Thus for Williamson the problem of slow growth was not one of

[6] R. Floud, 'Slow to Grow', Times Literary Supplement 19 July 1985, p.794.
[7] J. G. Williamson, 'Why was British Economic Growth so Slow During the Industrial Revolution?', Journal of Economic History 44 (1984); Williamson, 'Debating the Industrial Revolution', Explorations in Economic History 24 (1987); Williamson, 'Did English Factor Markets Fail During the Industrial Revolution?', Oxford Economic Papers 39 (1987).

supply-side constraints (as Crafts suggests) but of low capital formation and little change in the capital/labour ratio. The implication was that those increases which did occur in production and productivity arose more from ingenuity than abstention: from innovations and improvements in existing techniques and processes rather than from injections of capital. Thus, unlike Crafts, Williamson sees the period as one of widespread change and innovation even if the spread and impact of these changes was limited because of the diversion of capital to debt issues and because of localised labour shortages.[8]

Method and measurement
Current macro analyses depend upon national income accounting as a method of measuring economic activity. This has its critics when applied to modern economies, but it is inevitably more problematic when applied to earlier and less developed economies.[9] The national accounting framework is least appropriate where there is a low degree of occupational specialisation and considerable non-market interaction. In these circumstances, much activity is unrecorded and incapable of being captured in a single index of growth. Furthermore, in a period of fundamental change, the use of the national income accounting framework to capture growth may be less appropriate than at other times because of shifts in the proportion of total industrial and commercial activity showing up in the estimates. If, as seems likely, entry thresholds in most industries were very low, industrial expansion might take place first and foremost amongst the myriad of small firms which have left few records and whose contribution is lost to the historian who confines herself to easily available indices. In addition, periods of fundamental change are likely to incorporate technological shifts and innovations whilst the national accounts framework measures only the replication of goods and services. It cannot incorporate easily the appearance of new goods not present at the start of the time series nor improvements over time in the quality of goods, services or labour. New products distort efforts at national accounting particularly because they usually have very high prices at first which then decline rapidly as innovation proceeds. Finally, the national accounts framework cannot measure that technical change in the means of production which, by shortening hours or improving work conditions, is a necessary prerequisite to the enjoyment of economic growth. If the most sensible way to view the course of economic growth is through a comprehension of the timing and impact of innovation then, as Usher has argued,

[8] ibid.
[9] See G. R. Hawke, *Economics for Historians* ch.2; J. Hoppit, 'Counting the Industrial Revolution', *Economic History Review* XLIII (1990); D. Usher, *The Measurement of Economic Growth*, (Oxford, 1980).

it is at least arguable that the introduction of national accounting categories into the study of economic history and economic development, with the inevitable emphasis on saving and capital formation and the tendency to underemphasise science, economic organisation, new products and processes, and other aspects of economic life that have no independent place in the accounting categories, has on balance distorted our perception of economic history and misdirected policy to promote economic growth.[10]

The national income accounting approach is also fraught with measurement difficulties for this period simply because of the unreliability of data. Industrial output and GDP growth are necessarily based on the assessment of the growth of aggregates from the weighted averages of their components. The difficulties of assigning weights to industrial and other sectors of the economy, allowing for changes in weights over time and for the effects of differential price changes and value-added changes in the final product, are insurmountable. The relevant statistics are scarce or unreliable and always involve wide margins of error. These in turn become magnified in residual calculations like that of productivity growth. Jackson has argued, for example, that if the government sector is given the more realistic weight of 12% of GDP rather than the 8% which Crafts assigns to it (post 1760) this alone would double Crafts' estimate of the per capita GDP growth rate for the period 1760–1800.[11]

At the root of these problems concerning the composition and hence measurement of sectoral growth are the social and occupational tables of Lindert and Williamson upon which Crafts and others rely in their calculation of sectoral weights. These may well be more reliable than the earlier estimates of King, Massie and Colquhoun, but Lindert himself has cautioned that for the large occupational groupings of agriculture, commerce, and manufacturing, error margins could be as high as 60%.[12] Before the first tolerable indication of occupations in the Census of 1831, the sources, particularly parish registers, which historians use for occupational data are full of pitfalls. Most importantly, it is impossible to allow for composite occupations and multiple means of getting a living as these do not show up in the sources. Yet

---

[10] Usher, *Measurement*, p.10.
[11] R. V. Jackson, 'Government Expenditure and British Economic Growth in the Eighteenth Century: Some Problems of Measurement', *Economic History Review* XLIII (1990). A fuller critique of Crafts and Harley by Jackson and his alternative output and productivity results appear in *Economic History Review* XLV (1992).
[12] P. H. Lindert, 'English Occupations 1670–1811', *Journal of Economic History* 40 (1980), p.701. Their figures for agriculture and for certain categories in the service sector certainly give rise to concern as they contradict all indications available from contemporary qualitative evidence (Hoppit, 'Counting'). King and Massie did not separate agriculture from industry in their tables because they were concerned with social hierarchy rather than economic sectors.

they proliferated in the eighteenth century (and long after) and frustrate all efforts to categorise people neatly into sectoral groups. Lindert and Williamson rely on male burial records for occupational descriptions. This immediately underestimates those occupations carried out by younger males and poses problems where common 'occupations' like 'labourer' or 'gentleman' are not specifically attributable to a sector. More seriously, burial registers rarely record occupations for women and children despite their major contribution to all sectors of the eighteenth and early nineteenth-century economy and their predominance in many manufacturing and service occupations. This leads to gross underestimation of activity particularly in many proto-industrial occupations. Growth in multiple, part-time employments also adds to the problem of assigning occupations to agriculture or to industry before the mid nineteenth century. Yet this is a foundation of sectoral assessments in national income estimation. Sectoral indices and weights present further problems because they rely on broad occupational distributions (however accurate these may be) and are therefore more influenced by labour intensive than by capital intensive sectors.

Sources
Compounding the problems of macro estimates of the structure and functioning of the economy before the mid nineteenth century is the shaky nature of the output data currently available.[13] Crafts' estimates of industrial output are based on a sample of industries (see table 2.2) which omits many vital and growing manufactures such as pottery, glass, lead, distilling, brass, chemicals, furniture, coopering and coachmaking. In addition Crafts omits any direct assessment of a broad range of new and/or rapidly innovating industries including chemicals and engineering, food processing and metalworking and a

Table 2.2: Growth of real output in industrial sectors: Crafts' sample results (% per year)

	Cotton	Wool	Linen	Silk	Building	Iron	Copper	Beer	Leather	Soap	Candles	Coal	Paper
1700-60	1.37	0.97	1.25	0.67	0.74	0.60	2.62	0.21	0.25	0.28	0.49	0.64	1.51
1760-70	4.59	1.30	2.68	3.40	0.34	1.65	5.61	-0.10	-0.10	0.62	0.71	2.19	2.09
1770-80	6.20		3.42	-0.03	4.24	4.47	2.40	1.10	0.82	1.32	1.15	2.48	0.00
1780-90	12.76	0.54	-0.34	1.13	3.22	3.79	4.14	0.82	0.95	1.34	0.43	2.36	5.62
1790-1801	6.73		0.00	-0.67	2.01	6.48	-0.85	1.54	0.63	2.19	2.19	3.21	1.02
1801-11	4.49	1.64	1.07	1.65	2.05	7.45	-0.88	0.79	2.13	2.63	1.34	2.53	3.34
1811-21	5.59		3.40	6.04	3.61	-0.28	3.22	-0.47	-0.94	2.42	1.80	2.76	1.73
1821-31	6.82	2.03	3.03	6.08	3.14	6.47	3.43	0.66	1.15	2.41	2.27	3.68	2.21

Source: N.F.R. Crafts, *British Economic Growth during the Industrial Revolution* (Oxford, 1985), p.23.
(For the difficulties and potential pitfalls in making there estimates see Crafts, *British Economic Growth*, source notes for tables 2.3 and 2.4 and chapter 2.)

13 Hoppit, 'Counting'.

range of intermediate products. He may thus underestimate the role of innovativeness and change in his calculations of industrial performance.

Customs and excise figures used as evidence of production growth in cotton, linen, silk, beer, leather, soap, candles and paper are probably insufficiently reliable to support the edifice which Crafts erects upon them. Smuggling, evasion and corruption of officials were common. For other sectors, including coal, wool textiles, construction, iron and copper, Crafts builds up national estimates of output from separate industry studies many of which are partial and unrepresentative. In the case of coal output, Crafts' compound rate of growth in the first half of the eighteenth century is only half that of Flinn's and falls short of Flinn's by between 14% and 24% for the period 1750–1815. The root of such differences lies in the quality and representativeness of surviving and published data used as a basis for estimation.[14]

No sectoral or growth rate estimate by Crafts has caused so much controversy as that for agriculture. There is no direct evidence of output so historians must rely on inferences from population growth, agricultural incomes, and price and income elasticities of demand for agricultural goods. But our information on almost all of these is very shaky. Calculation of the size and nature of the service sector gives rise to similar problems with little direct evidence on its most innovating elements: transport, communications, financial services, retail and wholesale trading, the professions outside law, leisure and religion. Rubinstein's data on the generation of middle-class incomes and on wealth holding indicates that trade and finance had become the most profitable and dynamic growth sectors of the economy by the 1830s.[15] Yet the current consensus is dominated by the view that the tertiary (service) sector before the mid century grew at best no faster than manufacturing and that its dynamism was dragged down by the big employment and low productivity of domestic service.

In the calculation of national income it is vital not only to assign correct weights to specific industries and sectors, and to generate reliable output series, but also to use price information to calculate value added in each industry and sector. However, price data for the eighteenth century are scarce and estimates are based on indirect and very partial indicators with little possibility of allowing for major regional and local variations.

Having outlined why we are concerned about the reliability of the measures of output and growth derived from recent macro-accounting work, we can now say that, even if accurate measurement were possible, national output and factor productivity growth may not be

---

[14] *ibid.* and J. Hoppit, 'Understanding the Industrial Revolution', *Historical Journal* 30 (1987).
[15] W. D. Rubinstein, *Men of Property: The Very Wealthy in Britain since the Industrial Revolution* (London, 1981).

particularly good indicators of the sort of radical transition which lies at the heart of popular understanding of the industrial revolution. A clue to this is a recent statistical analysis of the industrial output series for Britain, Italy, Hungary, Germany, France, Russia and Austria which shows that Britain and Hungary were the only countries to exhibit a prolonged period of increase of trend growth in industrial production during the process of industrialisation. Although these increases were unspectacular, this is a remarkable finding in the light of qualitative evidence of the extent and speed of transformation in Germany and Russia in particular. It suggests that either the current macro estimates are so inaccurate to be worthless for this purpose and/ or that changes in the trend rates of growth at national level are not particularly helpful as a starting point for understanding economic transformation.[16]

Identifying the industrial revolution

Current aggregative studies have an inbuilt problem of identification in posing questions about the existence of an industrial revolution. As Mokyr has pointed out in the British case:

> Some industries which grew slowly were mechanising and switching to factories (e.g. paper after 1801, wool and chemicals like soap and candles) while construction and coal mining in which manual techniques ruled supreme with few exceptions until deep in the nineteenth century, grew at respectable rates.[17]

Clearly technical progress is not growth, and rapid growth does not everywhere imply the revolutionising of production functions. Industrial revolution and growth are not interchangeable terms and an industrial revolution is unlikely to be reflected in the short or even medium term by huge rises in productivity – a fact illustrated by the current wave of computer innovation. The industrial revolution is not a phenomenon which can be identified and measured solely or even primarily in a quantitative way, even if we restrict the concept to the history of industrial growth. As Landes argued some two decades ago:

> ...numbers merely describe the surface of the society – and even then in terms that define away change by using categories of

---

[16] N. F. R. Crafts, S. J. Leybourne and T. C. Mills, 'Economic Growth in Nineteenth-Century Britain: Some Comparisons with Europe in the Context of Gerschenkron's Hypothesis' *Warwick Economic Research Papers* 308 (1988). See also Crafts, Leybourne, and Mills, 'Trends and Cycles in British Industrial Production 1700–1913', *Journal of the Royal Statistical Society* 152 (1989), which suggests that, when cyclical influences are removed from the series, the trend rate of growth of industrial production in Britain was markedly more rapid between 1780 and 1830 than before or after.

[17] J. Mokyr, 'Has the Industrial Revolution Been Crowded Out?', *Explorations in Economic History* 24 (1987) p.314.

unchanging nomenclature. Beneath this surface, the vital organs were transformed; and although they weighed but a fraction of the total – whether measured by people or wealth – it was they that determined the metabolism of the entire system.[18]

With this in mind it is appropriate to examine the model of industrialisation which underpins the work of much macroeconomic theorising.

The slow-growth revisionist interpretations of the economic history of the period stress the divide between the traditional and the modern sectors, seeing the overriding size and primitive state of the former as a drag on the economy.[19] But the growing up process within the two sector model would (other things being held constant) have a contradictory effect on national accounting measures of the progress of industrialisation. The process would be faster the more backward and poor the industrialising country or region, even though the larger the traditional industrial sector, the longer the trajectory that an economy has to travel.[20]

In addition, clear-cut divisions between traditional and modern are impossible to maintain. Separate organisational forms, technologies, locations or even firms can rarely be ascribed to either. Eighteenth and early nineteenth-century cotton manufacturers serving domestic as well as foreign markets typically combined steam-powered spinning in factories with large-scale employment of domestic handloom weavers and often retained this mix long after the powered technology had become available. This was a function of risk spreading, the problems of early technology and the cheap labour supply particularly of women and children. Thus for many decades the modern sector was actually bolstered by and derivative of the traditional sector and not the reverse.[21] Artisans in the metalworking sectors of Birmingham and Sheffield frequently combined or changed occupations in such a way that they could be classified in both the traditional and modern camps. Artisan woollen workers in West Yorkshire clubbed together to build

[18] D. S. Landes, *The Unbound Prometheus: Technological Change and Industrial Development in Western Europe 1750 to the Present* (Cambridge, 1969), p.122.
[19] Crafts sees the major divide as that between high-productivity factory, mechanised industry along with agriculture on the one hand and a widespread industrial and service backwater on the other. A hallmark of the distinction between the two sectors is the divide between (internationally) tradeable products and non-tradeables. This section and the next draw heavily on Maxine Berg's work.
[20] J. Mokyr, 'The Industrial Revolution and the New Economic History', in Mokyr, ed., *The Economics of the Industrial Revolution* (London, 1985), p.5.
[21] See for example J. S. Lyons, 'Vertical Integration in the British Cotton Industry 1825–1850: A Revision', *Journal of Economic History* 45 (1985); M. Berg, 'Commerce and Creativity in Eighteenth-Century Birmingham', in Berg, ed., *Markets and Manufacture in Early Industrial Europe*; P. Hudson, *The Genesis of Industrial Capital* (Cambridge; 1986), ch. 2; P. Mantoux, *The Industrial Revolution in the Eighteenth Century* (London, 1928).

mills for certain processes and thus had a foot in both sectors. These so-called 'company mills' bolstered the success of the artisan structure.[22] Thus the traditional and the modern were most often inseparable and mutually reinforcing. Firms primarily concerned with metalworking diversified into metal-processing ventures as a way of generating steady raw material supplies. And manufacturers extended directly into marketing, especially during the Napoleonic Wars, to secure their returns.[23] Such cases of vertical integration provide further examples of the tail of 'tradition' wagging the dog of 'modernity'.

The revisionists argue that most industrial labour was to be found in sectors which experienced little change, such as the food and drink trades, shoemaking, tailoring, blacksmithing and trades catering for luxury consumption. But these supplied essential services on which town life, urban growth and hence much of centralised industry was ultimately dependent. Furthermore, early industrial capital formation and enterprise typically combined activity in the food and drink or agricultural processing trades with more obviously industrial activities, thus creating innumerable external economies.[24] This was true in textiles and in metal manufacture in Birmingham and Sheffield where innkeepers and victuallers were commonly mortgagees and joint owners of metal-working enterprises.[25] Such manufacturers also maintained joint occupations in the food and drink trades. In the south Lancashire tool trades Peter Stubs was not untypical. He first appears in 1788 as a tenant of the White Bear Inn in Warrington where he combined the activity of innkeeper, maltster and brewer with that of filemaker using barm bottoms (barrel dregs) to harden his blades.[26] There are many examples of this overlap between services, agriculture and industry which generated externalities and created the potential for increase in productive efficiency. These innovations get lost in the macro indicators.

Much of the macro work suffers from a narrow definition of technical innovation concentrating too much on machinery rather than processes. Product and process innovation, market creativity and organisational change get little attention. Neither do changing hand

[22] Hudson, *Genesis*, pp.70–80; Hudson, 'From Manor to Mill: The West Riding in Transition', in M. Berg, P. Hudson and M. Sonenscher, eds., *Manufacture in Town and Country Before the Factory* (Cambridge, 1983).
[23] H. Heaton, *The Yorkshire Woollen and Worsted Industries* (2nd edn. Oxford, 1965); H. Hamilton, *The English Brass and Copper Industries to 1800* (London, 1926); A. H. John, *The Industrial Development of South Wales 1750–1850* (London, 1950); S. Chapman, *The Rise of Merchant Banking* (London, 1984), ch.1.
[24] E. L. Jones, 'Environment, Agriculture and Industrialisation', *Agricultural History* LI (1977); P. Mathias, 'Agriculture and the Brewing and Distilling Industries in the Eighteenth Century', *Economic History Review* v (1952).
[25] Berg, 'Commerce and Creativity'.
[26] T. S. Ashton, *An Eighteenth-Century Industrialist: Peter Stubs of Warrington 1756–1806* (Manchester, 1939), pp.4–5.

tools, skills, dexterity and the knacks and work practices of manufacturing. Many of these would have had a delayed effect on aggregate productivity measures and taken separately only a modest effect. Cumulatively, however, they were as vital to the industrial revolution as the coming of factory production. Indeed, the latter was often dependent on them. The non-factory, non-tradeable and supposedly stagnant sector also experienced extensive technical and organisational change. Early textile innovations: carding and scribbling machinery, the dutch loom, the knitting frame, the flying shuttle and the Jenny, silk-throwing machinery and finishing techniques, especially in bleaching and calico printing, were all developed within rural manufacture and artisan industry. In the metal trades the stamp, press, drawbench and lathe were developed to innumerable specifications and uses, and new malleable alloys, gilting processes, plating and japanning were at least as important. Other 'traditional' industries experienced some form of transformation in materials or division of labour, if not in the artefacts of technological change. In the traditional textile industries there were many important product changes. The move from heavy serges to mixed stuffs, for example, considerably reduced finishing time, for many of these needed no fulling and were dyed in the wool rather than printed or vat dyed. And the success of the calico-printing industry in the later eighteenth century hinged not on new machinery or materials but on a cheap workforce prepared to carry out labour-intensive processes on a new scale and under new organisation and discipline in a competitive setting.[27]

New forms of putting out, wholesaling, retailing, credit and debt and artisan co-operation were devised as ways of retaining the essentials of older structures in the face of this new environment. Greater division of labour occurred in household manufacture, middle men were cut out, more work was done to order rather than for the open market, more women and children were employed on low wages, and the paying of wages was delayed or made in truck or kind rather than cash. Customary practices evolved to combat the needs of a more dynamic and market-oriented environment. The service sector employed more people and became more efficient, transactions costs declined and the turnover time of capital was speeded up. The result was considerable transformation even within the so-called traditional sector.[28]

Productivity and innovation
Productivity change is much discussed in connection with the industrial revolution but it is seldom broken down into its constituent elements.

[27] M. Berg, 'Women's Work, Mechanisation and the Early Phases of Industrialisation in England', in P. Joyce, ed., *The Historical Meaning of Work*; Berg, *The Age of Manufactures* (London, 1984).
[28] Mantoux, *Industrial Revolution*; Berg, *Age of Manufactures*; Hudson, *Genesis*; R. Samuel, 'The Workshop of the World', *History Workshop Journal* 3 (1977).

Productivity can be increased in at least five ways: by deployment of labour from lower to higher productivity sectors, by intra-sectoral shifts (often resulting from technological change), by changing participation rates, by capital investment, and by significant reductions in transactions inefficiencies and costs. We have plenty of evidence that all these were occurring in the industrial revolution period but their full impact on productivity is impossible to measure and was likely in any case to be less important in the short term than the long.

Total factor productivity (TFP) is the measure used by Crafts and others to conclude that productivity was slow to grow. It is usually calculated as a residual after the rate of growth of factor inputs have been subtracted from the rate of growth of GDP. There are several major problems with TFP measurement. First, as a residual calculation, it is subject to the magnified errors of any misestimations of sectoral outputs and factor inputs. Secondly, if factor reallocation from sectors with low marginal productivities to those with high ones was an important aspect of the period, it will not be possible to derive economy-wide rates of TFP growth simply by taking a weighted average across sectors. The factor reallocation effects must be added on and accurately incorporated in changing sectoral weights.[29]

Thirdly TFP embodies a number of restrictive assumptions: perfect mobility, perfect competition, neutral technical progress, no increasing returns and parametric prices. These conditions do not approximate to the reality of the eighteenth-century economy.[30] The assumption of neutral technical progress is suspect in the face of *long-term* empirical evidence of labour-saving technical change. And during the industrial revolution itself there may well have been a bias towards labour-intensive technical change. After all, if the key to the industrialisation process (in England at least) was the transference of labour into industry, then (assuming a relatively elastic labour supply) labour-intensive technical change may be more advantageous than labour-saving change although its potential impact on productivity would be less. Assumptions of constant returns to scale also conflict with evidence of increasing returns in many industries which necessitate adjustments in TFP calculations to allow for imperfect competition and changing elasticities of product demand and factor inputs.[31] In particular, those assumptions which imply that there were no under-utilised resources are misleading. Many industrial sectors experienced flooded labour markets particularly for the less skilled trades. These

[29] Williamson, 'Debating', p.270; Mokyr, 'Has the Industrial Revolution Been Crowded Out?', pp.305–12.
[30] For discussion of TFP see A. N. Link, *Technological Change and Productivity Growth* (London, 1987).
[31] B. Eichengreen, 'What Have We Learnt from Historical Comparisons of Income and Productivity?', *Ninth Congress of the International Economic History Association* (Berne, 1986), pp.26–36; Link, *Technological Change*, p.14.

were matched by massive immobile pools of agricultural labour in many southern and midland counties. Structural unemployment was endemic and chronic underutilisation of both labour and capital was aggravated by seasonal and cyclical swings.[32]

TFP takes no account of innovation in the nature of inputs or outputs; yet we know that both were marked features of the period. Labour input, for example, needs to be adjusted for changes in age, sex, education, skill and intensity of work. Output per worker is also a function of the relative power of employers to extract work effort and of the power of employees to withhold it.[33] Similarly, inputs were changing constantly in the period as product innovation affected the nature of raw materials and intermediate goods as well as final products. In the wool textile sector, for example, important innovations occurred with the introduction of cotton warps from the 1820s and with the use of cheaper imported wools and increasing amounts of recycled wool.[34]

The impact of innovation on productivity is conditioned by many things including rapidly altering macro economic circumstances and slowly changing institutional and cultural settings.[35] The problems of measurement of economy-wide productivity change as well as the disquiet in regarding such a measure as reflective of the extent of fundamental economic change are illustrated when one considers the nature of both industrial capital and industrial labour in the period. Massive redeployment from agrarian-based and domestic sectors to urban and more centralised manufacturing together with the widespread substitution of female and child labour for that of adult males may well have been accompanied by diminishing labour productivity in the short run. Green labour had to learn industrial skills as well as new forms of discipline and, within sectors, labour shifted into processes which were more rather than less labour intensive. The same tendency to low returns in the short term can be seen with capital investment. Early steam engines and machinery were imperfect and subject to breakdowns and rapid obsolescence. Gross capital investment figures (which include funds spent on renewals and replacements), when fed into productivity measures, are not a good reflection

---

[32] B. Eichengreen, 'The Causes of British Business Cycles 1833–1913' *Journal of European Economic History* 12 (1983); R. C. Allen, *Enclosure and the Yeoman* (Oxford, forthcoming), ch.12; E. H. Hunt, "Industrialisation and Regional Inequality: Wages in Britain 1760–1914', *Journal of Economic History* 46 (1986).

[33] Link, *Technological Change*, p.24; Eichengreen, 'What Have We Learnt?', pp.29–30; R. Elbaum and W. Lazonick, 'An Institutional Perspective on British Decline' in Elbaum and Lazonick, eds., *The Decline of the British Economy* (Oxford, 1986); W. Lazonick, 'Social Organisation and Productivity Growth in Britain and the US 1820–1913', *Ninth Congress of the International Economic History Association* (Berne, 1986).

[34] Hudson, *Genesis*, ch.6.

[35] See P. A. David, 'Computer and Dynamo: The Modern Productivity Paradox in the Not Too Distant Mirror', *Warwick Economic Research Paper* 339 (1989).

of the importance and potential of technological change in the period. Shifts in the aggregate measures of productivity growth are thus actually less likely to show up as significant during a time of rapid and fundamental economic transition than in times of slower and more piecemeal adjustment. This point was stressed by Hicks who suggested that the long gestation period of technological innovation might yield Ricardo's machinery effect: the returns from major shifts in technology would not be apparent for several decades and in the short term innovation would only increase unemployment and put downward pressure on wages.[36]

If patenting can be taken as a rough indication of inventive activity then we do have some evidence that the growth of TFP in the period 1760–1830 probably took place some 40 years after the acceleration of patents and patentable invention.[37] There is a similar disjuncture between the wave of innovations surrounding the electric dynamo in the late nineteenth century and the accelerating growth of GNP. And the current computer revolution which is transforming production, services and working lives across a broad front is not being accompanied by rapidly rising income, output or productivity within national economies. Resolving the apparent 'productivity paradox' involves recognising the limited nature of TFP as a measure of radical change and the long-time frame needed to connect fundamental technological and organisational innovation with productivity growth. Conventional productivity measures suggest that expenditure on computers during the 1980s has been misallocated. But are such measures failing to capture the contributions to economic welfare that can properly be attributed to the new technology and should we expect a surge in productivity so soon?[38]

The same difficulties occur in identifying the industrial revolution solely in terms of the immediate impact of change on macro-economic indicators. Just as it is possible to have growth with little change, it is possible to have change with little growth. In fact the more revolutionary the change technologically, socially and culturally the longer this may take to work out in terms of conventional measures of economic performance.

The state

The conventional view is that minimum state involvement and *laissez-*

[36] J. R. Hicks, *A Theory of Economic History* (Oxford, 1969), p.153; cf. M. Berg, *The Machinery Question and the Making of Political Economy* (Cambridge, 1980), ch.4.
[37] R. Sullivan, 'England's "Age of Invention": The Acceleration of Patents and Patentable Inventions During the Industrial Revolution', *Explorations in Economic History* 26 (1989); cf. C. MacCleod, *Inventing the Industrial Revolution* (Cambridge, 1988).
[38] David, 'Computer and Dynamo'.

faire produced a fertile environment for economic change in Britain. The British liberal tradition has always emphasised the importance for the economy and society of avoiding absolutism on the continental pattern, and this view continues to be fashionable in the present political climate with the dismantling of public ownership. By stressing the importance of *laissez-faire* in the past the state intervention that characterised British politics between 1945 and 1979 can appear like a temporary diversion from tradition.[39]

But in the eighteenth century Britain became a major military power, acquiring an extensive empire and dominating many branches of world trade. This was made possible by the emergence of a new kind of British state with a fully reorganised fiscal and military apparatus, heavy taxation, and a professional bureaucracy. The state and its activities came to affect civilians in every walk of life: it became the largest single actor in the economy with state expenditure rising well above the level of domestic capital formation. Short-term borrowing by the state and the conduct of war were responsible for virtually all of the financial crises and trade slumps of the century. Taxes rose to levels higher than elsewhere in Europe with the possible exception of Holland. As has recently been pointed out, 'This was no minor adjustment in the scope and priorities of government; it was a major commitment of resources'. The emergence of the 'fiscal-military state' marked a most important transformation in English government.[40]

The two different views of the role of the state, *laissez-faire* and interventionist, can be reconciled to the extent that increased state activity in the eighteenth century was almost all directed at external policy. Internally the maintenance of order and justice, and much economic and social regulation, were devolved locally and the power of the state was diluted by a patronage system which provided income and office for members of the landed classes. Internal economic regulations also declined. So the liberal interpretation is not incompatible with domestic policy. But military expansionism overseas was a different matter: the fiscal and borrowing implications had a major effect on the internal economy and on social and political life. The economic activities of the state were sufficient to create an important redistribution of income, to stimulate industrial and other sectors of the economy and to support institutions, such as those of the London money market, which were of long-term significance to the economy as a whole.[41]

Central government revenue

Between 1660 and 1815 the prosecution of war was largely responsible

[39] See discussion of this in J. Brewer, *The Sinews of Power* (London, 1989), Introduction.
[40] Brewer, *Sinews*, p.xvii.
[41] *ibid.*; see also P. K. O'Brien, 'The Political Economy of British Taxation 1660–1815', *Economic History Review* XLV (1988).

for an eighteen-fold increase in taxes in real terms. The share of national income appropriated in taxation rose from around 9% at the beginning of the eighteenth century to more than 18% by 1815, with most of the increase occurring from the American revolt onwards.[42] The bulk of wartime revenue needs was, however, raised on the London capital market and came principally from the Dutch and later from metropolitan and southern English investors. The role of the Bank of England and the close collaboration between the treasury and leading London financiers meant that, even in years when credit was tight, the government could raise funds. In peacetime, interest payments on the national debt which had accumulated from wartime deficit financing absorbed 40–50% of government revenue. Thus the bulk of tax revenue was trasferred to government stockholders. Debts had to be regularly serviced to maintain confidence in the credit of the state and specific taxes came to be earmarked to underpin specific stock issues. The capacity of the government to raise taxes was thus the foundation stone of the national debt and all that arose from it.[43]

It is important to examine this capacity as it set England aside from her contemporaries. The English tax burden far exceeded that borne much more reluctantly in other countries, particularly France.[44] Rising national income must have facilitated the peaceful acceptance of high taxation, but taxation rose three or four times faster than national income. Parliamentary consent lent legitimacy to government impositions and the formation of lobbies helped to limit the role of the state and rendered its institutions more public and accountable. The English system also looked fairer than those elsewhere because it did not have inequality built into its legal structure: administration was centralised and there were no legal exemptions for individuals. Rising taxation was also collected and administered with increasing efficiency as the system of farming was replaced by a predominantly professional body of state officials. This innovative efficiency was particularly marked in the excise administration. And the job of officials was helped by the existence of the commercial, transport and credit infrastructure of the relatively advanced economy.[45] Finally, the acceptance of the fiscal operations of the state was eased by the fact that taxation was indirect rather than direct. By 'an expedient tolerance of evasion and a prudent selection of the commodities and social groups "picked upon" to bear the mounting exactions of the state... rising taxation... [was made]... tolerable and politically manageable.'[46]

[42] O'Brien, 'Political Economy', p.3.
[43] O'Brien 'Political Economy', *passim*.
[44] P. Mathias and P. K. O'Brien, 'Taxation in England and France 1715–1810', *Journal of European Economic History* 5 (1976); Brewer, *Sinews*, p.91. French taxation was twice as high as English as a proportion of national income per capita.
[45] O'Brien, 'Political Economy'; Brewer, *Sinews*, pp.182, 189.
[46] O'Brien, 'Political Economy', p.6.

In assessing the role of state finance in economic growth it is important to ask who bore the brunt of increased state revenues. Direct taxes (largely the land tax) declined on trend as a proportion of revenue during the eighteenth century from over 40% to around 20% of the total, but rose again with the introduction of income tax from the 1790s reaching around 34% by 1810. Customs revenues (taxes on international trade, chiefly imports) followed the same trajectory, accounting for less than a third of revenue throughout the period and falling as low as a fifth during the middle decades of the century. It was the excise (duties on domestically produced commodities and services) which did most to sustain the increased tax burden of the eighteenth century, rising from a quarter of revenue to over a half between the 1730s and 1790 (see table 2.3).

Table 2.3: Sources of tax revenues in the eighteenth century

5 year averages centering on	Excises and stamps levied on domestic productions and services		Customs duties levied on retained imports		Direct taxes levied on manifestations of wealth and income	
	£m	%	£m	%	£m	%
1680	0.4	28	0.5	36	0.5	36
1685	0.4	36	0.6	55	0.1	9
1690	0.9	30	0.7	23	1.4	47
1695	0.8	27	0.8	27	1.4	47
1700	1.7	35	1.2	25	1.9	40
1705	1.8	34	1.5	28	2.0	38
1710	1.9	36	1.3	25	2.1	40
1715	2.4	44	1.5	28	1.5	28
1720	2.8	46	1.7	28	1.6	26
1725	3.1	53	1.6	27	1.2	20
1730	3.0	49	1.6	26	1.5	25
1735	3.2	55	1.6	28	1.0	17
1740	3.2	52	1.5	24	1.5	24
1745	3.1	48	1.3	20	2.1	32
1750	3.5	51	1.4	20	2.0	29
1755	3.8	54	1.7	24	1.5	21
1760	4.1	49	1.9	23	2.3	28
1765	5.5	55	2.2	22	2.3	23
1770	6.0	57	2.6	25	1.9	18
1775	6.3	58	2.6	24	1.9	18
1780	6.6	56	2.6	22	2.6	22
1785	7.8	57	3.3	24	2.7	20
1790	7.5	43	6.3	36	3.6	21
1795	8.9	44	7.2	36	4.0	20
1800	11.5	36	11.5	36	8.8	28
1805	19.4	41	16.4	35	11.2	24
1810	22.9	36	18.8	30	21.2	34

Source: P.K. O'Brien, 'The Political Economy of British Taxation 1660–1815,' *Economic History Review* XLI (1988).

There was no effective tax on wealth holders throughout the period. The Land Tax remained unrevised and bore lightest on those regions of the country (the north and west) where land values were increasing. Aristocracy and gentry resisted the revaluation of the land tax and the introduction of an income tax. They were also able in many regions to pass on the burden of the land tax to their tenant farmers and through them to farm labourers. Landowners and aristocrats as a whole paid a declining proportion of national taxation during most of the eighteenth century despite attempts to tax houses, windows and later riding horses, carriages, male servants and even dogs and hair powder! Not until the Napoleonic Wars when income tax joined the land tax (and then just until its repeal in 1816) did the upper classes make the sort of tax contribution that they had in the late seventeenth century.[47]

Those who made their fortunes in the expansion of shipping, the colonial and re-export trades, shipbuilding, and the servicing of international trade through banking and insurance also escaped lightly:

> From all the flourishing and visibly expanding activities of the City, Bristol, Liverpool, Glasgow and other ports, the state recouped (in the form of customs duties) only a fraction of the increasingly effective and expensive protection that British multinational enterprise received from the Royal Navy.[48]

There were of course difficulties in taxing this source of rising wealth through customs, not just because of the ease of evasion and the increased incentive for smuggling but because tariff policy was never merely a device for revenue raising. It had to be compatible with a number of objectives such as the fostering of exports, the regulation of imperial commerce and the formation of bilateral trade treaties. There were also powerful lobbies (the West Indian interest, the City, MPs on the payroll of the East India Company) which deflected the attention of revenue raisers from customs to excise.[49]

Many rapidly growing sectors escaped excise duty: banking, metallurgy, woollens, cottons, pottery, canals. This was partly because of lobbying, partly so as not to discourage production and also partly because of pressure to keep the costs of some basic necessities (such as plain cloths) at affordable prices. But there were excise taxes on many necessaries such as salt, candles, beer, cider, soap, leather, wire, coal, starch and malt as well as on luxuries, for example silks, printed muslins, tobacco, glass, paper, spirits and legal and commercial services. Taxation thus fell largely on necessities which were

---

[47] O'Brien, 'Political Economy', p.16; Brewer, *Sinews*, ch. 4; J. V. Beckett and M. Turner, 'Taxation and Economic Growth in Eighteenth-Century England', *Economic History Review* XLIII (1990).
[48] O'Brien, 'Political Economy', p.17.
[49] O'Brien, 'Political Economy', p.24.

relatively price-inelastic or on decencies and luxuries the consumption of which tended to rise faster than incomes. These commodities were a buoyant source of revenue, although their taxation excited some major opposition.[50] To deflect popular opposition and to accord with notions of egalitarianism, levies were often placed on a sliding scale so that more expensive varieties of a commodity were taxed more heavily: wax compared with tallow candles, soft compared with hard soap, printed compared with plain cottons. Also, parliamentary debate, by invariably advocating the need for luxury purchasers to bear the brunt of taxation, obscured any perception of where the main burden really lay. But the excise did impinge disproportionately harshly on those low down the income scale. This inevitably restricted the buoyancy of domestic demand for basic manufactures and may thus have slowed down industrialisation.[51] In addition, much of the excise revenue was immediately transferred as interest payments to the holders of government stock, so the tax system was doubly regressive. Thus it was indirect taxes which carried Britain to mercantile supremacy by underpinning the deficit financing of wars, and the investing classes were only lightly touched.

Government expenditure and war
For 75 years between 1692 and 1802 the country was involved in major military operations overseas or at sea. Despite the dislocative effects of war, particularly on coastal transport, on the labour and capital markets and in raising the prices of many consumer goods, eighteenth-century wars on balance had a multiplier effect throughout the economy because of the demand created for capital goods and military supplies. Iron smelting, coal mining, building, engineering, as well as horse rearing, grain and foodstuffs, sails, ropes, cannons, guns: all felt the stimulus of war-induced demand, investment and, often, technical change. By increasing the demand for metals, by making their import difficult and by raising the price of timber, wars set in motion cost and profit changes which speeded the search for methods of using coal for smelting. The War of Austrian Succession provided the turning point in iron production by stimulating improvements in coke-smelting technique. These made it possible to use domestic ores for pig as well as bar iron without which the nail trade would have perished. The Seven Years War had a similarly dramatic effect: the introduction of the iron railroad and the start of significant iron exports. And Cort's puddling and rolling process was perfected at the Cyfarthfa ironworks in the 1790s against the backcloth of heavily increased war demands. Coal and mining were also promoted in wartime, as was the

---

[50] Brewer, *Sinews*, ch. 4.
[51] Beckett and Turner, 'Taxation and Economic Growth'.

installation of Savery and Newcomen steam pumps in response to the problems of deeper mining of both copper and coal.[52]

The growth rates of many of the consumer industries were probably faster in peacetime, but certain branches of woollens, silk, linen and cotton, glass, pots, and hardwares felt a positive impact from war. Some benefitted from the absence of rival foreign goods, some benefitted from home and overseas demands for uniforms and supplies, while others felt the impact of increased domestic employment and consumer purchasing power. It is no accident that the Seven Years War saw the introduction of the fly shuttle in the cotton industry: it might have been more resented in the period when work was less plentiful.

The major prize of war, which stimulated employment levels and earnings in many regions and sectors, was the increase in export demand for British goods and in the carrying and re-export trades. It has also been suggested that the terms of trade moved in Britain's favour during periods of war and that this significantly contributed to the accumulation of mercantile and other profits. Most wars were accompanied by an initial loss of export impetus followed by steady gains, a post-war boom and then a settling down to higher levels than those obtaining pre-war. Substantial and permanent gains were made particularly at the expense of France. Britain's practical monopoly of the re-export trades ensured access to both distant and European markets and underpinned the marked expansion of shipping and ship building. By the end of the eighteenth century her mercantile marine was several times larger than the French, the nearest rival.

Study of enclosure and turnpike acts before 1763 indicates that wartime diversion of capital did not curtail domestic non-military activity. Building construction appears to have suffered in London during some periods of war, but in provincial centres, notably Liverpool, Bristol and Birmingham, it increased significantly. Outside London, those with capital likely to invest in industrial expansion, agricultural improvement or canal construction were not those likely to engage heavily in government stock. Thus, 'crowding in' may have occurred rather than 'crowding out': private capital formation was increasing at the same time as government expenditure. Thanks to southern English and Dutch capital, and the regionally fragmented nature of the capital market, England fought the eighteenth-century wars with a minimum of internal investment dislocation.[53]

Mobilisation was slight before the Napoleonic wars (less than 5% of the British male population). Most soldiers and sailors came from areas of significant underemployment and unemployment and so represented a net addition to employment. Compared with the much

52 A. H. John, 'War and the English Economy 1700–1763', *Economic History Review* VII (1955), pp.329–44. The following paragraphs rely heavily on this source.
53 John, 'War and the English Economy', p.340.

greater mobilisation of the Napoleonic period, the earlier wars do not appear to have created labour supply problems in other sectors of the economy. Nor was pressure placed on inputs in other industries since war demand largely resulted in the heavy metal industries turning to new sources of raw materials which did not compete with existing forms of economic activity. These developments in turn led to 'dynamic and historical reductions in costs' which bore fruit in the classic industrial revolution.[54]

The American War of Independence had more negative consequences, at least in the short term, than earlier wars. The financing of government demand had more impact on domestic investment and the fall in employment in the export industries and the rise in mercantile bankruptcies were marked. However, exports even to North America soon recovered. 'In the long run unquestionably the eighteenth century wars paid in a world of competing national economies. The proportionate volume of British trade was undoubtedly greater than it would otherwise have been.'[55]

The impact of the Napoleonic Wars

Interpretations of the effects of the Napoleonic wars have ranged widely. Crafts at one extreme attributes little to wartime dislocation or stimulus whilst some authorities stress the favourable impact of wartime demand on certain key sectors of the economy. Williamson attributes slow growth during the industrial revolution to the wars and their aftermath, to their effect on capital and labour markets in particular. Mokyr treads a middle ground estimating that there may have been some crowding out of civilian investment but not enough to bear the weight which Williamson attempts to place on it. He also plays down the impact of mobilisation and the war on relative prices. Whilst Heim and Mirowski find no evidence of crowding out, Black and Gilmore suggest that it did occur, even though a significant proportion of revenue came from abroad or from increasing the money supply, and despite the effect of high interest rates in encouraging the use of idle funds and less foreign speculation in favour of domestic investment, both public and private.[56]

The most recent assessment of the effect of the wars on the British economy eschews a rigorously quantitative approach. O'Brien argues

54 John, 'War and the English Economy', pp.340–3.
55 W. W. Rostow, *The Process of Economic Growth*, (Oxford, 1953), pp.159–60, quoted in John, 'War and the English Economy', p.344.
56 Crafts, 'British Economic Growth: Some Difficulties of Interpretation', *Explorations in Economic History* 24 (1987), pp.245–68. Williamson, 'Debating the Industrial Revolution'; Williamson, 'Why was British Growth So Slow During the Industrial Revolution?', *Journal of Economic History* 44 (1984); Mokyr, 'Has the Industrial Revolution Been Crowded Out?'; R. A. Black and C. A. Gilmore, 'Crowding Out During Britain's Industrial Revolution', *Journal of Economic History* 50 (1990). C. E. Heim and P. Mirowski, 'Interest Rates and Crowding-out during Britain's Industrial Revolution', *Journal of Economic History* 47 (1987).

that data constraints, together with the need fully to consider both short and long-term consequences, render the national accounts and equilibrium approaches unsuitable.[57] Growth rates of domestic output declined perceptibly between 1793 and 1819 and consumption standards were 10–20% below levels they *might have attained* if the economy had continued to grow at the pre-war rate. But one cannot assume that the growth rate of the 1780s would have been sustained indefinitely in the absence of war. Furthermore, assessment of these wars must include the impact of changes in government revenue raising and expenditure on different industries, on agriculture and on the pressure for innovation, technological, organisational and commercial. The *long-term* effects of the wars on capital formation, industrial production, agriculture and foreign trade must also be assessed in any balance sheet, but this has seldom been attempted.

As nearly 60% of the extra funds raised by the government to prosecute war between 1793 and 1815 came from taxes and not borrowing, O'Brien argues that these wars, unlike those earlier in the eighteenth century, should not be accused of raising interest rates or crowding out civilian investment. The tax strategy pursued by government imposed a major share of the burden on the consumption standards of the population and encouraged private capital formation to continue. Thus the share of national income invested during the war remained roughly constant, whilst private consumption fell sharply from over 83% of national expenditure in 1788–92 to around 72% in 1793–1812 and reached as low as 64% during the last years of the war.[58] Household incomes were depressed in two ways – by heavy taxes and by inflation. Public borrowing was maintained at high levels without significantly denuding private investment because the tax system (along with wartime inflation) redistributed income from wage earners to farmers, employers and property owners.

The wartime practices of the *rentier* classes encouraged the continuation of widespread government stockholding after the war, and the marketing and resale of government bonds encouraged the development and improved efficiency of institutional arrangements throughout the money market. London's registered dealers in bills and bonds rose from 432 in 1792 to 726 by 1812 and the Stock Exchange was formed in 1802. London banks increased in number from 63 to 80 and country banks from 280 to 660 over the war years. The efficiency of the London and provincial banking networks, and of the links between the

[57] P. K. O'Brien, 'The Impact of the Revolutionary and Napoleonic Wars, 1793–1815, on the Long-Run Growth of the British Economy', *Fernand Braudel Centre Review* xii (1989). The following paragraphs rely heavily on this source and on J. L. Anderson, 'Aspects of the Effect on the British Economy of the Wars against France 1790–1815', *Australian Economic History Review* xii (1972), and 'A Measure of the Effect of British Public Finance 1793–1815', *Economic History Review* xxvii (1974).
[58] O'Brien, 'Impact', p.347. For more detailed analysis of the effects on consumption see Beckett and Turner, 'Taxation and Economic Growth'.

two in dealing with both public and private investments, improved during the wars and this was further encouraged by expansive monetary policy. Thus the entire financial system benefitted.[59]

The wars also had a commercialising effect on agriculture, preventing the onset of diminishing returns. Wartime demands and induced inflation contributed significantly to the marked shift which occurred in the terms of trade between agriculture and other sectors of the economy. This added to the real incomes of landowners and farmers. The consolidation of land into larger farms was encouraged, as was the assertion of private rights to commons and wastes and the general improvement and extension of cultivable margins. In short, 'the upswing in agricultural prices associated with the war years pulled those who owned and managed British agriculture into a cage from whence escape from the imperatives to invest, innovate and exploit farm labour became more difficult'.[60]

The effect of the wars upon industry is more difficult to calculate in the absence of assessments of what might have occurred in the absence of war and better empirical material than is currently available. But it appears that wartime increases in customs and excise duties harmed only a handful of industries such as building and construction, malt, brewing, spirits, salt and the processing of tropical foodstuffs. Many major industries, including iron, metallurgical products, woollens, linens, candles, soap and leather, experienced no significant additions to taxation on their inputs or outputs, nor did they suffer from the rising costs of imported raw materials. Furthermore, reductions in demand for industrial goods which arose from the squeeze on consumption may have been considerably offset by army and navy purchases. This seems to have been the case in the West Riding textile industry which had firms supplying several of the major combatant forces of Europe.

The rate and scale of bankruptcies in both the industrial and trading sectors peaked during the war period. Initial attempts to exploit Latin American markets led to heavy losses in Buenos Aires in 1806 and in Rio de Janeiro in 1808–9, and the post-war flooding of the European market led to further losses in 1815–16 and 1819. In Manchester four out of five manufacturers, most with mercantile interests, disappeared during the twenty years or so of war. But such devastations were matched by the rise of new generations of fortune hunters and the introduction of new types of trading organisation. The settlement of foreign commission agents in the provincial centres of industry was a direct consequence of the French wars as was the development of the wholesale warehouse serving the exporter. These, together with the growing involvement of acceptance houses in the finance of trade, can

59 O'Brien, 'Impact', p.350.
60 O'Brien, 'Impact', p.359.

be seen as positive longer-term consequences of wartime commercial failures. Many of these houses maintained their headquarters in the northern trading centres until after mid century. There they advanced up to two-thirds of invoice to clients for three to four months in the North American markets and for up to 12 months in Far Eastern trade. These new structures did much to underpin the mid nineteenth-century growth of British trade and shipping.[61]

In the aftermath of war, monetary policy designed to protect bondholders is likely to have restrained the growth of trade and industry. It certainly depressed the employment and incomes of the urban poor. But low real incomes and regressive taxation may have raised the rate of saving and investment to the long-term benefit of economic growth and income levels. The considerable short-term costs of the wars and their aftermath must also be balanced against the capture of the carrying trade, unification with Ireland, the opening up of Latin America and the seizure of enemy colonies. In the longer term the wars probably inflicted much greater costs on the economies of rival European powers, whilst giving Britain a position for several decades which comparative advantage alone would not have achieved. As O'Brien has argued, the fiscal and financial policies adopted by Pitt to fund military expenditure may not have been given the credit they deserve for keeping the industrial revolution on course: 'the strategic decisions he took from 1797–99 – to suspend specie payments, to fund a far higher proportion of war expenditure from taxes, to introduce a non-progressive income tax, and to persist with the sinking fund – appear in retrospect to have sustained the economy through difficult times'.[62]

Economy, society and the fiscal military state
The fiscal military state affected perceptions of where political and economic power lay and of the relationship between different economic and social strata. Contemporaries suggested that the state had altered the balance of social forces in the country by penalising the landed classes, creating a new class of upstart financiers and laying a heavy burden of taxes on the ordinary consumer. Worries were voiced about the damage inflicted on the landed interest, the 'natural' rulers, by the Land Tax. It was also widely believed that all taxes, including those on commodities, eventually fell upon land whilst movable property and offices were untaxed. But a geater source of public disquiet in the early eighteenth century was the rise of a financial interest, whose wealth was derived from dealings with government as investors, contractors and remitters, and who had a vested interest in keeping the nation at war which in turn kept the Land Tax high.[63]

---

[61] S. D. Chapman, *The Rise of Merchant Banking* (London, 1984), ch.1.
[62] O'Brien, 'Impact', p.381.
[63] Brewer, *Sinews*, chapter 8.

Conflict between landed and financial interests was however toned down by the growing number of state offices open to the landed classes, both civilian and military. This not only bolstered incomes but also cemented aristocratic loyalty to the state's fiscal and military activity. Office holding had two other social consequences: it increased the number of gentry who were absent from their estates and it helped to erect a more sharply defined social distinction between the gentry and their social inferiors. Office holding was seen as more compatible with the gentlemanly ideal than trade, business or finance, but many landowners were drawn into speculation and investment in the Funds. In practice, few remained aloof from the spoils of the fiscal military state:

> Support for the debt paralleled its penetration into society at large. As the number of fundholders increased, so antipathy to public credit diminished...As Tories, country gentlemen and provincials invested in the funds, so they, in their minor way, became part of the financial interest.[64]

Although the specific incidence of taxation created divisions within and between economic interest groups, the system of public credit, by the late eighteenth century, tended to cement the interest and loyalties of capitalists whether they were landowners, merchants, financiers or industrialists. And the struggle over public revenue had a major impact on the evolution of the nineteenth-century state:

> ...the protestation of those who opposed standing armies and big government were more than the mere symptoms of an important change; they became an integral part of Britain's institutional transformation. The war against the state helped to shape the changing contours of government: limited its scope, restricted its ambit and, through parliamentary scrutiny, rendered its institutions both more public and accountable...[Paradoxically] this success made the fiscal military state stronger rather than weaker, more effective rather than more impotent. Public scrutiny reduced peculation, parliamentary consent lent greater legitimacy to government action.[65]

Conclusion

Just as current macroeconomic analyses underplay the extent and nature of radical change, so also traditional accounts of the role of the

[64] Brewer, *Sinews*, p.210.
[65] Brewer, *Sinews*, p.xix.

state have failed until recently to give full weight to the economic, social and political impact of the fiscal military regime. Assessment of the effects of war, and especially of the Napoleonic wars, on the process of industrial change, economic growth and social adjustment illustrate the shortcomings of studies which fail to incorporate long- as well as short-term elements and factors which cannot easily be quantified or modelled. If we adopt a broader perspective than growth-accounting in the task of assessing economic transformation, the notion of radical change in the classic industrial revolution period becomes more seductive. And if the full impact of state revenue raising and expenditure is considered, we draw nearer to an understanding of the broader process of economic change and its social and political corollaries.

3 AGRICULTURE AND THE INDUSTRIAL REVOLUTION

English agriculture between the late seventeenth and mid nineteenth centuries is usually regarded as a major success story from the point of view of the economy as a whole. Most accounts stress the innovations, the dynamism and the rising productivity of the sector and attribute to it a key role in stimulating the industrial revolution.[1] Its high productivity, compared with continental agriculture, is emphasised. This enabled the economy to support a large and growing non-agricultural labour force. In addition, the role of cheap food and buoyant agrarian incomes in the expansion of the home market for manufactured goods and services has been highlighted. And historians have shown how important landed capital was in the promotion of industry as well as urban and transport infrastructures.[2]

England certainly had a distinctive agricultural history compared with much of the rest of Europe. Although there was great regional

[1] This is so of Marx, Toynbee, Clapham, Tawney and other more recent authorities cited in chapter 1. The debate over if and when there was an agricultural revolution is now somewhat sterile as important developments can be found at many times between the sixteenth and the late nineteenth centuries. For recent surveys of this debate see M. Overton, 'Agricultural Revolution?; England 1540–1850', *Refresh* 3 (1986), repr. in A. Digby and C. Feinstein, eds., *New Directions in Economic and Social History* (London, 1989) and for detailed treatment Overton, *The Agricultural Revolution in England: The Transformation of the Rural Economy* (Cambridge, 1987). Also J. V. Beckett, *The Agricultural Revolution* (Oxford, 1990).

[2] On productivity and the release of labour see E. A. Wrigley, *Continuity, Chance and Change: The Character of the Industrial Revolution in England* (Cambridge, 1988), p. 14; Wrigley, 'Urban Growth and Agricultural Change: England and the Continent in the Early Modern Period', *Journal of Interdisciplinary History* xv (1985), pp.683–728, repr. in R. I. Rotberg and T. K. Rabb, eds., *Population and the Economy: Population and History from the Traditional to the Modern World* (Cambridge, 1986), pp. 123–86; Wrigley, 'Men on the Land and Men in the Countryside: Employment in Agriculture in Early Nineteenth-Century England', in L. Bonfield, R. Smith and P. Laslett, eds., *The World We Have Gained* (Oxford, 1985). See also N. F. R. Crafts, 'The New Economic History and the Industrial Revolution', in P. Mathias and J. K. Davis, eds., *The First Industrial Revolutions* (Oxford, 1989), p.39; Crafts, *British Economic Growth During the Industrial Revolution* (Oxford, 1985), esp. ch.4; Crafts, 'British Economic Growth 1700–1850: Some Difficulties of Interpretation', *Explorations in Economic History* 24 (1987), pp. 245–68. On agriculture and the home market see A. H. John, 'Aspects of English Economic Growth in the First Half of the Eighteenth Century', *Economica* 28 (1961), and in E. M. Carus-Wilson, ed., *Essays in Economic History* II (London, 1962), D. E. C. Eversley, 'The Home Market and Economic Growth in England', in E. L. Jones and G. E. Mingay, eds., *Land, Labour and Population in the Industrial Revolution* (London, 1967), pp.206–59; E. L. Jones, ed., *Agriculture and Economic Growth in England* (London, 1967), introduction, pp.36–46.

diversity and small farms remained common well beyond our period, there was, by the eighteenth century, no peasantry to compare with that of the continent. The century saw further concentration of land in the hands of commercial farmers, and a three-tier structure of landholding was becoming typical over large parts of the countryside: large landowners, tenant farmers and landless wage labourers. The structure appears to have been vital in facilitating the finance, enterprise and labour mobility necessary for marked technological innovation, productivity increase and the shedding of labour to industry.[3]

But it may be that this dominant verdict on English agriculture is too positive. It is appropriate to remember that the 'classical' view (which prevailed at least until the repeal of the Corn Laws) was that industrialisation occurred in Britain *despite* the obstacles created by a conservative, sluggish and sometimes hostile agrarian economy.[4] Claims concerning the positive role of agriculture must be set against the fragmentary and uncertain, though mounting, evidence of chronological and regional diversity in rates of growth and change: including a deceleration of output growth for several decades after 1760, and considerable pools of underemployed and unemployed labour in the countryside which did not move painlessly or efficiently into industry. Evidence that landlords invested some proportion of their savings in mining, housing or transport must be set against reverse flows of finance which occurred when merchants and industrialists invested in agriculture. Furthermore, increasing output of basic agricultural commodities created periods of declining prices and depressed incomes in the agrarian sector. Only if and when these depressive effects were exceeded in economic importance by the positive effect of cheap food on nutrition, on population expansion and mobility, and on non-agricultural real incomes, can agriculture be seen unequivocally as a positive element in the growth process.

There are two sets of issues involved in the debate about the contribution of agriculture. First, we will consider differing opinions regarding the extent and causes of output and productivity increase in the sector. How productive was agriculture? When did the main growth spurts occur? Did growth arise from extension of the cultivable area, from increases in the productivity of labour or from increased yields? Was the productivity of land and labour stimulated more by technological change (new crops, rotations, implements and capital

[3] *ibid.* and R. Brenner, 'Agrarian Class Structure and Economic Development in Pre-industrial Europe', *Past and Present* 70 (1976). For the debate surrounding this see n.18.
[4] Malthusian theories of population growth outstripping resources and Ricardian concepts of rent and the laws of diminishing returns reflect the fears of concerned contemporaries who for nearly a century expected economic progress to founder against serious supply constraints from agriculture. P. K. O'Brien has suggested these classical views may be ripe for rehabilitation in 'Agriculture and the Home Market for English Industry 1660–1820', *English Historical Review* 344 (1985), pp.773–800.

improvements) or by institutional change (for example, farm size, property rights, or employment relations). Secondly, we examine the force of various potentially dynamic links between agriculture and the rest of the economy: the supply of food and raw materials, the release of factors of production (labour and capital), the effects of agricultural development upon the demand for manufactured goods and services, upon real wages and consumption. Through these links, agriculture can act as a parent to industry (and the rest of the economy): a parent that can either stultify the offspring or nurture it to ever higher levels of economic development.

Productivity and innovation

Productivity estimates

As there is no direct evidence of agricultural output nationally, various assumptions have to be employed to estimate sectoral output and productivity change using trade statistics, price indices and labour force or population estimates.[5] Estimates of agricultural total factor productivity (ATFP) growth for the period c. 1700–1860 have varied widely depending on different methods of calculation and assumptions. Crafts suggests that ATFP grew faster than industrial productivity through much of the eighteenth century and that it sustained a level near 1% per annum in the first half of the nineteenth century. Other estimates, by Williamson, McCloskey and Mokyr, are much lower, varying between 0.02% and 0.45% per annum for the period 1780–1860.[6] Other controversial and rough estimates have been produced for English land and labour productivity separately. Output per acre measured in wheat yields may have risen from around 12–14 bushels per acre in the mid seventennth century to 20 and more by 1800 and then to about 36 by 1914. This increase did not, however, make England unusually productive, for wheat yields around 1800 were similar in Ireland, north-east France, Holland and probably also in

[5] For the most recently published estimates of output and capital investment with discussion of the pitfalls involved in calculation see B. Holderness, 'Prices, Productivity and Output', in G. A. Mingay, ed., *The Agrarian History of England and Wales* VI (Cambridge, 1989).

[6] Crafts, *British Economic Growth* p.84; J. G. Williamson, 'Debating the Industrial Revolution', *Explorations in Economic History* 24 (1987), pp.269–92. One of Williamson's main criticisms of Crafts is that he assumes the conditions of a closed economy in his calculations. If foreign trade is taken into account, the price elasticity of demand from agricultural products is likely to have been considerably more than the unity which Crafts allows. D. McCloskey uses a different method, comparing the prices of inputs with those of outputs: 'The Industrial Revolution: A Survey', in J. Mokyr, ed., *The Economics of the Industrial Revolution* (London, 1985), pp.53–74. The various methods are discussed and some reworked in J. Mokyr, 'Has the Industrial Revolution Been Crowded Out? Some Reflections on Crafts and Williamson', *Explorations in Economic History* 24 (1987), pp.293–319, esp. pp.305–12.

west Germany and Belgium.[7] As the calculation of national yields is full of pitfalls, recent work has looked instead at regional experience using the more reliable indicators of productivity obtainable from local records such as estate papers, probate inventories and local price series. Results for Norfolk and Suffolk suggest that, notwithstanding greatly improved stocking densities, there was little improvement on the best medieval grain yields, obtained in the fourteenth century, until the first half of the eighteenth century: livestock rather than crops emerges as the more dynamic sector.[8]

Labour productivity is more difficult to estimate, but Wrigley, using trends in urbanisation and population growth as a guide, calculates that each worker in agriculture was producing food for 1.5 non-agricultural workers in 1650, 2.5 by 1800 and 6.0 by 1911. His estimates show that labour productivity in England and France in 1500 and 1600 were similar but output per worker in English argiculture rose by between 60 and 100% over the period 1600–1800 (compared with less than 20% in France) and that it continued to grow about 1% per annum in the period 1811–51. By 1800 labour productivity in France was only 69% of the English level. Wrigley's calculations corroborate earlier estimates, by Bairoch and by O'Brien and Keyder of the labour productivity gap between French and English agriculture and show that it emerged in the seventeenth and eighteenth centuries. As output per acre was similar in England and France, England's higher labour productivity is shown to arise from lower employment per acre. Wrigley shows how these figures in fact understate the increase in labour productivity, because the land also sustained the raw material needs of far larger industries in 1800 than in 1600 and yielded the

---

[7] M. Overton, 'Agriculture' in J. Langton and R. J. Morris, eds., *Atlas of Industrialising Britain 1780–1914* (London, 1986), p.48; R. C. Allen and C. O'Grada, 'On the Road Again with Arthur Young: English, Irish and French Agriculture During the Industrial Revolution', *Journal of Economic History* 48 (1989); R. C. Allen, 'The Growth of Labour Productivity in Early Modern English Agriculture', *Explorations in Economic History* 25 (1988), p.117.

[8] For debate pointing at the need for local rather than aggregate studies see M. Turner, 'Agricultural Productivity in England in the Eighteenth Century: Evidence from Crop Yields', *Economic History Review* xxxv (1982), pp.489–510; M. Overton, 'Agricultural Productivity in Eighteenth-Century England: Some Further Speculations', *Economic History Review* xxxvii (1984), pp.244–51; M. Turner, 'Agricultural Productivity in Eighteenth-Century England: Further Strains of Speculation', *Economic History Review* xxxvii (1984), pp.252–7. For data on Norfolk and Suffolk see M. Overton, 'Re-estimating Crop Yields from Probate Inventories', *Journal of Economic History* 50 (1990), and relevant sections in B. S. Campbell and M. Overton, eds., *Land, Labour and Livestock: Historical Studies in European Agricultural Productivity* (Manchester, 1991).

fodder for the thousands of horses employed in industrial plants, mines and transport.[9]

Technical innovations

The roots of productivity increase on the land lay in changing husbandry and employment practices, but we are forced to build our picture of innovation from fragmentary local, estate and parochial data. Parochial returns of 1801 show the cultivation of seven arable crops, and similar information is available from the tithe files for the years following the 1836 Tithe Commutation Act.[10] The information we have suggests that the late seventeenth and eighteenth centuries saw the diffusion of new crops and rotational techniques which had first appeared decades if not a century earlier. The major innovations initiated in the sixteenth and seventeenth centuries were the floating of water meadows, the substitution of convertible husbandry for permanent tillage and permanent grass or for shifting cultivation, the introduction of new fallow crops and selected grasses, marsh drainage, manuring and stock breeding.[11] Convertible husbandry included temporary grass 'leys', sheep folding, arable and the use of fodder crops such as clover, sainfoin and ryegrass as a source of fertiliser both directly (fixing nitrogen in the soil) and indirectly (in providing animal feedstuffs). Common crop innovations in arable rotations were turnips and clover. So much so that an archdeacon took a rector to task for growing turnips even in the graveyard. 'This must not occur again', he said. 'Oh no, sir, next year it will be barley.'[12]

Specialist crops and livestock were also developed according to local market opportunities and to combat periods of declining cereal prices. Hops, vegetables (including potatoes), fruit, dyestuffs, commercial pig and poultry rearing, cattle raising and fattening, all expanded along with market gardening near to towns. Guano and coprolite were used as fertilisers from the late eighteenth century but, as with farm

[9] Wrigley, 'Urban Growth and Agricultural Change', pp.700, 720; Wrigley, *Continuity, Chance and Change*, pp.14, 35–44. There are problems in calculating labour productivity by looking at the size of the rural agricultural population compared with the rural non-agricultural population and the urban population because the occupational data on which these shares are based are likely seriously to underestimate the real degree of participation in agriculture. P. Bairoch, 'Niveau de développement économique de 1810 à 1910', *Annales Économies, Sociétés, Civilisations* 20 (1965), pp.1091–117. P. K. O'Brien and C. Keyder, *Economic Growth in Britain and France 1780–1914* (London, 1978), pp. 102–45.
[10] The available statistics are discussed in Overton, 'Agriculture'. This is also the best short survey of technical and organisational innovation c1780–1914.
[11] E. Kerridge, *The Agricultural Revolution* (London, 1967).
[12] G. T. Warner and C. H. K. Marten, *The Groundwork of British History* (London, n.d.), p.585, n.1, quoted in E. L. Jones, 'Environment, Agriculture and Industrialisation in Europe', *Agricultural History* 51 (1977), p.497. On this topic see M. Overton, 'The Diffusion of Agricultural Innovations in Early Modern England: Turnips and Clover in Norfolk and Suffolk 1580–1740', *Transactions of the Institute of British Geographers* 10 (1985), pp.205–21.

machinery, their spread and impact was probably slight before the 1830s and 1840s. Innovations proceeded slowly and patchily as a response to farm environment and local opportunities. The crop returns of 1801 suggest that the use of root crops in rotations may have been more limited geographically by that date than is suggested in much of the literature.[13] There was, however, an acceleration in the introduction of rotational techniques in the early nineteenth century as a response to rising prices. Innovations were pioneered as much by tenant farmers, small holders, open-field farmers and labourers as by aristocrats such as Bakewell, Townshend and Coke or leisured cranks like Jethro Tull who have been traditionally depicted as the heroes of an agricultural revolution. But innovations could also be retarded by the resistence of labourers, who feared unemployment, and even of farmers whose best interests were not always served by introducing labour-saving techniques which resulted in a shortage of labour at harvest time.[14]

As Jones, in particular, has demonstrated, it was the light soil areas of the south and east which adapted most easily to the new crops and rotations, especially Norfolk, Suffolk, Lincolnshire and Northumberland. These areas had a longer working season than the Midland clays, previously England's main granary, and had been earlier enclosed into larger farms, thus creating fewer institutional obstacles to innovation. The East Anglian areas had the additional benefit of being close to the major markets of London and the continent. The Midland clay areas could not compete in grain production with the south and east and instead shifted increasingly into pasture farming in the mid eighteenth century.[15]

Wrigley argues along with O'Brien and Keyder that a key element in the rise in labour productivity in England compared with the continent was the ratio between pastoral and arable activities. Innovations in mixed farming were increasing the role of cattle and sheep in field rotations. High pasture ratios are not only likely (through the use of animal manure) to have stimulated higher cereal yields, but the much greater use of draught animals was also vital in raising labour

[13] Overton, 'Agriculture', p.40.
[14] P. Mathias, 'Agriculture and Industrialization', in Mathias and Davis, eds., *First Industrial Revolutions*, pp.104–5; P. K. O'Brien, 'Quelle a été exactement la contribution de l'aristocratie britannique au progrès de l'agriculture entre 1688 et 1789?' *Annales Économies, Sociétés, Civilisations* 42 (1987); M. A. Haviden, 'Agricultural Progress in Open-field Oxfordshire', *Agricultural History Review* 9 (1962); E. J. T. Collins, 'The Rationality of "Surplus" Agricultural Labour: Mechanisation in English Agriculture in the Nineteenth Century', *Agricultural History Review* 35 (1987); S. Macdonald, 'Agricultural Improvement and the Neglected Labourer', *Agricultural History Review* 31 (1983).
[15] Jones, ed., *Agriculture and Economic Growth*, pp.9–10; E. L. Jones, 'Agriculture and Economic Growth in England 1660–1750: Agricultural Change', *Journal of Economic History* 25 (1965), repr. in Jones, ed., pp.152–71.

productivity. It seems possible that there was a rise of 27% in the horse power available per man on the land in the course of the eighteenth century. This facilitated many of the long-term improvements of farm land which depended on shifting and spreading loads of lime, shells, chalk, sand and the various forms of organic manure. More livestock also had a big impact on the supply of hides, skins, wools, and other raw materials to industry and in the efficient use of by-products from the industrial sector such as brewers' waste which was fed to pigs.[16]

Capitalist farming

There is a long tradition that attributes the dynamic role of agriculture in the English economy in particular to the system of enclosed, large-scale farming in contrast to the preponderance, in France and elsewhere on the continent, of small peasant proprietorships. The tradition derives originally from contemporary critics of enclosure who feared its depopulating and impoverishing effects and it was stressed by Marx who saw enclosures and the growth of capitalist agriculture pushing dispossessed workers off the land and propelling the newly proletarianised into industrial wage dependency or pauperism.[17] In an article which precipitated considerable debate in the 1980s, Brenner reasserted that the key factor which set England apart from much of the rest of Europe in the early modern period, and which uniquely underpinned her early industrialisation, was the absence of a significant peasant class in the countryside and the associated growth of large-scale capitalist agriculture. He attributed the decline of the peasantry to the outcome of class struggle from medieval times which in France resulted in legal protection of the peasantry (encouraged by the fact that they had become a major source of central government tax revenue). In England by contrast the mass of the peasantry never gained firm freehold rights and were more easily shifted, dispossessed and proletarianised in the process of enclosure, engrossment and the commercialisation of farming.[18] This had several potential effects not all of which are explored by Brenner. The commercialisation of

[16] Wrigley, *Continuity, Chance and Change*, pp.38–43; O'Brien and Keyder, *Economic Growth in Britain and France*, p.117.
[17] K. Marx, *Capital* I (London, 1976 edn.), chs.26–30. This perspective has remained a continuous theme in the historiography, notably in R. H. Tawney, *The Agrarian Problem in the Sixteenth Century* (London, 1912, repr. New York, 1967); M. Dobb, *Studies in the Development of Capitalism* (London, 1946), ch.6; R. C. Allen, *Enclosure and the Yeoman* (Oxford, forthcoming); K. D. M. Snell, *Annals of the Labouring Poor: Social Change and Agrarian England 1660–1900* (Cambridge, 1985); K. Tribe, *Land, Labour and Economic Discourse* (London, 1978).
[18] R. Brenner, 'Agrarian Class Structure and Economic Development in Pre-industrial Europe', *Past and Present* 70 (1976), pp.30–75. Many critiques and a defence by Brenner of his thesis were published in *Past and Present* 78, 79, 80, 85 and 87. The contributions are collected together and reprinted in T. H. Aston and C. H. E. Philbin, eds., *The Brenner Debate* (Cambridge, 1985).

farming could proceed relatively unhindered so that national agriculture could support a growing non-agrarian sector; the conservatism inherent in peasant culture had less effect on attitudes towards leisure, work and consumption than it had in France; and, finally, the push factors created by the development of agrarian capitalism ensured a ready supply of cheap landless and potentially mobile labour for non-agricultural pursuits.

Brenner has been criticised from many perspectives, particularly as much of his historical knowledge is that of a non-specialist. But he has been most taken to task for his emphasis on class struggle as the origin of differences in landholding patterns and property rights between England and much of the rest of Europe. Critics have stressed that cycles of demographic expansion (hence of labour supply and the demand for foodstuffs) are sufficient to account for the evolution of wage labour and farming innovations, whilst others suggest that the impulse of foreign trade and urban production was a more important source of dynamism in the growth of proletarianisation and commercial farming. What is at issue here is whether the proletariat was a 'natural' or a social creation: whether created by population expansion and economic growth or by a power struggle between different social groups and competing ideologies.[19]

The dominant view on the relationship between enclosure, large farms and labour supply in England has remained until very recently one which sees the institutional developments, particularly enclosure, creating more rather than less work on the land and resulting in innovations which increased yields and employment at the same time. The release of labour by the agricultural sector is seen to have arisen largely from demographic increase which occurred alongside the creation of a wage-dependent and hence more mobile work-force. Chambers provides the classic statement of this perspective.[20]

In the most recent contribution to the debate on the impact of the growth of capitalist farming using wage labour, Allen has rejected the importance of technical innovation, enclosure and demographic growth (in itself) in generating surplus rural labour. He calculates that in the seventeenth century corn yields rose which also raised labour productivity, but neither enclosure nor capitalist agriculture contributed significantly to this advance which occurred as much among open-field farmers as in the more restricted areas of large enclosed farms. In the eighteenth century, however, the changing institutional structure of farming in favour of larger farms employing wage labour reduced employment per acre sufficiently to account entirely for the observable

[19] Aston and Philbin, *The Brenner Debate*, Introduction, and discussion in Dobb, *Studies*, p.223.
[20] J. D. Chambers, 'Enclosure and the Labour Supply in the Industrial Revolution', *Economic History Review* v (1953), and Chambers, *Population, Economy and Society in Pre-industrial England* (Oxford, 1972).

Anglo/French labour productivity gap. Yields per acre nationally were largely unaffected in this century.[21]

Allen's interpretation relies upon new data regarding the size of farms in the eighteenth century which he derives from estate surveys and Land Tax figures. These show a marked shift in average farm size in both open and enclosed villages from 30–60 acres to well over 100 acres.[22] Allen judges this shift to be highly significant because family labour generally sufficed on farms up to 60 acres whilst farms over 100 acres necessarily employed a larger wage-dependent group and can therefore be defined as capitalist in structure.[23] Furthermore he identifies an important inverse relationship between farm size and employment per acre: specialisation of task and division of labour brought about considerable economies in the use of labour. The relative decline in employment was particularly marked in the case of women and boys; thus the sex balance of rural employment shifted as farms grew in size – a point emphasised by Snell in his studies of the rural south and east. The shift to large farms and wage labour meant that only the husbands in labourers' families tended to be employed; boys were more difficult to supervise on large farms and the decline in relative size of dairy herds reduced female employment. In addition, under the system of hired labour which was replacing service in the south and east, non-specialist and seasonal farm work tended to be offered to men to reduce the cost of poor families on the rates.[24] Wage labour rather than the yearly hiring of farm servants also reduced the overhead costs of labour – especially in those parishes where farmers were not the sole rate-payers supporting the poor relief that sustained families through seasonal slumps in employment.[25]

[21] R. C. Allen, 'The Growth of Labour Productivity in Early-Modern English Agriculture', *Explorations in Economic History* 25 (1988), pp.117–46. This fits to some extent with Jackson's chronology – that corn yield improvement became negligible from about 1740 – but is at odds with Overton's findings for Norfolk and Suffolk: R. V. Jackson, 'Growth and Deceleration in English Agriculture 1660–1790', *Economic History Review* xxxvii (1985), pp.333–51; Overton, 'The Diffusion of Agricultural Innovations'.

[22] Allen, 'Labour Productivity', pp.120–4. This is consistent with some accounts of the decline of the English peasantry but not with that in G. Mingay, *Enclosure and the Small Farmer in the Industrial Revolution* (London, 1968). Allen suggests that the disagreement arises because Mingay relies on Gregory King's social tables for 1688 which have been shown to be highly inaccurate for farmers and freeholders. The account in F. M. L. Thompson, 'Landownership and Economic Growth in England in the Eighteenth Century' in E. L. Jones and S. J. Woolf, eds., *Agrarian Change and Economic Development* (London, 1969), pp.41–60, also conflicts with Allen but this is largely because Thompson is concerned with ownership and not land occupation.

[23] Of course the optimal size for family working varied between arable and pasture areas: Allen, 'Labour Productivity', p.127.

[24] Snell, *Annals*, chs.1, 3 and 4. See also A. Kussmaul, *Servants in Husbandry in Early Modern England* (Cambridge, 1981).

[25] Allen, 'Labour Productivity', p.133; Kussmaul, *Servants in Husbandry*, pp.18–20.

In contrast to Chambers, Allen's results show that enclosure reduced rather than increased the demand for farm labour when it was accompanied by the conversion of arable to pasture; otherwise it had no effect. Allen thus accords farm reorganisation, rather than enclosure *per se*, the greater role in changing agrarian social relations.[26] This is a thought-provoking finding but the shift away from farm service and the increasing preference for male labour in arable regimes (which arose partly from the poor relief system) occurred alongside both reorganisation and enclosure. It is difficult to separate out definitively the influence of all these factors by using multiple regression techniques on the aggregate national figures, as Allen does. Regional and local diversity, particularly the experience of areas in the north and west (which did not witness major growth in farm size or an early decline in farm service) and the precise mechanics of change at grass roots level are obscured by such analysis.

Enclosure
We have known for some time that the heavy emphasis which earlier historians placed on parliamentary enclosure in the late eighteenth century and its neat coincidence with industrial change was misplaced because enclosure by act was merely the tail-end of a long process which had been going on since medieval times with similar spurts of activity. Yet the very specific nature of parliamentary enclosure and its timing demand that we assess its impact carefully. In the century or so after 1750 virtually all the remaining open-field arable areas were enclosed. Village rules and regulations governing crops, livestock and farm techniques were abolished in favour of the management of farms by individual farmers or landlords. Rights of ownership were now recognised through parliament as exclusive rights to use, so that common lands and common usage declined dramatically.[27]

There were two peaks of parliamentary enclosure activity which differed in their underlying motives: the late 1760s–1770s and the period of the French Revolutionary and Napoleonic Wars. The first peak was largely the result of enclosure going on in the remaining open-field areas concentrated in the Midlands. It was associated with a shift from arable to grazing to take advantage of soils which were

---

[26] In contrast to Marx, *Capital*, chs. 27 and 29, and to some extent Snell, *Annals*, ch. 4, and also J. Saville, 'Primitive Accumulation and Early Industrialisation in Britain', *Socialist Register* VI (1969).
[27] C. Dahlman, *The Open-Field System and Beyond* (Cambridge, 1980), M. Turner, *Enclosures in Britain 1750–1830* (London, 1984); Snell, *Annals*, ch.4.

better suited to grass than crops.[28] This involved the switch to less labour-intensive farming and to larger farms, thus contributing to a significant growth in rural labour surplus.

The second peak after 1790 concentrated on improving arable output on lighter soils, and it also brought into cultivation much marginal land: the commons and wastes of the uplands, fenlands, heaths and moors as well as residual wastes in lowland areas. Chapman has recently calculated that the amount of open or common land abolished by parliamentary enclosure was 7.25–7.35 million acres, a bigger area than was previously thought. Overwhelmingly the parliamentary enclosure movement, especially after 1790, was about land reclamation. Even at its peak the enclosure of arable land never accounted for more than 60% of total enclosure activity. It is thus strange that study of the motives for enclosure at macro level has generally revolved around debate about the relative inefficiency or otherwise of open fields.[29] This debate is somewhat inconclusive with open fields being shown to have been remarkably flexible in adjusting to changing economic circumstances and to innovations. Enclosure does however appear to have opened the door to a more efficient balance between arable and animal farming.[30] But if commons and waste dominated the movement, as Chapman's work suggests, then other explanations must be sought to account for the extension of the cultivated acreage. Agricultural prices and rents loomed large in these particularly in the inflation of the war years.

The logic of enclosure, where it involved the reclamation of wastes and the privatisation of the commons, was the shift to larger farms. Evidence showing that the number of owner occupiers actually increased around enclosure time is probably an illusion because owners of common rights were recorded for the first time as owners only when their rights were transformed from customary to real. Many small owners sold up at or shortly after enclosure. Small plots carried a heavy burden because they were disproportionately costly to enclose. They were also often too small to support families without the aid of customary use rights for grazing, hunting and gleaning which had been

[28] Turner, *Enclosures*, p.81, suggests that this was related to improved living standards and dietary demands in favour of meat but there is no firm evidence that the living standards of the masses were improving significantly in the later eighteenth century. We have evidence of a decline in the per-capita consumption of agricultural goods (Jackson, 'Growth and Deceleration', p.351) and there appears to be no shift in the terms of trade between livestock and arable husbandry, although considerable local variations may have occurred (O'Brien, 'Agriculture and the Home Market', p.780). Enclosure for grass is more likely to have been a defensive response to competition from new grain growing areas with which the Midlands could not compete.

[29] J. Chapman, 'The Extent and Nature of Parliamentary Enclosure', *Agricultural History Review* 35 (1987). See also J. R. Wordie, 'The Chronology of English Enclosure 1500–1914', *Economic History Review* xxxvi (1983), pp.483–505.

[30] M. Turner, 'English Open Fields and Enclosures: Retardation or Productivity Improvements', *Journal of Economic History* 46 (1986), pp.669–92.

integral to the ancient usages of the common lands. Small holders after enclosure became easy prey to being bought out by larger landowners particularly in periods of depression of agricultural prices. It is thus not surprising that the most vocal and radical opponents of enclosure were small farmers and landless labouring families who stood to lose most from the enclosure of commons and feared unemployment and dependent pauperism.[31]

Thus, although the relationship between enclosure in itself and increased labour productivity is debatable, enclosure appears to have been accompanied by an increasing turnover in the land market and a rationalisation of tenancies at the poorer end of the scale. Life on the land was made considerably more difficult for smallholders, cottagers and squatters. In addition, the loss of common land took away much employment (such as pig and poultry keeping, grazing cows, gleaning) which was specifically considered women's work or that of juveniles and children. Hence an important pillar of family earnings was removed, making families less secure and creating pools of under-employed female and juvenile workers. These were often the first to be soaked up by manufacturing by-employments or by intermittent labouring or service trades in nearby urban centres. With such points from recent research in mind, it is not perhaps surprising that enclosure is again receiving the attention of historians as a major factor in the industrialisation process.[32]

The marketing of agricultural produce

Compared with advances in production, much less is known about the increasing efficiency of the internal market for agricultural commodities in the eighteenth and early nineteenth centuries. Yet this is an area which also witnessed considerable innovation. According to O'Brien, the integration of domestic markets through transport improvements was the factor which activated the already latent ability of agriculture to feed a growing population off the land.[33] In judging the ability of the agrarian sector efficiently to supply inputs to the rest of the economy, consideration of market innovation is very important. If demographers are presently looking at reductions in mortality rates, particularly in towns, as a major stimulus to population increase from the late eighteenth century (see chapter 5), then changes in the efficiency of food supply to industrial towns must be addressed. And if the notion of increasing specialisation of regions on the basis of comparative advantage is relevant, we must consider how trade

[31] J. Neeson, 'The Opponents of Enclosure in Eighteenth-Century Northamptonshire', *Past and Present* 105 (1984). For social effects of enclosure see J. L. and B. Hammond, *The Village Labourer 1760–1832* (London, 1911, repr. 1980), and Snell, *Annals, passim.*
[32] Notably by Snell, *Annals,* ch.4; see also M. E. Turner, 'Parliamentary Enclosures: Gains and Losses', *Refresh* 3 (1986); P. King, 'Gleaners, Farmers, and the Failure of Legal Sanctions in England 1750–1890', *Past and Present* 125 (1989).
[33] O'Brien, 'Agriculture and the Home Market', p.785.

between areas specialising in commercial agriculture and those specialising in manufactures was conducted. The greater the margin between farm gate prices and prices to the final consumer, the less responsive agriculture was likely to be to changes in demand.

Transport improvements and competitive pressures placed a strain on old markets and fairs: some declined and disappeared while others benefited. Fairs remained the centre of the livestock trade and there was a major development in the droving trades especially for cattle, with Scotland joining Wales as a major supplier well integrated into English markets. At the same time, in other trades, private marketing grew in importance, thus reducing the significance of public institutions. 'Inn yards and parlours and shop doorways became the effective places of trade, together with the farm gate as the wholesale and retail trades diverged.'[34] The role of women in formal market trading in the towns appears to have declined with the growth of private deals in the male social world of the inn and public house. Rules governing weights and measures also favoured regularised and large-scale dealing.[35] More efficient marketing structures came into existence in both foreign and domestic trades, and there was a proliferation of middlemen and specialist dealers who spread information, extended credit and speeded up transactions. The result was improved networks of supply for the growing urban populations. London's population grew about 70% in the century after 1650, inducing agricultural specialisation in its supplying regions from the home counties to the Scottish lowlands.[36] As middlemen and factors became more numerous they enjoyed greater freedom from regulation, but this could have had a detrimental effect on markets as some trades virtually became oligopolies with their abuses the subject of much criticism. It was difficult for small farmers to deal with powerful factors. Trade was conducted on credit and often the farmer was forced to be both risk taker and creditor. In the cheese trade, for example, producers involuntarily extended six months credit to London factors in the 1700s.[37]

Improvements in post services, legal and illegal, speeded up and broadened information flow. Investment in roads and the greater efficiency of stagecoach services and road carriers made road transport

[34] J. Chartres, 'The Marketing of Agricultural Produce', in J. Thirsk, ed., *The Agrarian History of England and Wales* v (Cambridge, 1985), p.501. This section relies heavily on this excellent survey. See also R. Perren, 'Markets and Marketing', in Mingay, ed., *Agrarian History of England and Wales* vi.
[35] M. Prior, 'Women and the Urban Economy: Oxford 1500–1800', in Prior, ed., *Women in English Society 1500–1800* (London, 1985), pp.93–117; W. Thwaites, 'Women in the Market Place: Oxfordshire 1690–1800', *Midland History* ix (1984).
[36] Chartres, 'Marketing', p.406; E. A. Wrigley, 'A Simple Model of London's Importance in Changing English Society and Economy 1650–1750', *Past and Present* 37 (1967).
[37] Chartres, 'Marketing', p.487.

'a dynamic force in agricultural marketing in the century before 1750'.[38] Improved inland navigation and coastal shipping services also speeded the integration of markets in wool, grain, cheese and other products. But enclosure and the tighter administration of highways in the eighteenth century probably raised costs in the droving trades: various tolls had to be paid, wayside pastures were harder to find, and overnight halts had to be formalised and rented.

To what extent had efficient and integrated markets for agricultural commodities been achieved by the industrial revolution period? This is a difficult question. Thorold Rogers was of the opinion that before the third quarter of the eighteenth century there were six separate price regions for cereals.[39] More recent work has shown that national rather than local disequilibrating factors were dominant in the wheat market by the years 1753–62, and Chartres has demonstrated the possibility that the wheat market was fairly well integrated as early as the 1690s.[40] However, wheat seems to be unrepresentative of cereal markets as a whole because it was a major cash crop with a wider market, including exports, than other commodities. Most markets remained regionally fragmented until fuller integration of the national economy through the development of the canal networks and later the railways. But even then there is some debate about the extent to which both canals and railways served their local regions better than interregional flows.[41] The supply of livestock, dairy produce and fruit and vegetables to towns certainly improved in the canal era and received a major boost with the coming of the railways.

Despite the shift to greater freedom in trading, the state still intervened in a great deal of commercial activity through bounties, Navigation Laws, and export and import prohibitions. It is likely, for example, that the Corn Laws between 1819 and the late 1830s bolstered the price of bread grain internally.[42] Local authorities including JPs, parish and manorial bodies could also be very active in enforcing rules about marketing hours, forestalling and regrating, weights and measures, and even price levels. But although they were

[38] Chartres, 'Marketing', p.446.
[39] Quoted in A. H. John, 'The Course of Agricultural Change 1660–1760' in L. S. Presnell, ed., *Studies in the Industrial Revolution* (London, 1960), pp.126–7.
[40] Chartres, 'Marketing', p.460.
[41] J. Langton, 'The Industrial Revolution and the Regional Geography of England', *Transactions of the Institute of British Geographers* 9 (1984), pp.145–67; G. Turnbull, 'Canals, Coal and Regional Growth During the Industrial Revolution', *Economic History Review* XL (1987). See also M. Freeman, 'Transport', in Langton and Morris, eds., *Atlas of Industrialising Britain*.
[42] Perren, 'Markets', p.213.

often resurrected in times of dearth, these internal rules had generally fallen into decline by the late eighteenth century.[43]

It is impossible to quantify what all these changes in efficiency, large, small and faltering, implied for the dynamic role of agriculture. However, the proliferation of specialist factors, the greater freedom of trading, the expanded use of credit instruments and continual improvements in transport and communications can only have speeded the turnover of trade, aided the growth of towns and made agriculture potentially more responsive to market signals.[44]

The dynamic links

Having discussed agrarian change in the century or so before and during the industrial revolution we must now ask what effect this had on the rest of the economy. Was agriculture the prime mover in economic growth and structural change, or did it merely react to stimuli from elsewhere? How responsive was the secotor and what role did it play in industrialisation?

The release of labour
The number of workers employed in agriculture continued to rise until the third quarter of the nineteenth century. But the increase in labour productivity was associated with a marked *relative* decline in the recorded agricultural labour force. This decline was probably greater in the case of women and juveniles than adult males, who show up more accurately in census returns and other records. It is now time to ask what happened to this labour and to assess the claim that its availability as a cheap labour source for industry was of key importance in industrialisation.

There are two sorts of theories regarding labour release from the primary sector and its absorption into secondary and tertiary activities in the process of industrialisation. Dominant in much current and past literature are supply-side theories which imply that labour will automatically be absorbed by industry and that, in accordance with neo-classical economic theory, no significant structural unemployment will occur. This is implicit in Crafts' model, and Chambers' view was

---

[43] Thwaites suggests that in times of dearth, conflict between the free-trade ideals of central government and the pressures of scarcity upon local authority policy resulted in a broad consciousness of the moral and social effects of changing marketing practices: W. Thwaites, 'Dearth and the Marketing of Agricultural Produce: Oxfordshire c.1750–1800', *Agricultural History Review* 33 (1985).

[44] It is possible that before the 1840s the improvements in supply of food to towns was only consistent with stable per capita consumption and that innovations in marketing structures were limited in the early nineteenth-century decades of rapid urbanisation: G. Shaw, 'Changes in Consumer Demand and Food Supply in Nineteenth-Century British Cities', *Journal of Historical Geography* 11 (1985).

that even where the rate of growth of the rural population (and hence the release of labour) exceeded the growth of demand for manufactures this merely caused manufacturing wages to collapse to a point at which manufactures became cheaper and hence more attractive, stimulating increased employment.[45]

The second sort of theory revolves around the role of labour *demand* and concentrates therefore on the rate of absorption of labour by industry. Its most notable exponent was W. Arthur Lewis who developed a model of industrialisation based on unlimited supplies of labour.[46] For Lewis the major feature of most underdeveloped economies is a perfectly elastic supply of labour at the income level obtainable in agriculture and other 'traditional' 'unskilled' occupations such as petty retailing or domestic service. With the supply of labour unlimited, industrial employment will depend on the demand for labour in industry which, in his hypothetical 'closed' economy, Lewis saw as largely linked to capital formation. Unlike Chambers and others who ascribe a large role to population growth in the expansion of industrial employment in eighteenth-century England, Lewis stressed the labour surplus endemic in many sectors before the eighteenth-century demographic advance. This is consistent with what we know from Poor Law records about unemployment and underemployment in pre-industrial England. Lewis identified four specific sources of surplus labour at zero marginal product: labour retained on small family farms, labour on the margins of petty retailing, workers in domestic service and women in general.[47]

Bearing the rival supply-and demand-side models in mind, we must now ask whether surplus agricultural labour did move significantly into manufacturing. Since Redford's classic study we have known that the long distance migration of population from largely agricultural to provincial industrial regions was small and occurred in waves mostly

---

[45] Chambers, *Population, Economy, and Society,* p.431.
[46] W. A. Lewis, 'Economic Development with Unlimited Supplies of Labour', in A. N. Agarawala and S. P. Singh, eds., *The Economics of Underdevelopment* (Oxford, 1958), pp.400–49.
[47] The demand-side model of Lewis has three important implications for the study of the precise role of labour release from eighteenth-century English agriculture. First, it allows for the possibility of structural (demand deficient) unemployment and of chronic unemployment arising from labour market rigidities. Secondly, the manufacturing wage in the Lewis model is dependent on, and tends to be the equivalent of, the wage in the 'traditional' sector. This is interesting because of the declining demand for, and hence 'opportunity cost' of, women in some areas of agriculture and because of the comparatively low agricultural wages in the north and west before the late eighteenth century. Finally, the Lewis model draws our attention to the small family farm sector and petty trading as well as to female labour within these as a source of labour surplus. In view of the nature of expansion and labour use in various proto-industries and in urban sweating during industrialisation these points are most important.

between towns and their immediate hinterlands.[48] At the same time
we know that the major expansion of proto-industries and urban or
centralised manufacturing production occurred outside commercialising agricultural regions which are likely to have been shedding labour.
It is thus impossible to explain industrial growth simply in terms of the
release of labour from agriculture, particularly from areas that seem to
have been increasing their labour productivity most.

London was certainly a magnet for rural labour in the home counties
and also much further afield, although there is some evidence that the
'labour pull' of the capital outside of the home counties was reduced by
the later eighteenth century with the formation of more regionally
insulated labour markets. According to Allen, after 1750 the south
Midlands developed into a self-contained labour market no longer
linked by migration to the rest of the country.[49] Hunt's work on
regional wage differences also supports the notion of the strengthening
of growth pole effects in the decades after 1770, i.e. the clustering of
market forces locally or regionally rather than the growth of national
integration or a national equilibrium of supply and demand.[50] As we
have seen, Williamson suggests that labour market failure may have
cost the country about 3% of GNP in the industrial revolution
period.[51]

If labour did not readily migrate from southern agricultural areas
into urban industries or industrial regions, were agrarian by-employments the beneficiaries? Though not exclusively so, protoindustries
tended to expand in districts with small farms, often concentrating on
livestock rather than arable because pasture was less labour intensive.
Where household manufacturing did develop in areas of commercial
grain or pasture farms it tended to utilise female labour or slack season
workers and usually failed to achieve the firm base necessary for long-
term success. Jones has suggested that this was a natural result of the
marked regional specialisation occurring in the eighteenth and early
nineteenth centuries on the basis of comparative advantage: 'the early
modern European countryside did gradually separate out into two
broad categories of regions with two sorts of ecosystem and economy,

[48] A. Redford, *Labour Migration in England 1800–1850* (Manchester, 1926); P. Deane
and W. A. Cole, *British Economic Growth 1688–1959* (Cambridge, 1962; 2nd edn 1967),
pp.106–22; P. Clark and D. Souden, eds., *Migration and Society in Early-Modern
England* (London, 1987), chs.1, 7, 10.
[49] Allen, *Enclosure and the Yeoman*, ch.12. See also Deane and Cole, *British Economic
Growth*, p.118, table 27.
[50] E. Hunt, 'Industrialisation and Regional Inequality: Wages in Britain 1760–1914',
Journal of Economic History 46 (1986).
[51] J. G. Williamson, 'Did English Factor Markets Fail During the Industrial Revolution?', *Oxford Economic Papers* 39 (1987), pp.641–60.

one agricultural, the other proto-industrial, linked by trade'.[52] The crop-growing areas most competitive in terms of new farming systems became more purely agricultural, their manufacturing dying back, whereas less competitive areas sought other sources of income, especially industrial by-employments. As manufacturing regions became more successful, benefiting from the build up of specialist infrastructures and associated external economies, it became more difficult for the remaining rural manufacturers in lowland arable regions to survive in competition (aside from those catering for purely local markets). With the advent of powered processes this interregional competition and specialisation reached a logical conclusion. On the clays and lowland heaths of the south and east 'with little or no alternative to "mother and daughter power", no escape from the spinning wheel or handloom, cottage industry contracted in the wake of competition from machines'.[53] The improvement of agricultural techniques between 1650 and 1750 did boost industry by stimulating regional specialisation. But the major physical separation between commercial agricultural regions and the most successful proto-industrial centres meant that the boost to industry arising out of the release of labour from the land into manufacturing may have been more limited than is often supposed.

One region which has always been cited as an illustration of the expansion of proto-industry alongside commercial agrarian production, especially during the significant shift to less labour-intensive pasture farming in the eighteenth century, is the Midlands. This region saw the expansion of straw plaiting, lace making, nail making and framework knitting, so it provides a good test case for the links between agricultural labour supply and industry. But Allen has calculated that for the south Midlands at least, between 1676 and 1831, the jobs created for men in proto-industries were less than the decline in full-time agricultural jobs and even less than the increase in the agricultural work-force. The biggest increase in employment was in petty production and retailing for local markets and in construction. For those workers who remained in agriculture the labour market was glutted so that competition for jobs was intense, hours were long and wages a pittance. The most striking feature of the eighteenth-century labour market was the growth of unemployed surplus labour, concentrated, as in the Lewis model, in the small farm sector, in petty retailing and among women and juveniles. The female proto-industries of straw plaiting, spinning and pillow lace making eventually declined in the

[52] Jones, 'Environment, Agriculture and Industrialisation', p.494. For a formal model of this regional specialisation see J. Mokyr, 'Growing Up and the Industrial Revolution in Europe', *Explorations in Economic History* 13 (1976), pp.371–96.
[53] Jones, 'Environment', p.498. Jones argues that there was a marked shift in comparative advantage as a result of the improvement of agricultural techniques c. 1650–1750.

face of competition with other industrial regions and with the factory elsewhere. Clearly proto-industry failed to expand to absorb surplus labour at low cost: such labour supplies were not a sufficient condition for successful rural or factory industry. Low wages do not necessarily translate into low labour costs if the labour is unskilled and lacks a manufacturing tradition. Labour quality was of key importance in the siting of industry and in its long-term success, as were the external economies (in the form of the accumulation of urban and tertiary services) gained by the sectoral specialisation of a region.[54]

The experience of the south Midlands alerts us to the fact that probably in many regions agricultural reorganisation and population growth created a society of paupers not proletarians. Surplus labour lay in pools unconnected with labour markets where there was demand for unskilled industrial labour. In the south Midlands (and elsewhere) industrialisation came a century or more too late to absorb the cheap newly released labour surplus which features so much in the accounts of historians anxious to explain the timing of the industrial revolution.

Switching freely from skilled land work to skilled work in industry was in any case scarcely possible. '...in-door and out-door habits, the loom and the plough, the shuttle and the sickle, the soft hand and the hard hand, cannot be interchanged at pleasure', noted a Wiltshire observer as late as the mid nineteenth century.[55] Dairying could be combined with industry, as each used the softer hands of women and juvenile workers, but hard field work could not. Industrialists could not therefore draw quickly on reserves of rural labour, a fact exacerbated by the obstacles to migration. Migration was not only discouraged by lack of information, inertia and the loss of neighbourhood and kinship ties, but by aspects of farm employment policy particularly in the rural south and east and by the nature and administration of poor relief. We have some evidence that a key determinant of levels of poor relief and of labour-intensive employment practices was the need to retain an agricultural labour force within a parish through the slack seasons in order to ensure an adequate supply of workers in times of peak demand.[56] The Settlement Laws may have been an additional deterrent to mobility, as entitlement to poor relief was usually lost with migration.

Finally, industry was slow to gain from surplus rural labour because agricultural workers often strongly resisted being sucked into industry. They were accustomed to a social life conditioned by the harvest year,

[54] Allen, *Enclosure and the Yeoman*, ch.12. See also S. Pollard, *Peaceful Conquest: The Industrialisation of Europe 1760–1970* (Oxford, 1981), p.106.
[55] J. Wilkinson, 'History of Broughton Gifford', *Wiltshire Archaeological Magazine* vi (1860), p.37, quoted in Jones, ed., *Agriculture and Economic Growth*, p.24.
[56] G. Boyer, 'The Old Poor Law and the Agricultural Labour Market in Southern England: An Empirical Analysis', *Journal of Economic History* 46 (1986); Snell, *Annals*, ch.3; Collins, 'Rationality'; Mathias, 'Agriculture and Industrialisation', p.112.

their higher earnings at harvest time and by perquisites such as the gleaning of fallen ears for the making of winter flour. Such important social markers and valuable traditional supplements to family incomes were lost with the movement to industrial jobs. Throughout the eighteenth century iron furnaces and forges were brought to a seasonal halt by workers who went harvesting, and early textile factories suffered the same interruptions. Established rural habits were frustrating to manufacturers anxious to stockpile goods for sale after harvest to satisfy the peak of internal demand. Thus, even where surplus rural labour involved itself in industry, its priorities often lay in the traditional rhythms of the agrarian cycle.[57]

Obviously, where successful proto-industrial regions depended on the integration of agrarian and industrial employments, the shifting balance of activites in favour of manufacturing owed much to the decline in labour-intensive agrarian pursuits. This was particularly the case where women turned to manufacturing alongside declining dairy farming and common land activities. But because of the under-developed nature of the labour market, the separation between labour surplus and industrial regions, the policies of farmers and the resistance of labour, industrial regions were often short of workers. This has sometimes been stressed as a major reason for the innovation of mechanical substitutes. But it would be wrong to praise agriculture because its inability to release enough labour (in the right places and at the right times) prompted invention and innovation.

The supply of food, raw materials and exports
Until recently, the success of English agriculture in providing food for the expanding population and raw materials for industry was unquestioningly stressed by historians: 'agriculture more than adequately supplied the country's wants until the mid eighteenth century (without fatally depressing farm gate prices) and failed to do so afterwards by only a short head'. So successful was agriculture that, until the 1760s, England exported more and more grain and was the main grain surplus area in western Europe. This was reversed during the third quarter of the eighteenth century but the 1780s were years of plenty again. Shortages returned during the French wars with starvation among the poor in 1795–6 and 1800–1. But these shortages spurred heavy agricultural investment and after 1813 there followed another period of adequate provision. This was the chronology of success charted by Jones in the late 1960s.[58]

To examine this success story more carefully let us first take the case of exports. Exports of wheat and other products ensured command

[57] E. P. Thompson, 'Time, Work Discipline and Industrial Capitalism', *Past and Present* 38 (1967); H. Heaton, *The Yorkshire Woollen and Worsted Industries* (Oxford, 1920), p.342; T. S. Ashton, *Iron and Steel in the Industrial Revolution* (Manchester, 1963 edn.), p.197.
[58] Jones, ed., *Agriculture and Economic Growth*, pp.18–19.

over foreign currency in the first half of the eighteenth century when the European demand for manufactured goods was sluggish.[59] But if agriculture was so efficient compared with the continent, why did these exports dry up? Why did they not continue, alongside the supply of food to the growing population internally? Crafts answers this question by saying that patterns of international trade are based on relative efficiency and as England became so much more efficient than her neighbours in producing manufactures, especially cotton textiles, agricultural goods became importables much more quickly than elsewhere in Europe.[60] In this explanation industry emerges again as the main source of dynamism dictating agriculture's role, but exports of grain actually dried up before a clear efficiency advantage in the production of cotton cloth emerged. It may just be that agriculture, though capable, did not respond quickly enough to the demands of the 1750s and 1760s. Arthur Young argued that in Norfolk 'for 30 years from 1730, the great improvements of the north western part of the county took place...For the next 30 years to about 1790 they nearly stood still; they *reposed on their laurels*'.[61] This sort of response failure may have been important in prompting legislation to admit Irish tallow meat and dairy produce, and in diverting resources to industrial expansion.[62]

It must also be remembered that exports were bolstered by a subsidy before the mid century and the strength of British grain exports owed much to government intervention. Furthermore, export bounties may have had the effect of raising domestic grain prices by as much as 19%.[63] The bounties on exports potentially benefited farmers and certainly benefited both landowners and merchants. But the domestic consumer paid a high price and the purchasing power if not the nutrition of the wage-earning population must have suffered as a result. Bread rioters particularly resented the way in which grains for

---

[59] A. H. John, 'Agricultural Productivity and Economic Growth in England 1700–1760', *Journal of Economic History* 25 (1965), repr. in Jones, ed., *Agriculture and Economic Growth*, pp.172–93.

[60] N. F. R. Crafts, S. J. Leybourne and T. C. Mills, 'Economic Growth in Nineteeth-Century Britain: Comparisons with Europe in the Context of Gerschenkron's Hypotheses', *Warwick Economic Papers* 308 (1988), p.180: forthcoming as 'Britain' in R. Sylla and G. Toniolo, eds., *Patterns of Industrialisation in Nineteenth-Century Europe; N. F. R. Crafts, 'British Industrialisation in an International Context', *Journal of Interdisciplinary History* xix (1989), pp.415–28.

[61] A. Young, *General View of ... Norfolk* (1804), quoted in Jones, ed., *Agriculture and Economic Growth*, p.42.

[62] John, 'The Course of Agricultural Change', pp.152–5.

[63] M. Combrune, *An Enquiry into the Prices of Wheat, Malt and Occasionally Other Provisions* (London, 1768), pp.50–98, quoted and discussed by Chartres in 'Marketing', pp.448, 454, 497–501.

export sold at a premium could lead to shortages and high prices for consumers in the grain-growing counties themselves.[64]

The importance of industrial raw materials derived from the agricultural sector has been stressed by a number of historians. Efficiently produced (and therefore relatively cheap) inputs for the clothing and footwear industries, as well as for soap and candle making and for brewing and distilling, were important in minimising the upward movement of manufacturing costs in certain industries. Economies in the use of materials were also introduced. For example, waste grains from processing plants in starch making, distilling and brewing were used in the fattening of pigs and cattle for urban markets. These forms of 'industrial agriculture' reused most of their by-products and subtly changed production methods as a response to the costs of different feedstuffs from one season to the next.[65] But it must be remembered that few of England's leading industries, particularly those producing exportables, relied heavily on domestic raw materials. Industries like cotton and silk, which were first to innovate in terms of machinery and the concentration of production, were entirely dependent on imports of their main raw material, and imported wool was increasingly used in wool textile production from the 1780s and 1790s.

We now turn to the provision of food and the effect of agriculture on nutrition. The population of 1850, although three times that of 1750, was still largely fed by home production. But is this the best we can say – that agriculture provided sufficient food to allay large-scale starvation and a mortality crisis? This level of agricultural development had probably been achieved well before 1750. O'Brien suggests that the potential for supporting an accelerating proportion of the population off the land had lain dormant for generations.[66] In Allen's view that position had been achieved in the previous century or so (during what he has termed the yeoman's revolution in farming which increased productivity by improved cropping yields). The shift to larger farms which occurred in the later eighteenth century did not increase yields any more than small farms had. Therefore, Allen argues, this institutional change cannot be held responsible for nourishing the population explosion. It was the proletarianisation associated with the shift to larger farms which played a major role in demographic increase and not the effect of food supplies on nutrition.[67]

The weakness of Allen's argument is that yields of livestock are not sufficiently considered, nor is the achievement of agrarian change in the eighteenth century in supplying a better balance of livestock and

[64] E. P. Thompson, 'The Moral Economy of the English Crowd', *Past and Present* 50 (1971); Thwaites, 'Dearth and Marketing'.
[65] P. Mathias, 'Agriculture and the Brewing and Distilling Industries in the Eighteenth Century', *Economic History Review* v (1952).
[66] O'Brien, 'Agriculture and the Home Market', p.785.
[67] Allen, 'Labour Productivity', p.143.

grain for food. As Wrigley has pointed out, the growing number of farm animals implied a lesser dependence on corn, hence a better balanced diet and a reduced risk of catastrophic variation in supplies (not only because farm animals are a living food source but also years that were bad for cereals might be good for grass).[68] However the problem of considering the impact of livestock ratios and yields on nutrition and demographic growth is that we know little about the social distribution of meat eating. The connection between agriculture, population growth and improved diet requires further research.

Jackson agrees with Allen that agriculture's achievement for the economy as a whole was greater in the century or more before 1750 than during the industrial revolution itself. He has shown that between 1740 and 1790 agricultural growth slowed just as population growth began to accelerate. Increases in agricultural output lagged well behind the increase in population, and falls in the level of output and consumption per head of agricultural products resulted. This highlights the fact that the 'Malthusian trap' may have been avoided by a smaller margin than is often supposed and that the onset of population growth after the middle of the century had serious consequences for the per capita supply of food and agricultural raw materials. Thus the agricultural innovations of the late seventeenth and early eighteenth centuries were not the beginnings of a simple success story. In spite of 'the eulogy British agriculture has received from its historians, its capacity for change (when measured against the additional supply required to maintain stable prices) does not seem all that impressive.'[69]

Incomes, real incomes and the home market

Several historians have been concerned to stress the size and dynamism of the home market during England's industrialisation and the role of agriculture in underpinning that dynamism.[70] Agricultural change could widen the domestic market for industrial goods in three ways: through rising agricultural incomes which might be spent on manufactures, through movement of workers out of agriculture into higher paid jobs with more disposable income, and finally through shifts in the intersectoral terms of trade which altered expenditure on manufactured goods. If agricultural prices fell relative to industrial prices (i.e. if the terms of trade favoured industry), wage earners might be encouraged to spend more on manufactured goods while investment in manufacturing might also be stimulated. If agricultural prices rose relative to industrial prices, the reverse would happen as the terms of trade would shift to favour agriculture. Measuring the impact of

---

[68] Wrigley, *Continuity, Chance and Change*, p.42.
[69] Jackson, 'Growth and Deceleration', *passim*, P. K. O'Brien, 'Agriculture and the Industrial Revolution', *Economic History Review* xxx (1977), p.175.
[70] See n.3 above.

changing terms of trade has generated much debate partly because the assessments involve making rather arbitrary assumptions about the elasticity of demand for different sorts of goods. Elasticities are necessary in order to calculate how much industrial or agricultural demand might be affected by particular changes in relative prices.

John gathered evidence of a major growth in demand for processed foods and for manufactures in the 1730s and 1740s and linked this to the conjunction of increased efficiency in agriculture and slow population growth which resulted in declining bread prices and increasing disposable incomes for the mass of the population. The effect of increasing disposable incomes on the demand for manufactures would of course only be significant if the prices of industrial goods were not rising to offset the fall in foodstuff prices. John implies this although industrial and agricultural price data are shaky and unreliable for the period. A further necessary part of John's argument was to stress that farm incomes themselves held up so that the growing purchasing power of the non-agricultural population was not offset by declining incomes and purchasing power on the land.[71] However it is possible that increasing disposable incomes (if they were generated) were spent on the growth of imported products such as tea and sugar with little stimulus being felt by the industrial sector. Or they may have been reflected, not in the purchase of manufactures, but in workers taking more time off, preferring leisure to increased consumption.

In another key contribution on the positive effect of agriculture on the home market, Eversley argued that demand for industrial goods continued to deepen in the third quarter of the eighteenth century, despite rising prices for foodstuffs, because food was sufficiently cheap not to erode disposable incomes nor to affect the demand for manufactures among the middle income groups. Farmers also became more prosperous and bought more manufactures, especially household utensils, clocks and draperies. Even more positively, Jones argues that it is unlikely that higher food prices ever seriously eroded the expansion of the home market for consumer goods among the working population in the late eighteenth century. During the Napoleonic Wars, for example, the removal of workers into the armed forces and the need to produce more food combined to increase the demand for agricultural labour relative to supply and put an upward pressure on wages. This, Jones argues, sustained real incomes and promoted the introduction of threshing machines to save labour.[72]

A less rosy picture of the links between agriculture and the home market has recently emerged from new indices of secular swings in the relative prices of agricultural and industrial commodities and hence of the intersectoral terms of trade. O'Brien has found that for a century

[71] John, 'Aspects'.
[72] Eversley, 'Home Market'; Jones, ed., *Agriculture and Economic Growth*, pp.46–6.

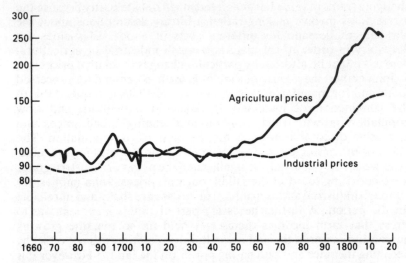

Figure 3.1: Indices of agricultural and industrial prices 1660–1820 smoothed by 9-year moving averages

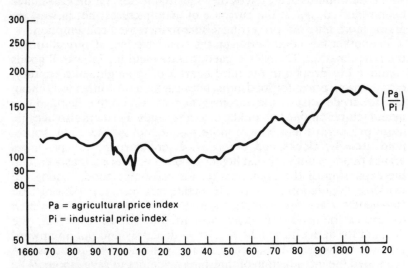

Figure 3.2: Terms of trade between agriculture and industry 1660–1820.

Source for figs 3.1 and 3.2: P.K. O'Brien, 'Agriculture and the Home Market for English Industry 1660–1820', *English Historical Review* 394 (1985), p.776.

before 1745 both industrial and agricultural prices fluctuated around a stable trend. In the second half of the seventeenth century there was a slight tendency for the net barter terms of trade to move against agriculture but this was followed by four decades when the terms of trade moved to favour neither industry nor agriculture. From 1745 to 1810 farm prices increased more rapidly than industrial prices and there was a decisive and almost continuous shift in the terms of trade against the industrial sector (see figures 3.1 and 3.2). The century from the 1640s to the 1740s stands out from the experience of relative prices throughout the period from the fifteenth to the late nineteenth century as the only time when the intersectoral terms of trade did not move consistently in favour of agriculture! But O'Brien calculates that the slight swings in favour of industry during this period (between 1666 and 1746) may only have increased expenditure on industrial goods between 3 and 8%. The reverse swing (1745 to 1815) probably reduced home demand for manufactured goods by 8–20% below the level it would (hypothetically) have attained with stable net barter terms of trade. And at the same time it probably sucked significant resources of labour and capital back into grain-growing.[73]

O'Brien's calculation of the impact of changing agricultural incomes on the demand for manufactures, and of the release of labour into higher paid jobs, is similarly very modest. The wages of labourers and husbandmen failed to keep pace with the rise in food prices after 1760. Farmers, freeholders and landowners fared better but, at most, the increased income of all farming groups *and* the effect of shifting employment structures added 68% to total expenditure on manufactures during the whole eighteenth century when industrial output expanded by a factor of around 3.7.[74] O'Brien concludes that although most of the increase in industrial output was sold to the home market, it is difficult to see agricultural productivity as a primary source behind the growth of domestic purchasing power for manufactures. This

[73] O'Brien, 'Agriculture and the Home Market', p.783. To make these calculations O'Brien has to rely on various assumed levels of elasticity of demand and of cross elasticity (the predicted change of expenditure on industrial goods for a unit change in the average price of farm produce). Furthermore, inference from direct analysis of price trends ignores the positive effect of prices in stimulating agricultural investment and innovation in the late eighteenth century and assumes market orientated 'rational' behaviour on the part of workers who were perhaps as likely to respond to lower food prices by taking more time off for leisure as they were to use higher real income to buy manufactured goods. On the possible threat to the growth of industry from the labour needs of increased grain-growing see A. Kussmaul, *A General View of the Rural Economy of England 1538–1840* (Cambridge, 1990). Kussmaul uses changing patterns of marriage seasonality as an indicator of shifts between mixed farming, arable, pastoral, and industrial pursuits in different areas of the country.
[74] O'Brien, 'Agriculture and the Home Market', p.780. These figures involve various assumptions: that real agricultural incomes rose by 81% 1700–1800; that agriculture's share of national expenditures was about 36%, and that the income elasticity of demand for manufactured goods lies between 1.0 and 1.5.

conclusion is endorsed by the recent calculations of Allen who has shown that increasing agricultural incomes accrued largely to landlords (not to those with a high propensity to consume domestically produced manufactures) and that much of the labour released from agriculture flowed not into higher paid jobs but into pauperism.[75]

Thus after the mid eighteenth century agriculture may well have started to act as a brake on industrialisation. Despite the fact that exports of domestically produced agricultural products virtually ceased and imports of food rose, especially from Ireland, agricultural prices still increased at a pace not witnessed since the sixteenth century because population was rising rapidly and agricultural output growth was decelerating, even stagnating. The mid century price rise restrained potential gains in real wages in the non-agricultural economy (thus dampening purchasing power). It was accompanied by a decline in the per capita consumption of agricultural products and this in itself suggests some downward pressure on living standards later in the century.[76] The price rise also tended to push up money wages and raw material costs in industry, thus eroding profit margins and reinvestment and increasing risks (entrepreneurs were compelled to sell higher proportions of their goods in more volatile markets abroad). The shift in the trend terms of trade after the middle of the century was an important negative development: it favoured investment in agriculture at a time when investment opportunities in industry were not only greater in number but likely (through scale economies, technical progress and advances in productivity) to yield more medium-term profit, and also more long-term value to the economy as a whole.

Agriculture as a consumer of goods and services

Activities in the agricultural sector placed direct demands upon other areas of the economy – through backward linkages (the demand for inputs) and lateral linkages (the demands for transport and other services) as well as through forward linkages (the supply of raw and semi-processed material inputs from agriculture to manufacturing) which we have already considered. The most important impulses were probably felt by the tertiary sector. Much canal construction was initially geared to the transport of grain and coal but the canals had a

---

[75] Allen, *Enclosure and the Yeoman*, chs. 12 and 14: 'productivity growth creates the possibility to raise the income of everyone in society. Who actually benefits depends on the particular institutions of the society. In England the market system and the law of property were the principal institutions that determined the division. Reliance on the market meant that most of the benefits accrued to landowners, and the law of property ensured that there were not many.'

[76] Jackson, 'Growth and Deceleration'. See also O'Brien, 'Agriculture and the Home Market', p.776. Jackson avoids the problem of unknown elasticities in commenting on consumption by taking the latter to be equal to the market clearing quantity demanded; cf. E. L. Jones, 'Agriculture 1700–1780' in R. C. Floud and D. McCloskey, eds., *Economic History of Britain since 1700* (Cambridge, 1981) I, pp.66–86.

major effect in the diffusion of industrial goods and raw materials of all kinds. Similarly the demands of the farming sector for legal services, estate stewardship, the mortgaging of land and the preparing of evidence for parliamentary enclosure helped create a body of professionals and clerks of use to the industrialising economy more generally. The export trade in grain provided a bulk outward cargo and thus contributed to greater efficiency in the use of ships and was also a spur to shipbuilding. Coastal and canal traffic in agricultural commodities had a similar effect. The growth of country banking owed much to agricultural demands, as did the development of credit instruments like the bill of exchange. Drovers were especially important in performing intermediate banking services and their traffic made Smithfield a major market for inland bills for internal trade generally by the late seventeenth century.[77] The marketing practices as well as the finance of interregional trade were mostly pioneered by agricultural traders.

Agriculture also provided a market for producer goods, although growth here was very protracted because of the slow innovation of improved tools and machinery. Iron ploughs, chaff-cutting, winnowing and threshing machines were not introduced on any scale until the Napoleonic wars. During the crucial decades of the late eighteenth century most agricultural implements continued to be made largely of wood and to be manufactured in local forges and workshops. In the 1830s and 1840s demands increased for machinery, tiles and drains, building materials, guano imports and improved implements associated with the period of 'high farming'. But this spurt in demand was linked more to the maturing of the industrial economy than to the industrial revolution itself. It may well be that from the 1830s and 1840s the stimulus from agriculture to the rest of the economy came into its own, not only via backward linkages but also because the railway era improved mobility and information flow, easing the process of migration and labour transfer. The period of high farming did, however, make agriculture more capital intensive and we need to consider the direction of net flows of capital between the land and the rest of the economy in this period and earlier.

The release of capital

It can be argued that agriculture performed a valuable role in providing much of the revenue for central and local government and finance for industry, transport and urban developments. But this aspect of the role of agriculture is perhaps more fraught with problems of estimation and the disparate nature of evidence than any other. In summarising the analyses available in 1965, Crouzet was moved to remark that 'landed' capital 'seems to have played an altogether minor

77 Chartres, 'Marketing', p.481.

part in financing the industrial revolution'.[78] In more positive vein Jones wrote that 'Landowners did play a noteworthy role in fostering industry ... the balance of probabilities is that agriculture did make a net contribution to the formation of industrial capital'.[79] Twenty-five years on we are still little nearer to resolving this question largely because of the range of possible avenues for the flow of funds, different types of finance, the reverse flow of industrial and commercial funds into agriculture, and great local, regional and sectoral variation.

We know that some landlords were closely involved in coal and mineral mining on their estates. The north-east coalfield and the Cornish tin-mining region illustrate this well. Others invested in transport, notably in local canals: in many canal companies between 1760 and 1815, for example, landed finance represented about a third of shareholdings.[80] In some areas, like Liverpool and Birmingham, landowners also put capital into urban housing. But on close inspection it appears that much of the landed investment in industry was of a *rentier* type, although historians have found direct enterprise and investment more common in the early stages of exploration and exploitation of mines. This was certainly the case in the Black Country in the late eighteenth century.[81] And in the brewing industry it appears that landed finance played a major role both at the initiation and during the later expansion of concerns.[82] There are also examples of landowners becoming involved in textile businesses but here the involvement was usually one of leasing mills to fullers or to manufacturers. Lord Dartmouth, for example, owned and leased out 19 mills in the Leeds/Huddersfield area in the early nineteenth century. He was just one of several landowners in the West Riding who made a contribution to the provision of fixed capital for local industry. Some like Sir James Graham encouraged domestic clothiers to settle on their estates by providing cottages and agricultural plots as well as building mills.[83]

The leasing of mineral rights, mines, farm plots and other industrial premises by landowners was most often clearly seen as an aspect of estate improvement. Extension and improvements to installations or premises were accompanied by rising rents which in some cases

[78] F. Crouzet, ed., *Capital Formation in the Industrial Revolution* (London, 1972), p.178.
[79] Jones, ed., *Agriculture and Economic Growth*, pp.35–6.
[80] J. T. Ward, *The Finance of Canal Building in Eighteenth-Century England* (Oxford, 1974).
[81] T. Raybould, 'Aristocratic Landowners and the Industrial Revolution: The Black Country Experience, *c*.1760–1840', *Midland History* IX (1984).
[82] Mathias, 'Agriculture and Brewing'.
[83] For details of these and other examples of landed finance in the West Riding textile industry see P. Hudson, *The Genesis of Industrial Capital* (Cambridge, 1986), ch.4. Landowners owned about 6% of all wool textile mills traced in the West Riding before 1850.

creamed off profits and deprived industry of funds for reinvestment. Industry often paid a high price for the capital transferred from the landed sector.[84]

There are also examples of landowners who were opposed to industrial development and took steps to prevent it. Some regarded canals with suspicion because they feared that an easier flow of grain would glut markets and depress prices and rents. In Nottinghamshire and Derbyshire some magnates tried to exclude textile mills from access to water power and on the Durham coalfield decisions regarding wagonways, pits, tips and colliery buildings were determined by a desire to minimise the visual impact from the landowners' mansions.[85] Landowners sometimes sold off their industrial assets to finance farm improvements. Sir Christopher Sykes sold his interests in stock and shipping in order to develop the Yorkshire Wolds at the end of the eighteenth century. As we have seen, the terms of trade at that time would favour such shifts of investment, while the heavy costs associated with enclosure might compel such a shift on the part of landowners determined to raise the efficiency of their estates through consolidation and privatisation. Landed estates often carried a heavy burden of mortgage debt, supposedly raised from professional and commercial sources, and this must be added to the substantial dowries brought to the land by the heiress daughters of merchants.[86] Landes has suggested that 'in the early decades of heavy enclosure, that is the very years that also saw the birth of modern industry, British husbandry was taking as much capital as it was giving; while in the period from 1790–1814, when food prices rose to record levels, the net flow of resources was probably towards the land.'[87]

It is not clear from case studies of the careers of industrialists whether industry benefited from agricultural capital or the reverse. Joseph Wilkes (1735–1805), who came from a farm family, prospered by promoting transport improvement, became a cotton manufacturer and then a landowner in Staffordshire. Richard Arkwright provides a spectacular example: his Hampton Court Estate in Herefordshire cost £229,000 which equalled nearly 60% of the fixed capital in the centralised cotton industry in 1809! More generally, Jones has argued that 'a man's descendants commonly bled his factories to subsidise their life as country gentlemen and the improvement of their estates'.[88]

[84] Hudson, *Genesis*, pp.86–7, 90–1.
[85] Jones, ed., *Agriculture and Economic Growth*, pp.26, 32–3.
[86] Jones, *Agriculture and Economic Growth*, p.26, n.2; Allen, *Enclosure and the Yeoman*, ch.14; J. M. Martin, 'The Cost of Parliamentary Enclosure in Warwickshire', in Jones, ed., *Agriculture and Economic Growth*, pp.128–51.
[87] D. S. Landes, *The Unbound Prometheus: Technological Change and Industrial Development in Western Europe from 1750 to the Present* (Cambridge, 1969), p.77.
[88] Jones, ed., *Agriculture and Economic Growth*, p.28; Jones, 'Industrial Capital and Landed Investment: The Arkwrights in Herefordshire 1809–43', in Jones and Mingay, eds., *Land, Labour and Population*, pp.48–71.

There is some evidence of a slow down in the land market in the late eighteenth century which may have reduced the numbers of newcomers to landownership and thus changed the course of industrialists' career patterns. And Stone has argued that the landed élite was not so open to newcomers throughout the eighteenth and nineteenth centuries as earlier accounts suggest; but his research concentrates on entry to the highest ranks and his results almost certainly underestimate the movement of persons and capital into landed society at lower levels.[89] What is certain is that both old landed families and new arrivals included those prone to spend a great deal of their wealth in conspicuous consumption rather than industrial or commercial investment. Stylish country mansions were a feature of the age, most larger landowners possessed fine art collections, a well-stocked wine cellar, armies of household retainers, and spent a great deal of money in spa towns, in the capital or on the continent. Improving landlords were also conspicuous in the breeding of animals, usually an exciting and costly hobby rather than a commercial investment.

The flow of finance from industry into landowning and vice versa is also complicated by differential regional patterns in the two sectors. It is possible that in southern England industrialists more readily left older industries for agriculture and speeded their contraction. The decline of the Weald of Kent was accompanied by such shifts. And the movement of capital from the south-east textile sector into agriculture was not just for the prestige of landownership but out of a recognition that local industrial investment was no longer viable.[90] The considerable regional specialisation occurring during the industrial revolution suggests that there were marked spatial variations in the size and direction of the flow of funds. In general, as with the flow of labour, it is worth bearing in mind that the rural areas with the greatest potential surplus of funds in the form of high profits and farm rents were often those most removed geographically from industrial concentrations. Thus it is necessary to consider improvements which were occurring in interregional as well as in local capital markets.

Although the network of country banks was expanding in the second half of the eighteenth century and these institutions were capable, via the London clearing banks, of effecting a transfer of funds from areas of surplus to areas of need, it is likely that their impact in this respect was slight until into the nineteenth century. The development of specialist bill brokers during the Napoleonic Wars did facilitate the transfer of short-term funds interregionally via the discount

[89] H. J. Habakkuk, 'The English Land Market in the Eighteenth Century', in J. S. Bromley and E. H. Kossman, eds., *Britain and the Netherlands* (London, 1960); L. Stone and J.F.C. Stone, *An Open Elite? England 1540–1880* (Oxford, 1984).
[90] Jones, ed., *Agriculture and Economic Growth*, pp.28–9; B. Short, 'The Deindustrialisation Process: A Case Study of the Weald', in P. Hudson, ed., *Regions and Industries: A Perspective on the Industrial Revolution in Britain* (Cambridge, 1989).

market. Agriculture therefore played a role in financing trade. But the liquidity needs of both arable and industrial sectors peaked at the same time – in the summer months and just before harvest – leaving only limited surpluses to be shifted to industry in the crucial times of greatest need. Furthermore, the capital flow created by the growth of the insurance business may have been a major factor in ensuring a reverse drift of capital from industry and trade to the land. Premiums from the rising insurance companies were most often invested in the secure arena of the mortgage market for farmers and landowners.[91]

The informal and formal capital market at local level appears to have been the most important in linking agriculture and industry. Small agricultural holdings, or just access to common lands on the part of domestic workers, subsidised artisan households or enabled putting-out employers – those who farmed out work to households – to pay industrial wages below subsistence level. Thus capital from land and industry was intimately linked in the functioning of rural domestic manufacturing concerns. Ownership of a farm or smallholding could also facilitate the entry of entrepreneurs into larger-scale undertakings. At a time when such a large proportion of total wealth was in agricultural assets, it is not surprising that land was the major security upon which loans could be raised and upon which financial status, respectability and credit worthiness rested. So important was the mortgage of land in raising industrial capital in the West Riding that the Registry of Deeds was established in 1725 specifically to document ownership transfers and thus promote the finance of industry.[92] Raising finance on the security of land was also of crucial importance in Lancashire, the West Midlands and other areas. The sale and mortgage of farms and fields, from the evidence of title deeds and business papers in Yorkshire and elsewhere, appears to have been a major channel for the transfer of capital into industry; but as most of the mortgagees were merchants, manufacturers and, later, banks one can see that land mortgage and sale was acting more as a means of transferring wealth within the commercial and industrial classes than shifting capital from agriculture to industry.[93]

Also important to industrialists in the period was the increasingly efficient transfer of local funds between landowners (particularly widows and spinsters) and industrialists via local and regional capital markets. Attorneys were especially important in arranging loans within regions and localities, and their legal role in estate agency and

[91] P. G. M. Dickenson, *The Sun Fire Insurance Office 1710–1960* (London, 1960), pp.244ff. Williamson ('English factor markets') estimates that capital market failure may have cost the economy 4% of GDP during the industrial revolution; cf. C. E. Heim and P. Mirowski, 'Interest Rates and Crowding Out during Britain's Industrial Revolution' *Journal of Economic History* XLVII *(1987)*.
[92] Hudson, *Genesis*, chs.3 and 4 and pp.96ff.
[93] This was certainly the case in the West Riding textile industry: Hudson, *Genesis*, pp.96–104.

trusteeship placed them in a good position to learn about and be trusted with the disposal of surplus funds arising from estate ownership. However, if the West Riding is at all representative of industrialising regions, it seems that landowners were less important as a source of loans for manufacturers than were local wool staplers or merchants.[94]

There is some evidence of an acceleration of the transfer of finance from the land into industry during the profit inflation of the Revolutionary and Napoleonic Wars. Jones cites a number of account books which indicate that farmers became serious local lenders only on the strength of their windfall gains in the 1790s and 1800s.[95] Thus it may be, as O'Brien suggests, that 'High prices had to be paid to those who had charge of English agriculture and its investable surplus in order to persuade them to lend serious and positive support to industrialisation'.[96]

Conclusion

Current interpretations of the role of agriculture in the English industrial revolution do not reflect a consensus, but more cautious and negative analyses are now appearing than at any time since Ricardo. Some historians still place agricultural change at centre stage in accounting for the structural shift in employment during industrialisation.[97] Others stress a sequence akin to the classical scenario: rising living standards followed by accelerating population growth and, in the long run, by a lack of supply response in agriculture.[98] Resolving the issue is difficult given the sources and data: the lack of direct output figures, the problems of estimating the sectoral shift in the working population over time, the relative absence of information about the female population, assumptions which have to be made about living standards and demand elasticities, and the problem of allowing for great regional variations of experience and of sectoral interaction.

Capital flowed in both directions between industry and agriculture via national taxation, local rates, investment by landowners in government stock, and via the formal and informal capital markets. It is impossible to quantify all these flows, but few historians place the emphasis on industry as overwhelmingly the major recipient. The size of the agricultural sector inevitably meant that its impact on the rest of the economy in supplying and demanding goods and services would be

94 Hudson, *Genesis*, p.101.
95 Jones, ed., *Agriculture and Economic Growth*, p.32.
96 O'Brien, 'Agriculture and the Home Market', p.785
97 Crafts and Wrigley in particular.
98 Jackson, O'Brien and Allen.

important.[99] But did the sector become *more* significant as a stimulus to the economy in the eighteenth century as industrialisation got underway, or did it respond only shakily to the demands placed upon it? Estimating agricultural productivity change is important because it is the key to assessing how the sector affected the supply of labour and food to industry. However if the labour force in factories and in urban industrial centres came mainly from the industrial regions themselves or from areas with a long history of industrial by-employment, the role of commercialising agriculture in determining the opportunity costs of these workers appears less important. Similarly, lower productivity would have led to greater imports, but without estimating the supply elasticities facing England it is difficult to be sure how much domestic agriculture really mattered to the rest of the economy during the industrial revolution.[100] On balance, the current evidence suggests that we should turn from attributing to agriculture the major dynamism of the period and instead re-examine the notion that the industrial revolution was primarily industrial, urban and commercial.[101]

[99] In 1800, after decades of relative contraction, the sector still contained around one-third of the labour force, two-thirds of the national capital stock and directly accounted for about one-third of national income.
[100] Mokyr makes these points in 'Has the Industrial Revolution Been Crowded Out?', p.305. The importance of a flexible supply of food from abroad, especially from Ireland, is stressed by Brindley Thomas in 'Escaping from Constraints: The Industrial Revolution in a Malthusian Context', *Journal of Interdisciplinary History* xv (1985), pp.729–53.
[101] A reaffirmation is needed according to O'Brien in 'Agriculture and the Home Market', p.786.

II

The Industrial Revolution

4 REGIONS AND INDUSTRIES

An identifying feature of the industrial revolution was the marked dynamism of certain industrialising regions while in others manufacturing activity and its offshoots stagnated or declined. Slow-moving national indicators of growth and change obscure the unevenness of development and thus underplay fundamental shifts in economic and social life occurring in most regions of Britain. The markets for food and for manufactured goods were not fully integrated in the eighteenth century and interregional flows of labour and capital were even less well developed, particularly the movement of labour which involved so many cultural, institutional and social rigidities. There were marked regional price and wage differentials, different units of weights and measures, different mixes of agriculture and industry, and hence different terms of trade between the two sectors. Technological developments in industry, the changing nature of work, gender and age structures in work, labour relations, urban living standards and social class relations all varied enormously from one region to the next. Thus studies of the role of agriculture, the pace of industrialisation, the extent and causes of population growth, and the changing nature of social relations may all yield very different insights when focused on specific regions rather than the nation as a whole. A regional perspective is particularly important in examining the causes and the dynamics of change.[1]

The regional perspective

There are several reasons why a regional perspective is more important for studying the industrial revolution than, perhaps, almost any other period in British history. First, there was something unique about the process of regional specialisation taking place in the late eighteenth century and in the first half of the nineteenth. Industrialising regions came to be dominated by particular industrial sectors (principally by various combinations of textiles, coal, engineering, metalwares and shipbuilding). Thus cotton textiles became more exclusively the business of south Lancashire; the West Riding gained a marked ascendancy over East Anglia and the south-west in the production of wool textiles; the Midlands became the noted home of

[1] See S. Pollard, *Peaceful Conquest: The Industrialization of Europe 1760–1970* (Oxford, 1981), pp.3–41, 111–23; J. Langton and R. J. Morris, eds., *Atlas of Industrialising Britain 1780–1914* (London, 1986); P. Hudson, *Regions and Industries: A Perspective on the Industrial Revolution in Britain* (Cambridge, 1989).

the small metalwares and hardware trades; and coalfields increasingly dictated the location of iron processing and, later, steel manufacture and, in turn, shipbuilding. This marked geographical concentration of whole sectors of production had never been experienced before. Nor has it been observed since, because sectoral specialisation by region began to break down after the nineteenth century, a process accelerated during the 1920s and 1930s and after the Second World War. The twentieth century has seen the growth of intrasectoral spatial heirarchies. High-order capital-intensive and research activities for each major sector tend to be sited in metropolitan and urban centres, often far removed from the location of more labour-intensive or low-grade activities which need cheap labour and add less value. This process has of course been facilitated by the use of electric power (which freed energy consuming industries from the necessity of coalfield siting) and also by the greater international division of labour following transport improvements and the growth of multinational capital.[2]

Thus the industrial revolution created regions different in kind to those existing now and also to those earlier. Before the eighteenth century similar pre-industrial regions existed side by side, largely cut off from one another because of poor communications and lack of the economic complementarity which might stimulate major transport improvements. These sorts of regions disappeared from the mid eighteenth century to be replaced by distinct, internally integrated and economically more specialised regions whose extraregional export base became an important foundation of their success.[3]

Secondly, the most important spatial unit regarding markets for factors, especially capital and labour, for information flow and for commercial and credit networks in the pre-railway period was undoubtedly the region. And the construction of the improved waterway and canal systems did much to cement the existence of regional economies. Waterway networks were largely regionally constructed (at first almost entirely regionally financed and promoted) and somewhat inward looking.[4] As Langton has argued,

Dense patches of the [canal] network ... developed highly integrated economies largely separate from one another ... As they developed on the basis of comparative advantages and the external economies of scale available to particular industries

[2] D. Massey, 'In What Sense a Regional Problem?', Regional Studies 13 (1979); Massey, Spatial Division of Labour: Social Structures and the Geography of Production (London, 1984); D. Harvey, The Limits to Capital (Oxford, 1982).
[3] This is argued more fully in Pollard, Peaceful Conquest, pp.3–41 and Hudson, Regions and Industries, ch. 1.
[4] M. Freeman, 'Transport', in Langton and Morris, Atlas, p.86.

within them the canal-based economies became more specialised, more differentiated from each other and more internally unified.[5]

Nor were railways quick to destroy regionally integrated transport systems. Most companies found it in their best interests to structure freight rates so as to encourage the trade of the regions they served. In Freeman's view, 'where companies exhibited discrete territorial identity this acted to cement existing resource grouping, almost forming a policy of regional development'.[6]

The regional nature of factor markets is illustrated by the case of labour. In his work on regional wages Hunt has gathered evidence of a major and widening shift in regional differentials between 1760 and the 1790s in favour of the northern industrialising areas. This is not consonant with the assumption of current macroeconomic work, that industrialisation is accompanied by more efficient markets which reduce spatial price differentials. Hunt sees his findings as more consistent with a growth pole interpretation (compatible with a regional perspective and analysis). The growth-pole approach predicts that market forces may operate to reinforce the initial advantages of industrialising regions. The development of external economies and economies of scale will encourage the clustering of new economic activities creating backwash effects in more peripheral regions which prove unable to compete and may lose their most vigorous populations through migration.[7] Recent work by Souden on regional patterns of migration endorses this view of the regionally specific nature of labour supply and labour needs and of the largely short-distance sex-specific flows of migrants which this precipitated.[8]

[5] J. Langton, 'The Industrial Revolution and the Regional Geography of England', *Transactions of the Institute of British Geographers* 9 (1984), p.162. See also G. Turnbull, 'Canals, Coal and Regional Growth in the Industrial Revolution', *Economic History Review* XL (1987).

[6] Freeman, 'Transport', p.92. See also G. Hawke, *Railways and Economic Growth in England and Wales 1840–1914* (Oxford, 1970).

[7] E. H. Hunt, 'Industrialisation and Regional Wage Inequality: Wages in Britain 1760–1914', *Journal of Economic History* 46 (1986); Hunt, 'Wages' in Langton and Morris, *Atlas*, pp.60–8.

[8] D. Souden, ' "East, West – Home's Best"? Regional Patterns in Migration in Early Modern England', in P. Clark and D. Souden, eds., *Migration and Society* (London, 1987), pp.292–332. See also P. Deane and W. A. Cole, *British Economic Growth 1688–1959* (Cambridge, 2nd edn, 1969), pp.106–22.

The markets for industrial capital and commercial credit were also primarily regional before the 1830s and 1840s.[9] In the eighteenth and early nineteenth centuries capital rarely flowed outside industrial regions where it was generated, and the bulk of finance raised by industrialists came from within a network of commercial, social and familial links where face-to-face knowledge and trust were important. Regional networks of capital supply were articulated in the eighteenth century through the role of attorneys active at the level of the county legal circuit. Land-tax collectors, with their important seasonal balances, were also regionally based. Both had detailed knowledge of the landed or other security of potential borrowers. The banking system of the period also had distinctive regional features. It was quite common for private banks within each industrial region to bail each other out in times of crisis with declarations of support. And the basis of the developing banking system – agreements and recognition, the acceptance of notes and cheques – was much denser within the region than beyond. The banking system did also transfer funds from areas of capital surplus to areas of capital need, a function which increased in importance after the development of specialist bill brokers during the Napoleonic wars. In the discount of foreign bills in particular the London acceptance houses of the late eighteenth century and the metropolitan bill brokers of the nineteenth century were vital. But London's pivotal role here served to endorse regional difference by bolstering the supply of capital and credit in the industrial regions, particularly where those regions were receiving an influx of foreign bills in return for exports. And the differential interest rates which provided a motive force for this transfer were themselves an illustration of the existence of specifically regional capital markets.[10] The regional nature of many commercial crises and waves of bankruptcies provides further testimony of the intra-regional level of the great bulk of financial links during the industrial revolution.[11]

[9] P. Hudson, *The Genesis of Industrial Capital: A Study of the West Riding Wool Textile Industry c. 1750–1850* (Cambridge, 1986); B. L. Anderson, 'The Attorney and the Early Capital Market in Lancashire', in J. R. Harris, ed., *Liverpool and Merseyside: Essays in the Economic and Social History of the Port and its Hinterland* (Liverpool, 1969); T. S. Ashton, 'The Bill of Exchange and Private Banks in Lancashire 1790–1830', in T. S. Ashton and R. S. Sayers, eds., *Papers in English Monetary History* (Oxford, 1954); L. S. Presnell, *Country Banking in the Industrial Revolution* (Oxford, 1956).

[10] B. L. Anderson, 'The Lancashire Bill System and its Liverpool Practitioners: The Case of a Slave Merchant', in W. H. Chaloner, ed., *Trade and Transport* (Manchester, 1977); Presnell, *Country Banking*, pp.223, 254, 556.

[11] Hudson, *Genesis*, pp.127, 203, 232–3; cf. J. Hoppitt, *Risk and Failure in English Business 1700–1800* (Cambridge, 1987), pp.59–63. Also cf. I. Black, 'Geography, Political Economy and the Circulation of Finance Capital in Early Industrial England', *Journal of Historical Geography* 15 (1989), who stresses the metropolitan-dominated flow of mercantile finance – as opposed to manufacturing capital – which underpinned the regionally fragmented series of export-based economies.

Thirdly, it can be argued that, despite the continuing influence of London, the industrial regions of this period were freer of metropolitan economic, social and political influence than they had been in the seventeenth and early eighteenth centuries or were to become from the late nineteenth century with the greater integration of the national economy. This had much to do with sectoral specialisation and the ·development of export trades which were conducted not through London, as in the past, but direct from the industrial regions themselves through their own ports and mercantile facilities. Thus, for example, less and less of the export trade in woollen cloths from the West Riding passed through Blackwell Hall factors but was increasingly conducted by Yorkshire merchants dealing direct through Hull and, later, through agents in Liverpool. Less of the inland trade in consumer goods also flowed through London by the late eighteenth century. The rapid growth of provincial industrial towns resulted in greater dispersal of the specialist factors and middlemen involved in the manufactures, food and droving trades than had been the case when the major markets of London had fewer significant competitors.[12] Furthermore, with increasing sectoral specialisation by region, slumps in the markets for particular goods and the effects of specific state policies often led to the formation of regionally based lobbying groups and political and social protest movements. Such oppositional politics between London and the provinces was not of course new. In a sense it was inherent in the formation of the nation state from Tudor times and was heightened by the Civil War. However, there appears to have been as increasing gulf of interests between economically powerful groups in London and the industrial regions during the industrial revolution, endorsed in the second quarter of the nineteenth century, if not before, by provincial opposition to central interference in local government.[13] The London/provincial cleavage was also marked within the skilled trade unions and only started to be bridged from 1851 with the formation of the Amalgamated Society of Engineers.[14]

It has even been suggested that there were two fundamentally different patterns of growth during the industrial revolution which reflected a dualism between the metropolitan economy and the centres

[12] R. G. Wilson, *Gentlemen Merchants: The Merchant Community in Leeds 1700–1830* (Manchester, 1971), ch. 3; R. B. Westerfield, *Middlemen in English Business, particularly between 1660 and 1760* (New Haven, 1915; repr. Newton Abbot, 1968).

[13] This opposition was endorsed by the Municipal Corporation Act of 1837 which placed many urban centres under the control of local liberal élites. See E. P. Hennock, *Fit and Proper Persons: Ideal and Reality in Nineteenth-Century Urban Government* (London, 1972) and Hennock 'Central/Local Government Relations in England: An Outline 1800–1950', *Urban History Yearbook* (1982).

[14] H. Southall, 'Towards a Geography of Unionization: The Spatial Organization and Distribution of Early British Trade Unions', *Transactions of the Institute of British Geographers* 13 (1988), p.473.

of provincial industry. Growth in the industrial areas was based largely on exports requiring low wages to keep down costs and prices. This had the effect of limiting the development of consumer goods industries and the personal service sector. By contrast, growth in the metropolitan economy (despite the mass of casual poor) generated significantly higher per capita incomes. Based 'on the twin pillars of accumulated wealth from trade and finance and the land',[15] the metropolitan economy generated demand for services, especially domestic employment, but also for lawyers, bankers and financial advisers. The affluence of the metropolitan market also extended to construction and consumer goods manufacture. Lee argues that the economic and geographical separateness dividing land and commerce from industry (and dividing the economy of London and the south-east from that of the industrialising north) was reinforced by 'the social links between London financiers and the landed gentry, the Anglican church, the public schools, the ancient universities and conservative political interest ... The industrial provinces ... remained largely outside this network of influential institutions and interest, and adhered to nonconformist denominations, liberal politics and their own educational institutions'.[16] It is easy to overplay these distinctions between industry, finance and the land; and between the culture and authority of provincial businessmen and the older élites.[17] But the thesis that the metropolitan economy was structurally different and geographically separate from that of the industrialising provinces is an important one.

Fourthly, the period saw a growing identification among all social groups with the economic, social and political interests of their region. Although it may have been no more important than other identifications based on class, religion, nation or community, it certainly grew with them and reacted upon them. Regional identities are obvious in the growth of regionally based clubs and societies, employers' associations, trade unions and radical movements, including Luddism, food rioting and the arming and drilling of the war years. Employers depended on regional co-operation to control such matters as unreasonable credit practices and embezzlement and to blacklist and otherwise curtail the role of labour activists. Even Chartism, despite its national formation and cohesion, is difficult to understand without close attention to marked regional differences in support, outlook, motives and policies. Industrialisation accentuated the difference between regions by making them more functionally distinct and specialised. This gave them very particular occupational and income distributions and varying degrees of dependence on specific markets or

[15] C. H. Lee, *The British Economy Since 1700: A Macroeconomic Perspective* (Cambridge, 1986), pp. 136–41.
[16] Lee, *The British Economy*, p. 141.
[17] See discussion in ch. 7.

technological changes. Economic and commercial circumstances were thus experienced regionally in the first instance. While it would be unwise to employ a crude economic determinism here, it is clear that social or political movements with their regional fragmentation can only fully be understood in relation to economic and social structures at regional level.[18]

Gregory has argued that the structural transformation of labour and of the labour process during the industrial revolution was a regional affair and that struggles over the control and character of work were undertaken largely at regional level.[19] And Randall has shown that workers in the West Riding and the West Country, which were both dominated by wool textile production, found it difficult to link their interests in a common cause (such as opposition to the deregulation of the woollen industry in the early nineteenth century) because of differences in expectations and experiences which arose from fundamental differences in regional class structures and social relations.[20]

Likewise, issues of national political reform came to be identified with particular regions, for example, factory reform with Yorkshire, the anti-Poor Law campaign with Lancashire, currency reform with Birmingham. Langton has argued that 'These regional differences of preoccupation generalised beyond particular issues, entered people's consciousness ... and became one of the major currencies of English literature when the regional novel emerged as an important genre in the 1840s'.[21] Often the clearly identifiable industrial region was created by links with provincial centres – Manchester, Liverpool, Birmingham, Bradford, Leeds or Newcastle – and made complete by the intraregional nature of most migration and by the growth of the provincial press.

Sectoral specialisation and the relative efficiency of intraregional, compared with interregional, transport and communications largely explains the distinctive social and class relations found in the industrial areas. As a result regional difference in political attitudes, trade union membership, voting behaviour and cultural activities lasted long after late nineteenth-century innovations in communications and in business and financial institutions began to dissolve some of the material

[18] Langton, 'Industrial Revolution', pp. 150–5; see also D. Read, *The English Provinces 1760–1960: A Study in Influence* (London, 1964). For studies of working class political movements adopting this perspective see A. Briggs, *Chartist Studies* (London, 1959); J. Foster, *Class Struggle in the Industrial Revolution* (London, 1974); D. Gregory, *Regional Transformation and Industrial Revolution: A Geography of the Yorkshire Woollen Industry* (London, 1982).
[19] Gregory, *Regional Transformation*, p.292.
[20] A. Randall, *Before the Luddites* (Cambridge, 1991); Randall, 'Work, Culture and Resistance to Machinery in the West of England Woollen Industry', in Hudson, *Regions*.
[21] Langton, 'Industrial Revolution', p.156.

underpinnings of regionalism.[22] This was one of the most important legacies of the industrial revolution as a social and political as well as an economic process.

Finally, a regional perspective on the industrial revolution can help in understanding the dynamic of industrialisation more generally. Pollard has argued that the influence of Britain as a pioneer industrial nation 'was grounded on the existence of ... relatively limited regions providing, as it were, a system of walls within which the new ideas could reverberate and gain reinforcing strength ... instead of being diffused ineffectively across the length and breadth of a mostly unreceptive island'.[23] Thus, for Pollard, the industrial region of the late eighteenth and nineteenth centuries had a dynamic and operative function and not just a descriptive meaning. Industrial regions, he argues, generated an interaction which would have been absent if their component industries had not been juxtaposed in that way. And the dynamism of these industrial regions eventually spread out to influence other manufacturing areas. The Sheffield area, for example, could tap capital, technological aids, commercial information, and foreign markets and rely on the protection of the British navy, all of which had been built up for the use of the earlier-advanced export regions.[24]

The industrial region of the nineteenth century differed from its proto-industrial predecessor in requiring a minimum critical mass to maintain the momentum of growth. By contrast proto-industrial concentrations were of very mixed size and structure: sometimes small towns, most often dispersed in hamlets and villages, but over areas varying greatly in size from relatively isolated pockets to entire counties. Proto-industry clearly did not require the same sorts of external or scale economies as we find in centralised, more capital-intensive production.[25] Thus the interactions and self-reinforcing drive created by the development of industry in its regional concentration must lie at the heart of analyses of the industrial revolution in Britain and elsewhere.

National considerations

In making a case for the importance of a regional perspective on the industrial revolution we must not undermine those national aspects of economic and social development which were of significant and even growing importance and which must remain a major focus of our attention. For example, new and intense forms of competition and

[22] See for example, M. Savage, *The Dynamics of Working Class Politics: The Labour Movement in Preston 1880–1940* (Cambridge, 1987); H. R. Southall, 'The Origins of the Depressed Areas: Unemployment, Growth and Regional Economic Structure in Britain Before 1914', *Economic History Review* 41 (1988).
[23] Pollard, *Peaceful Conquest*, p.19.
[24] Pollard, *Peaceful Conquest*, pp.28–9.
[25] Pollard, *Peaceful Conquest*, pp.33–9, 106.

changing power relations between employers and workers affected all regions and a mass of trades across the spectrum from farm to factory and to workshop, sweatshop and garret. The nature and role of the central state is also of crucial importance. Its activities impinged across a broad front although most policies had a regional, sectoral or class-specific emphasis and had often arisen from pressure group activity at that level. Taxes and bounties usually endorsed existing tendencies to the unequal distribution of regional (as well as class) development. The Land Tax, for example, fixed approximately in line with late seventeenth-century land values, tended to favour the advancing northern industrial districts by not raising their share as industrial property values rose. There was however, more to state activity than taxes and bounties. The 'fiscal military state' had an overall effect on the national economy by providing military support for colonial development, by engaging in costly trade wars which stimulated certain sectors of the economy, by the creation of the National Debt which ensured loyalty of an important group of state creditors, by promoting a legal system which protected private property and by activities which expanded state bureaucracy and hence tertiary sector employment in London in particular.[26]

Neither must one underemphasise the economic and cultural role of London in the life of the country as a whole. A large proportion of the English population (perhaps one sixth) had regular and immediate contact with the capital through trade, training, social life or travel routes. The capital was a centre of commercial intelligence and conspicuous consumption influencing fashion and tastes far and wide. And the demand of the London market created regional specialisation in the production of both agricultural and industrial goods. The flow of commerce to the capital did much to develop the tertiary sector, particularly interregional transport and financial services. Thus, although industrial capital markets in the provinces were largely regional, the role of London in underpinning and providing the extension of credit involved in trade, especially international trade, cannot be overemphasised. For example, when the value of Liverpool's foreign trade overtook that of London for a period in the early nineteenth century, this development was dependent on the London

---

[26] J. Brewer, *The Sinews of Power: War, Money and the English State 1688–1783* (London, 1989); P. O'Brien, 'The Political Economy of British Taxation 1688–1815', *Economic History Review* XLI (1988), and see chapter 3 in this volume. On taxes endorsing unequal regional development see Pollard, *Peaceful Conquest*, p.38 and Pollard 'Regional Markets and National Development' in M. Berg, ed., *Markets and Manufactures in Early Industrial Europe* (London, 1990).

money market. This and other links between London and the rest of the economy were crucially significant in national development.[27]

Markets for many consumer goods were becoming more nationally integrated: the same sorts of fashion items in clothing, metalwares, draperies, pottery could be found in homes throughout the country, though with some interesting regional variations. If a 'national' culture was formed as much through consumption as through production, one could argue a case for the disintegration of distinctively regional habits during the industrial revolution, although this would be largely confined to those classes with an ear to the pulse of national fashions and a level of income enabling them to participate in conspicuous consumption.

Even the mass of the population were more mobile and had wider geographical horizons than is often suggested by migration studies. Many workers, especially male artisans, travelled to complete their training or in search of work. Travel broadened outlooks, and tramping artisans became major conduits of information flow. Some tramps even became the active and vocal inspiration for political and national consciousness. The role of the outsider and the travelling orator was important in early nineteenth-century radicalism, providing a catalyst for debate and dissention whilst informing about similar conditions and interests elsewhere in the country. The long-standing importance of tramping and mutual aid amongst artisan groups cemented interregional solidarities and was important in the formation of nationally organised friendly society and trade union activities as well as in Chartism and other political movements. This was particularly so by the 1830s and 1840s.[28]

Neither should the importance of popular nationalism and royalism in the national psyche be ignored. Colley has emphasised the nationalistic vocabulary of popular radicalism in the early nineteenth century and has argued that this gave a unified edge to the articulation of class interests. But this must be set against the regional operation and fragmentation of political movements, particularly before the 1830s. Furthermore, after 1815 the state began to foster local customs and regional traditions as a means of combating the possibilities of

---

[27] E. A. Wrigley, 'A Simple Model of London's Importance in Changing English Society and Economy, 1650–1750', *Past and Present* 37 (1967), pp. 44–70; I. Black, 'Geography, Political Economy and the Circulation of Capital in Early Industrial England', *Journal of Historical Geography* 15 (1989); S. D. Chapman, *The Rise of Merchant Banking* (London, 1984), ch. 1.

[28] E. J. Hobsbawm, 'The Tramping Artisan', in Hobsbawm, ed., *Labouring Men* (London, 1964); H. R. Southall, 'Mobility, the Artisan Community and Popular Politics in Early Nineteenth Century England', in G. Kearns and C. W. J. Withers, eds., *Urbanising Britain: Essays on Class and Community in the Nineteenth Century* (Cambridge, 1991).

nation-wide opposition. This was obviously made possible only by existing popular identification with locality and region.[29]

This chapter provides a regional perspective on the industrial revolution in Britain. It does not argue that this is the only legitimate perspective but merely suggests that the approach uncovers elements of discontinuity and uniqueness which are hidden in more nationally orientated studies. We consider in what way and why economic development varied between regions. We also consider the implications for our understanding of the industrialisation process as a whole of reassembling the national picture from regional building blocks.

Regional diversity

Much industrial locational analysis implies an almost mechanical relationship between the siting of natural resources and economic development. The presence of coal or surplus labour can of course be of crucial importance in determining where industries take root and grow successfully. But the relationship between location and investment in industry depends also upon factors such as mutable systems of land ownership, the power and influence of local elites, the nature of local government, the strength of entrenched customs or traditions and a host of other variables not comprehended by straight locational analysis.[30]

Proto-industrialisation: the location
A body of literature about proto-industrialisation has helped to take regional analysis away from traditional locational theory. By establishing the possible links between the nature of industrial change, peasant ecosystems, family life, demography and culture and by seeing these as integrated rather than separate fields of study, the concept of proto-industry has significantly changed the way in which the region is perceived in the analysis of industrialisation. No longer are those wishing to analyse the mainsprings of industrial growth in a region satisfied merely to explore a shopping list of locational factors. It is now necessary to consider how manufacturing meshed in with agriculture through the seasons, how systems of landholding, inheritance and wealth distribution conditioned the nature, organisation and finance of industrial activities in an area, how urban production

---

[29] L. Colley, 'Whose Nation? Class and National Consciousness in Britain 1750–1830', *Past and Present* 113 (1986) and Colley, 'The Apotheosis of George II: Loyalty, Royalty and the British Nation 1760–1820', *Past and Present* 102 (1984).
[30] Location theory 'fails to make a clear distinction between the causes for concentration of industry in regions as such and for the growth of particular industrial regions'; Pollard, *Peaceful Conquest*, p.113. For a particular view of locational factors of a political kind within Britain see M. Hechter, *Internal Colonialism: The Celtic Fringe in British National Development 1536–1966* (London, 1975).

functioned in relation to rural manufacturing, how the family, household and personal life adapted to changes in work regimes and market opportunities, how these were reflected in demographic behaviour and how all these variables related to one another.

In accounting for the growth of rural domestic manufacturing in certain regions of Western Europe from the seventeenth century, Mendels, building on the work of Thirsk and others, initially stressed the importance of areas of high ground and infertile soils where loose systems of inheritance and population growth created an increasingly proletarianised group whose livelihood could only be supported by manufacturing sidelines.[31] The part-time nature of much early proto-industry allowed farming and other activities of the rural calendar effectively to subsidise low manufacturing piece rates. The separation of regions into those more favoured to become commercial agricultural producers and those which turned to manufacturing alongside rural pursuits was a feature stressed in earlier writings, most notably by Jones. He cites eighteenth-century English examples of lace making in Devon and the South Midlands, nail making in Buckinghamshire (stimulated by the relaxation of manorial controls on common pasturage), and framework knitting in Nottinghamshire, Derbyshire and Leicestershire (promoted by the switch to pastoral farming which resulted in movement of labour into open manufacturing parishes).[32]

Considerable empirical work in the last two decades has unearthed a more complex picture of the regional environments which favoured the extension of manufacturing. By no means all dynamic proto-industry occured in regions where agriculture was poor, neither were populations everywhere driven to manufacturing out of dire necessity.[33] Commercial manufacturing successfully existed alongside commercial farming in some cases, especially where the gender or age division of labour or the seasonality of agricultural work created a pool of available labour at low cost. There were also areas where rural industry emerged, not as a substitute for high-cost cereal farming but because cheap food actually underwrote a low supply price of labour.[34]

[31] J. Thirsk, 'Industries in the Countryside' in F. J. Fisher, ed., *Essays in the Economic and Social History of Tudor and Stuart England* (Cambridge, 1961), pp.70–88; F. F. Mendels, 'Proto-industrialisation: the First Phase of the Industrialisation Process', *Journal of Economic History* 32 (1972).
[32] E. L. Jones, 'Agricultural Origins of Industry', *Past and Present* 40 (1968), pp.62–3; See also Jones, 'Environment, Agriculture and Industrialisation in Europe', *Agricultural History* 51 (1977).
[33] See for example, D. Hey, *The Rural Metalworkers of the Sheffield Region* (Leicester, 1972) which is an expanded version of 'A Dual Economy in South Yorkshire', *Agricultural History Review* xvii (1969).
[34] Jones cites German examples of this but it is likely to have been a feature of some English regions as well: 'Environment', p.501. See also R. Houston and K. D. M. Snell, 'Proto-industrialization? Cottage Industry, Social Change and Industrial Revolution', *Historical Journal* 27 (1984); R. A. C. Allen, *Enclosure and the Yeoman* (Oxford, 1992).

Clearly there is more to explain here than can be comprehended within the theory of comparative advantage.

Proto-industrialisation: dynamic influences

At issue among proto-industrial theorists and their critics is not just the environment of proto-industry but also the limits and the possibilities of the transition of proto-industrial regions into more fully developed industrialism. Mendels stressed that the transition from proto-industrialisation to factory and urban-based industry was never automatic but would, he implied, usually occur in the absence of institutional obstacles, because of increasing marginal costs and lack of control over the work-force.[35] Kriedte is much more explicit in recognising a disjunction between the proto-industrial consumer-goods phase of industrialisation and a second phase based on producer goods and heavy industries, necessarily involving different sectors, skills, resources and often therefore different locations. Competition from factory production elsewhere would also place strict limits on the possibilities of successful movement beyond proto-industry.[36] The fact that only four out of ten English proto-industrial regions, identified by Coleman, witnessed an early industrial revolution proves very little about the importance of the concept of proto-industrialisation (or the research which it has stimulated). But it does alert us to the need to consider the changing locational demands occasioned by shifts in technology and material inputs.[37]

Coleman argues that coal supplies were a more important determining factor than prior proto-industry in the successful industrialising of regions. And Wrigley has recently stressed that the whole question of Britain's industrial revolution revolves around the shift from organic to inorganic sources of energy and raw materials (with its obvious effects on industrial relocation).[38] But the eclipse or success of many proto-industrial regions had mostly been assured before coal became a major locational influence as a source of power and had been precipitated by quite different factors as the Weald of Kent, the West Country, the West Riding, and other examples reveal (see pp.115–

---

[35] Mendels, 'Proto-industrialization'.
[36] P. Kriedte, H. Medick and J. Schlumbohm, *Industrialization before Industrialization: Rural Industry in the Genesis of Capitalism* (Cambridge, 1981), ch. 6.
[37] D. C. Coleman, 'Protoindustrialization: A Concept Too Many?' *Economic History Review* xxxvi (1983).
[38] E. A. Wrigley, *Continuity, Chance and Change: The Character of the Industrial Revolution in England* (Cambridge, 1988); see also B. Thomas, 'Towards an Energy Interpretation of the Industrial Revolution', *Atlantic Economic Journal* 8 (1980).

31).[39] Turning away from interpretations which concentrate on resource endowments or employ the notion of comparative advantage, Berg places major stress on the social and institutional factors influencing locational shifts in manufacturing industry in the eighteenth century, particularly in explaining the decline of formerly buoyant manufacturing regions. Certainly the way industry was organised, the regional institutions and practices of finance and commerce, and the traditions of organised labour could radically influence the sources of capital, entrepreneurship and labour for expanding industry. Sometimes regional trades could become dominated by a clique of large powerful employers who militated against injections of initiative and new methods. This was often crucial in regions where a single sector dominated.[40] Sometimes capital came largely from outside the region (as was the case with the Weald, and later South Wales), or the power over markets was held outside the region (witness the control of Blackwell Hall factors over the textile trades of East Anglia and the south-west). It is often argued that the master clothier and worker structure in the textile industry of the south compared unfavourably with the socially more uniform and technologically more flexible small weaver communities of the north. The organisation of trades affected innovation, not just because of its implications for entrepreneurship and capital supply but also because resistance to mechanisation occurred where innovation most upset the established structures of the trade and of labour hierarchies. Local and regional traditions of community solidarity and protest in promoting resistance to innovation by the work-force were also important.[41]

The successful expansion of an industrialising region during the industrial revolution period and beyond also depended on the achievement of critical mass. According to Pollard:

What was important was interdependent diversity, in terms of backward and forward integration, service trades, infrastructure including a good transport system and close linkage with markets and suppliers to enable the region to react quickly to changing costs and prices or fashion. Where these elements were present the tendency would be for the region to pull ahead of the rest and

[39] On the demise of protoindustry in the South Midlands see Allen, *Enclosure*. On the importance of canal transport in the regional use of coal see G. Turnbull, 'Canals, Coal and Regional Growth'. J. V. Beckett and J. E. Heath argue that in the East Midlands it was the undeveloped state of communications before the railway period which placed limits on the dynamism of the extractive industries and on the diversification of opportunities. Thus although the East Midlands had coal and pioneered various advances in cotton, silk and worsted manufacture, these industries came to fuller fruition elsewhere in the early nineteenth century: 'When was the Industrial Revolution in the East Midlands?', *Midland History* 13 (1988).
[40] M. Berg, *The Age of Manufactures*, pp.118–22.
[41] Randall, 'Work', in Hudson, *Region and Industries*.

for regional inequality to increase cumulatively for very long periods.[42]

The major industrial regions of Britain which survived into the twentieth century were those which saw a succession of distinctive economic bases. Both Lancashire and Yorkshire had coal and iron to take them through from the phase of textile domination to the broader bases of economic diversification into engineering, services and chemicals. Similar sequences of mixed industries characterised the growth of the north-east, whereas the array of different metal and hardware trades of South Yorkshire and the West Midlands served to create a balanced growth quite apart from the existence of coal in both regions. These conditions arose from the achievement of critical mass and eluded North Wales, the West Country and East Anglia. This was by no means mere accident nor, as North Wales proves, was it dependent on the absence of coal.[43]

Capital, labour and innovation

Only by considering the nature of developments in contrasting regions can the complex interplay of competition, capital formation, technology, and changes in the labour process be explored. The rest of this chapter focuses on specific regions using each as a case study to illustrate particular aspects of regional transformation. In Britain it is clear that industrialisation in Scotland, Northern Ireland and Wales has been influenced particularly by the concentration of finance and of political and economic power in England. Aspects of what has been termed 'internal colonialism' and the effect of client status on the nature and development of industrial capitalism, though vitally important, are not the main concern here.[44] The following case studies are English and explore those sources of regional difference which operated within and alongside of state formation.

The West Riding of Yorkshire

An increase in the output of the British wool textile sector of 150%

[42] Pollard, *Peaceful Conquest*, p.39.
[43] The nature and survival of industrial regions also owed much to the structures of political and economic power at regional, national and international levels. These are discussed in Hudson 'The Regional Perspective', in Hudson, *Regions and Industries*, pp.30–8.
[44] For further reading on this see Hechter, *Internal Colonialism;* T. Dickson, *Scottish Capitalism: Class, State and Nation from before the Union to the Present* (London, 1980); Gwyn A. Williams, 'Imperial South Wales' and 'When was Wales', both in Williams, *The Welsh and their History* (London, 1982). T. M. Devine, 'The Union of 1707 and Scottish Development', *Scottish Economic and Social History* 5 (1985); P. Hudson, *Regions and Industries: A Perspective on the Industrial Revolution in Britain* pp.33–8, and chs. 6 and 8; on the development of Ulster see L. Kennedy and P. Ollerenshaw, *An Economic History of Ulster 1820–1939* (Manchester, 1985).

during the entire eighteenth century seems very modest, but this conceals dramatic relocation taking place in favour of the West Riding of Yorkshire whose share of national production rose from around 20% to around 60%.[45] From the aggregate perspective, 150% increase over a century could have been achieved simply by gradual extension of traditional commercial methods and production functions. But Yorkshire's intensive growth necessarily embodied a veritable revolution in organisational patterns, commercial links, credit relationships, the sorts of cloth produced and (selectively) in production techniques. The external economies to be achieved when one region took over more than half of the production of an entire sector were also of key importance to say nothing of the social implications. The West Riding thus provides an interesting example of the dynamics of concentration and sectoral specialisation by region and of proto-industrialisation followed by the gradual centralisation and mechanisation of the major production processes.

In the eighteenth century different rural environments within West Yorkshire gave rise to different forms of industrial organisation and divisions of labour both within and between households. The independent artisan woollen manufacturer who employed his own family and one or two journeymen survived and flourished in areas of small farms where family labour could balance activities throughout the year and where landholding provided not only a cushion against difficult times in the textile trade, but also a source of collateral for raising loans and credit. By contrast, the putting-out system which characterised worsted production in the West Riding was dominant in the north and west where proletarianisation and pauperisation had occurred in an area of more marginal agricultural potential. Here yeomen emerged as putting-out merchants in the process of social polarisation. They had sizeable farms which they used to raise capital and credit and they let cottages and plots to some of their employees. They distributed raw materials to large numbers of spinners and weavers working on piece rates in their own homes.

The resilience the landholding artisan imparted to the woollen branch in the West Riding has been seen as a major source of dynamism especially in comparing the rise of Yorkshire with the relative stagnation of the West Country by the late eighteenth century. There clothiers in the woollen trade worked on a putting-out basis and were often large employers.[46] Josiah Tucker, writing in 1757, believed that the 'domestic system of the West Riding produced better value products and better industrial and social relations. In the West Country journeymen 'deprived of the Hopes of advancing themselves ... think it no Crime to get as much Wages, and do as little for it as they

[45] Hudson, *Genesis*.
[46] Hudson, *Genesis*, ch. 2; Wilson, *Gentleman Merchants:* A. J. Randall, *Before the Luddites* (Cambridge, 1991), ch. 1.

possibly can, to lie and cheat, and do any other bad Thing'.[47] The basic difference in structure certainly appears to have been important in the receptiveness of the two regions to innovation in the late eighteenth century. Early innovations (the jenny and scribbing engines) were willingly incorporated in Yorkshire without upsetting the traditional structure, while worker opposition to technological change in the West Country·was a major factor in the region's decline. Resistance was strengthened in the West Country by traditions of solidarity and collective action in earlier industrial and food riots. Furthermore, the West of England produced a variety and quality of cloths unmatched elsewhere which gave specialised workers a strong sense of craft pride and solidarity. In the West Riding the domestic system's relative lack of specialisation meant that new technologies of the late eighteenth century did not threaten vested interests in the same way.[48]

A further aspect of the institutional structure of cloth production and sale in both woollen and worsted branches of the West Riding was the presence of specialist resident merchants closely in touch with changing tastes and fashion in European and transatlantic markets as well as on the domestic front. Also, which was important, these merchants bought for cash or short bills (particularly before the Napoleonic wars) which placed manufacturers quickly in funds and enabled them to benefit from the long credits extended to them on the purchase of raw materials. Thus the West Riding illustrates the complex nature of regional difference and the extent to which 'comparative advantage' lay in social and institutional as much as strictly economic factors.[49]

West Riding clothiers feared the effect of the changes of the late eighteenth century: the bypassing of the cloth halls by large merchants, the growth of working to order, and early factory development by capitalist employers. The innovation of the powered integrated factory met with the same response from established workers in both Yorkshire and the West Country because it represented the same drastic extension of capitalist control over them and the pace and nature of their work. Mills like Bean Ing in Yorkshire and Staverton, Twerton and Uley in the West Country were few and far between in the early nineteenth century but the fear which they aroused was immense and common to the two regions. Opposition in Yorkshire and in the West Country was expressed in the same set of values: belief in the importance of apprenticeship, regulation of production methods, and controls over capital to protect the legitimate rights and

[47] J. Tucker, *Instructions for Travellers* (London, 1758) quoted in Randall, 'Work and Resistance', p.181.
[48] Randall, 'Work and Resistance', pp.181–5.
[49] R. G. Wilson, 'The Supremacy of the Yorkshire Cloth Industry', in N. Harte and K. G. Ponting eds., *Textile History and Economic History. Essays in Honour of Miss Julia de Lacy Mann* (Manchester, 1973), p.240; Hudson, *Genesis*, ch. 8.

autonomy of different trades.[50] There was a common distrust in the textile districts as elsewhere of the intentions of innovators who wished to restructure industry through machinery and the factory system. The textile areas saw a clash between those merchants and large-scale master clothiers who demanded repeal of the old regulatory statutes and those workers and small masters who demanded their full reinstatement in the name of social justice. The market economy faced the moral economy quite distinctly. As the *Leeds Mercury* reported in 1803, the uncontrolled introduction of machinery would polarise the woollen industry into overgrown rich monopolists and impoverished subservient workers with fatal consequences for the 'spirit, energy and patriotism' of the country.[51] The clash was not straightforwardly between capital and labour but between large-scale innovating employers and the rest of the industry. The same happened in the worsted sector where, for example, larger employers forced legislative compulsion in the policing of embezzlement in 1777.[52] The state rejected pleas for renewed state regulation and endorsed the Worsted Acts.

The gender division of labour was also important in the West Riding, as elsewhere, in facilitating industrialisation. Several estimates of the early eighteenth century suggest that there were eight or nine women and children for every man employed in wool textiles. In 1774 it was estimated that (female) worsted spinners outnumbered weavers and combers (the main male occupations) by four to one and female workers in the woollen branch can scarcely have been less important.[53] Worsted spinning extended into Lancashire, Cheshire and the Yorkshire Dales through the medium of shopkeepers and other agents geared to supplying the female work-force. The industry was able to take advantage of a cheap female labour supply spread over a wide geographical area which had few alternative work opportunities. Agriculture was either limited or subject to change which reduced the demand for female labour.[54] In the artisan structure of the woollen trade female and child workers carried out spinning and assisted in all other processes. They were also vital in the livestock keeping characteristic of the clothier smallholding. Women supplemented family income with home supply of butter, cheese, eggs and

---

[50] Randall, 'Work and Resistance', p.184; Randall, 'New Languages or Old? Labour, Capital and Discourse in the Industrial Revolution', *Social History* 15 (1989).
[51] Quoted by Randall, 'New Languages', p.203.
[52] J. Styles, 'Embezzlement, Industry and the Law in England 1500–1800', in M. Berg, P. Hudson and M. Sonenscher eds., *Manufacture in Town and Country before the Factory* (Cambridge, 1983).
[53] John James, *The History of the Worsted Manufacture in England* (London, 1857), pp.211, 218, 281; I. Pinchbeck, *Women Workers and the Industrial Revolution 1750–1850* (London, 1969), p.124.
[54] Enclosure and the decline of dairying were important here.

garden produce; their dairying was done in the intervals of carding, spinning and preparing the wool for the loom.[55]

The transition to machine spinning in both woollen and worsted industries did little to change and everything to endorse the high female input. In the worsted mills of Bradford and Halifax in 1835, 60% of the work-force were women of whom 70% were under the age of 21. Only a quarter of the factory work-force in the woollen branch at this time was female but as hand spinning declined more women took up handloom weaving.[56] The factory manufacturer seems to have been anxious to employ women wherever possible: they were equally efficient 'slaves to his machinery' and men were more likely to cause trouble by combinations.[57] At the same time women were desperate to work: the breakdown of the family unit in woollen production and the threat to male handloom weaving posed by mechanisation in that sector placed many young girls in a position where they had to find work, particularly as agricultural service was on the wane.

By the mid 1830s there were over 600 mills in Yorkshire compared with only 242 in 1800. Admittedly most employed only a handful of workers or were sublet to very small concerns who rented room and power. Average mill horsepower in 1838 was 16 and the average number of workers just 45 in woollen mills, and 76 in worsted. Most mills relied wholly or in part on water rather than steam power. But averages belie the fact that there were sufficient sizeable powered and mechanised establishments to begin to transform the landscape and the skyline of manufacturing towns. By 1851 more than 10% of worsted mills employed more than 200 workers and these included a significant number which had over 1000 employees. Spinning, carding, and scribbling as well as fulling were largely mechanised processes and the progress of the power-loom just across the Pennines showed a way to the future. Factory workers were young and largely female whilst male employment suffered. Cycles of boom and slump in both domestic and export markets radically affected employment and incomes in the entire region, and the scale of resistance to innovation and of mass protest from the Luddites and the arming and drilling during the Napoleonic Wars to the violence of Chartism was wholly unprecedented. Small-scale production and hand technology remained a permanent feature in several parts of the industry: it existed alongside the factory and often in conjunction with it. All establishments were subjected to more intense cost-cutting competition and market rivalry. Thus, in important ways, the sector and the

---

[55] Pinchbeck, *Women Workers*, p.127.
[56] Hudson, *Genesis*, pp.81–4.
[57] P. Gaskell, *Manufacturing Population of England* (1833), quoted in Pinchbeck, *Women Workers*, pp.187–8. For statistical and other information on the woollen and worsted industries in this and the next paragraph see Hudson, *Genesis*, pp.40–8.

region had been fundamentally transformed in the classic industrial revolution period.

Lancashire

Much of what has been said here about the West Riding has a parallel in the Lancashire cotton region.[58] The pace of factory development there was unusual but, even so, mixed development was the major characteristic and, again, female and child labour played an increased role in both centralised and small-scale production. In the proto-industrial period, cotton, woollen, linen and silk industries were all significant in different parts of the region and each industry had internal subdivisions with differences in products, organisation, markets, the labour process and relationship with agriculture. In the rural areas where woollen and cotton manufacture developed most rapidly, the importance of farming alongside spinning and weaving in the family economy declined. As in the West Riding, the subdivision of holdings was a feature of the seventeenth and eighteenth centuries in areas not only of partible but impartible inheritance (where the need to provide cash portions for younger heirs because of primogeniture led to the break up of farms and small holdings).

The industrial revolution gave cotton primacy in the region. And where cotton supplanted wool, as in the Pennine areas, the sources of capital and enterprise shifted. In fact, in the later eighteenth century, woollen manufacturers in Lancashire more often became landowners or bankers than moved into cotton.[59] Thus not only was proto-industrialisation in south Lancashire a mixed and complex affair, but the transition to more centralised production was far from straightforward in terms of any continuity of entrepreneurship, capital or the labour force. Even in the nineteenth century the industrial and employment structures in towns which concentrated on spinning were very different from those in predominantly weaving centres. Mechanisation and centralisation was a slow process which was by no means completed even for the weaving process by mid century. As piece-rate wages for handloom weaving fell sharply in the 1830s and 1840s (because of competition from mechanisation and the flooding of the labour market by displaced spinners and by Irish immigrants), many family incomes became dependent on factory work for children and young women. Lyons suggests that the availability of factory work for some family members alongside domestic industry made the decline of handloom weaving much more protracted and ensured that it was by no means confined to older men or to women by the second quarter of the nineteenth century. Male handloom weavers often became a

[58] For the classic study see A. P. Wadsworth and J. de L. Mann, *The Cotton Trade and Industrial Lancashire 1600–1780* (Manchester, 1931); for a recent survey of subsequent research see J. K. Walton, 'Proto-industrialisation and the First Industrial Revolution: the Case of Lancashire', in Hudson, *Regions*, upon which the following remarks draw.
[59] Wadsworth and Mann, *Cotton Trade*, p.280.

reserve army of labour for factory employers and this economised on fixed capital. Employers hedged their bets by installing enough power looms to cope with normal demand and using domestic workers when demand temporarily increased.[60]

The viability and durability of merchant capital and putting-out production compared with centralised industrial production was reflected in the structure of property and in the urban politics of early nineteenth-century Manchester. The Manchester rate books show that most property investment in 1815 was in warehousing, and there was even more capital invested in public houses than in factories in 'cottonopolis' at this time. The dominant influence economically and politically until well into the nineteenth century was the merchant group who owned and operated Manchester's vast warehouses and provided the mercantile services for its manufacturing hinterland.[61]

Like the West Riding, south Lancashire is a major example of the sectoral concentration of industry from which considerable external economies accrued because of the specialist services of the regional infrastructure. The transport system, the supply of raw materials and machinery, the availability of specialist mercantile, legal, financial and credit facilities were all important. The import of raw cotton and the need to find export outlets for much of the output of the industry necessitated the generation of substantial mercantile capital, expertise and credit. The bill of exchange system was developed to its most sophisticated level in south Lancashire. It underpinned the transatlantic economy and provided good access for Lancashire manufacturers to short- and long-term funds, often drawing on London finance houses and merchants.[62]

Birmingham and the West Midlands

Most studies of this region suffer from using the factory textile districts of Lancashire and Yorkshire as a reference point, implying that there is a 'normal' path of industrial development towards capital-intensive centralised units of production. This is the implication of much proto-industrial literature, which tends to underplay the combined and uneven character inherent in the development of industrial capitalism in favour of a linear path from dispersed to centralised production. By the linear yardstick the history of Birmingham and the metalwares district has been successively seen as an aberration, an alternative and a late developer. These approaches are all inferior to one which

60 J. S. Lyons, 'Family Response to Economic Decline: Handloom Weavers in Early Nineteenth Century Lancashire', *Research in Economic History* 12 (1989).
61 R. Lloyd-Jones and M. I. Lewis, *Manchester in the Age of the Factory: the Business Structure of Cottonopolis in the Industrial Revolution* (London, 1988).
62 See ch. 6 in this volume.

attempts to place the history of the region in the context of its own products, processes and markets.[63] The West Midlands of the eighteenth century had a marked degree of sub-regional specialisation. The presence of coal and iron made the region the country's largest mining and iron producer after the north-east and these resources also underpinned a wide range of metal manufactures. Ironmakers and primary manufacturers were concentrated on water-power sites around the Birmingham plateau, particularly the western rim close to the Severn. The nailing industry expanded rapidly in the eighteenth century around the edges of the coalfield in communities like Darleston, West Bromwich and Sedgley, whilst holloware, edge tools and glass were made in Walsall, Wolverhampton, Wednesbury and Stourbridge. As in the West Riding and Lancashire, organisational structures of pre-factory industry owed a great deal to the patterns of landholding and of wealth distribution in the sub-regions.[64]

The Digbeth district of Birmingham had witnessed major growth in nailing, cutlery and edge-tool making in the seventeenth century, but after substantial removal of these trades to the countryside and villages in the eighteenth century the city concentrated on newer industries and innovative products mainly directed to 'luxury' markets both domestic and foreign: brass wares, jewellery, enamelled and plated goods, 'toys', buttons, buckles. Birmingham was also the centre of the gun trade with its clear regional division of labour between processing and intermediate manufacture in the hinterland (Bilston, Wednesbury, Darleston) and finishing and assembly in the urban setting. The Birmingham trades were export orientated and depended on a complex network of merchants and agents in Birmingham, London, Liverpool and abroad who organised the extensive movement of goods to many European, American and African markets. The well-developed banking network served the region but also underpinned much of the credit needed for longer-distance trades. Similarly, although the canal network was very dense intraregionally by the late eighteenth century, important links had also been made, by 1790, with the Thames and with Lancashire.

[63] M. Berg, 'Commerce and Creativity in Eighteenth Century Birmingham', in Berg, ed., *Markets and Manufactures in Early Industrial Europe* (London, 1990); C. Behagg, *Politics and Production in the Early Nineteenth Century* (London, 1990) and 'Myths of Cohesion: Capital and Compromise in the Historiography of Nineteenth Century Birmingham', in *Social History* 11 (1986). Cf. Briggs, *Chartist Studies;* Briggs, *Victorian Cities* (Harmondsworth, 1968); C. Sabel and J. Zeitlin, 'Historical Alternatives to Mass Production', *Past and Present* 108 (1985); M. Rowlands, 'Continuity and Change in an Industrialising Society: The Case of the West Midlands Industries', in Hudson, *Regions*.
[64] Berg, 'Commerce and Creativity'; Rowlands, 'Continuity'. The account of Birmingham and the Black Country presented here relies heavily on these articles and on the work of Behagg (see note 63).

Because the trades of Birmingham itself were so nationally and externally orientated, Berg has argued that the growth and nature of the city cannot be seen as an adjunct to rural proto-industrialisation: 'it stood in no simple continuity with industrialisation from below'.[65] The city was peculiarly vital in its own right: its inventive activity became legendary. Products and raw materials were changed and adapted, divisions of labour were introduced. There was also a range of new inventions and innovations in tools, metal compositions, metal finishes and scientific instruments as well as the widely quoted introduction of the stamp, press, draw bench and lathe. The city and its region benefitted from economies of agglomeration arising out of the specialisation of trades and markets and this made a fertile environment for small firms to flourish. Small firms were also encouraged by demand for a very varied set of products and by the fact that there was little economic or technological advantage in producing on a large scale in the industries concerned.

Briggs, writing in the 1960s, identified Birmingham as possessing a particular and peculiar tradition. Here industrialisation had resulted in the multiplication of small workshops, continuing close connection between masters and men, opportunities for social mobility, and a relatively skilled work-force. The classes did not become 'separated from each other by the gaunt walls of the factory'. The social cohesion which resulted was reflected in the apparent weakness of trade unionism and political movements, from the Birmingham Political Union to Chartism. These exhibited class co-operation rather than class conflict.[66] Briggs' interpretation encouraged a body of studies, some employing a crude structural functionalist or economic determinist approach in identifying small-scale industry with harmony of interests between employers and employed, and factories with conflict. This is particularly contentious when so many factories actually represented a collection of workshops under one roof and when artisan unrest was legion.[67] Sabel and Zeitlin, with rather different emphasis, have claimed that the Birmingham region represents an alternative path to industrialism based on flexible labour-using technology and market specialisation rather than mass production. This was furthered, they argue, by an institutional framework which emerged from the community ethos, aided small employers with technological, financial and marketing contacts and balanced competition and co-operation between firms. The Birmingham alternative was based on

[65] Berg, 'Commerce and Creativity', p.183.
[66] Briggs, quoted by Behagg, 'Myths', p.375.
[67] For a fascinating case study of the sharing of factory space and of the relationships of dependency and independence involved see L. D. Smith, 'Industrial Organisation in the Kidderminster Carpet Trade 1780–1850', *Textile History* 15 (1986).

consensus between employers and on a 'terrain of compromise' between skilled workers and masters.[68]

These theses about the Birmingham tradition have recently been criticised by Behagg in research which has shown that the political, social and economic cohesion which features in the rhetoric of Birmingham industrialists was a myth.[69] The typical unit of production in Birmingham (as in the rest of the economy) remained the small workshop, but there was also a sizeable large-scale sector which had not emerged from the self-made struggles of small masters (as the spokesmen of the area liked to suggest). On the whole, small firms remained small because larger concerns controlled their credit and marketing facilities. While they remained small they served the needs of large firms without threatening them in the market-place. With the rules of competition dictated by large-scale capital, it was as imperative for small concerns to maintain economic viability via work reorganisation as it was for the large concern. And despite the destructive nature of their relationship with larger concerns, small producers increasingly adopted the value systems of large-scale capital because they too needed to exert control over labour. Increasingly, running a small firm involved the rejection of artisan notions of production with labour dictating the nature and pace of work. The result was conflict in the work-place with small firms just as likely to be hit as the larger concerns. The alliance between the classes in the Birmingham Political Union can be seen as little more than the working-class need for respectable support and the middle-class requirement of numerical strength.

An important part of the restructuring of the labour force and labour process in the metalware trades involved the expansion of female and child labour, increased division and specialisation of labour by sex and an unprecedented intensification of the pace of work. This paralleled the increasing use of female and child labour in the factory districts. In the Black Country the expansion of women's work was facilitated by the traditional prominence of women and children in many trades. Furthermore, innovation did not often displace the household work-place in the region, and in trades such as nailing and the making of chains, nuts, bolts, files and stirrups, expansion was tied up entirely with the use of low paid female workers and children from the age of five or six upwards.[70] That this passed unnoticed throughout the agitation against young children working in factories and mines was because workshops and domestic premises were so much less

[68] Sabel and Zeitlin, 'Historical Alternatives'.
[69] C. Behagg, Politics and Production; Behagg, 'Myths'.
[70] M. Berg, 'Women's Work, Mechanisation and the Early Phases of Industrialisation in England', in P. Joyce, ed., The Historical Meanings of Work (Cambridge, 1987); Pinchbeck, Women Workers, p.273.

visible to the public eye; also the moral issue of the decline of parental authority with work outside the home was not so relevant. The adoption of machines for stamping and piercing and the expansion of the japanning process extended the range of employment for young girls. The burnishing, piercing and hand painting of buttons and buckles was regarded as specially suited to the deftness of women and girls. Women also worked beside men in the heavy industries of mining, holloware, harness, saddlery and chainmaking, but in these as in the lighter trades there were clear status divisions between the sexes. Women's work was regarded as inferior and their wages were much lower. Men made high-class jewellery and women gilt articles and chains at the cheap end of the trade. In the button trade there was a division between the old 'more skilled' metal and pearl button section, which employed some men, and the new covered and linen button section which employed women. By the mid nineteenth century the division of labour by sex and age was enabling employers to take advantage of cheapness, dexterity and what was almost a production line setting. In pearl button manufacture, for example, men cut the pearl from the shell and turned it on a lathe, women drilled holes and polished, boys filled edges and girls carded. In the metal button trade girls from the age of nine were employed as 'putters in', feeding the press with metal strips. Women worked a range of presses large and small, though skilled male tool makers earning three or four times as much fixed the tools into the presses.[71]

Thus, changes in the Black Country and Birmingham trades were not so different from those in the textile districts. As in Manchester the trade and service sectors dominated the structure of Birmingham's insured assets at the end of the eighteenth century, but in both cities this belies the level of transformation and expansion of both manufacture and commerce. And inventive activity in Birmingham was provoked more by competition between firms, by patenting, by quality controls and by secrecy than by the mutuality of small firms stressed by Sabel and Zeitlin. The object was not to create institutions to ensure freedom of invention and transmission of ideas, but to legitimise and shape trading and manufacturing practices within a corporate structure which favoured a particular group of well-established industrialists. The introduction of controls over patent rights and quality was a subject of conflict between those manufacturers and artisans who set them and those who bypassed them.[72]

Explanations of Birmingham's success have ranged from lack of institutional regulation, to religious toleration, skill traditions, artisan mutuality and economies of agglomeration. But conflict and competition between large and small manufacturers was an important

---

[71] Berg, 'Women's Work'.
[72] E. Hopkins, 'The Trading and Service Sectors of the Birmingham Economy', *Business History* xxviii 3 (1986); Berg, 'Commerce and Creativity' pp.190–95.

dynamic, as was diversification of products and markets which left a place for smaller firms in the industrial structure. With few exceptions, similar technologies were used in large and small firms alike and both were involved in restructuring the labour process and in increasing the intensity of labour which provoked major unrest in the 1830s and 1840s.

Coalfield industrialisation: the case of Northumberland and Durham

The north-east was the pioneer of the coal trade and of industrial society in Britain. Yet it has been neglected in studies because of a search of an industrial revolution emanating from proto-industrialisation and linked to textiles and canals.[73] The region had none of these. But by the sixteenth century there was a detailed division of labour and a large wage-earning proletariat. The region also had good sea contact with London and Newcastle, and its close international mercantile links with Danzig and the Netherlands. By the seventeenth century relations between landlords and tenants were contractual rather than dependent and the development of coal mining and improving agriculture went hand in hand, making for particularly close ties between landed and mercantile interests. Coal output and export grew in the eighteenth century. And the incomes it generated were bolstered by the monopoly arrangements of the powerful cartel of coalowners who imposed a limit on entry to the trade in order to preserve prices. A succession of these arrangements dominated the trade, culminating in the Limitation of the Vend of 1770 to 1845, an agreement between producers to limit sales and so maintain prices. Although this appears to have made only a small difference to the price of coal to London consumers, it did have an important impact in protecting the profits of producers.[74]

Coal attracted other industries to the region from the seventeenth century: salt, glass and chemicals. Steam pumps were used in the mines as greater depths began to be worked by the mid eighteenth century. The problems posed by coal transport, particularly as the industry moved away from the coast, resulted in the region being the major area of railway development in the early nineteenth century. The growth of output, incomes, profits and other measures in the classic industrial revolution period in the north-east may have been modest; possibly some of the linkage effects of coal supply were weakened by exporting so much of it. But the region was witnessing the build up of an important series of interconnected developments: the invention of the

---

[73] This section draws heavily on N. Evans, 'Two Paths to Industrialisation: Wales and the North East', in Hudson, *Regions*.

[74] Evans, 'Two Paths', pp.211, 226; P. M. Sweezy, *Monopoly and Competition in the English Coal Trade, 1550–1850* (Cambridge, Mass., 1938); W. J. Hausman, 'Market Power in the London Coal Trade: The Limitation of the Vend 1770–1845', *Explorations in Economic History*. Between 1700 and 1830 annual coal output in the north-east increased fivefold.

steam ship and the railway, the tapping of deeper coal seams, the building of docks on the Durham coast, and the foundation of Armstrong's and Palmer's major shipbuilding firms. These set the stage for the swiftest and most remarkable period of industrial expansion in the third quarter of the nineteenth century.

Coal became the basis for a diversified economy which included iron shipbuilding and engineering with associated spin-offs. These were supported by a prosperous and improving agriculture, particularly in Northumberland which was one of the regions to adopt new rotational techniques. The enclosure of arable had largely occurred by the seventeenth century and there was considerable growth of grain output in the eighteenth century with productivity gains of five to sevenfold being recorded in some areas. This did much to support urbanisation in the area in the nineteenth century and, interestingly, capital for agrarian improvement appears to have come from local landowners and farmers. These commercially oriented landowners were also the crucial suppliers of capital for mining and manufacturing. There seems to have been little import of capital into the region.[75]

The importance of local supplies of capital, entrepreneurship and the balanced nature of change has been highlighted in a recent study comparing the north-east with South Wales. In the latter, improving agriculture was absent, markets and urbanisation were retarded, and local supplies of capital had to be supplemented by considerable 'imports' which took control of Welsh industry away from the region itself. Thus, although by 1840 the Dowlais iron works was the largest in the world with 5000 employees, lack of diversification continued to hold back development in South Wales: coal mining became dominant at a stage where the key innovations it was likely to produce had already been made elsewhere. By contrast, the pioneer role in coal production gave the north-east a key place in engineering and shipbuilding.[76]

As in other industrialising regions, the north-east experienced changes in the division of labour by sex. Although women and girls worked extensively down the pits and on the surface in the seventeenth and eighteenth centuries, their employment underground ceased around 1780. The transport of coals to the surface was taken over by tramways and horses.[77] Women continued to work as part of family groups in iron-working areas into the nineteenth century, but the really big expansion of female work occurred in agriculture. Clearly the bias in the demand for male labour for heavy coal and metal working reduced the availability of men in the more sparsely

[75] M. W. Flinn, *The History of the British Coal Industry* II: *1700–1830* (Oxford, 1984), pp.267–9; M. Sill, 'Landownership and Industry: the East Durham Coalfield in the Nineteenth Century', *Northern History* 20 (1984).
[76] Evans, 'Two Paths', p.215.
[77] Pinchbeck, *Women Workers*, pp.241, 271.

populated areas which were turning to commercial agriculture. Northumberland pioneered the substitution of female and child labour in the hoeing of turnips at half the expense ('and better than by men').[78] By 1790 it was reported in Northumberland that 'all our girls are employed in agriculture'.[79] The crucial importance of women and girls in underpinning agricultural innovation in Northumberland and Durham is illustrated by the prominence of the bondage system in the two counties in the later eighteenth century. Each male labourer had to supply a female worker to work at daily rates (paid to him) whenever required by the farmer. Both were paid in kind: in oats, barley, wheat, beans, cow pasture and in wool for women to spin into yarn which was then either knitted into stockings or sent to be woven into blankets. 'This system would seem to have been introduced along with the new cultures and the large farm; the one provided, the other demanded, women's employment.'[80]

Thus long-term success in the industrialisation of the north-east came from interdependent diversity and a supportive landholding and agricultural sector which provided capital, food supplies and industrial labour. This was bolstered in the industrial revolution period by shifts in gender specific labour and by monopoly structures in the coal export trade to London. Coal was vitally necessary to the industrialisation of the north-east, but the presence of coal in itself was not a sufficient determinant of the region's sustained growth.

Deindustrialisation: the case of the Weald

In 1600 the Weald was one of England's leading industrial areas, producing iron, glass, timber products and textiles, almost all for extraregional markets. More than half of the total number of English blast furnaces was located in the region. Yet the Weald deindustrialised and industry was not replaced by commercial agriculture. It is thus an example of 'failed transition' from proto-industry to full industrialisation and one that defies any simple model of comparative advantage. The decline of the Weald occurred before coal became a major locational influence: in the iron industry, several generations separate the peak of Wealden production from the use of coal-fired bellows at Coalbrookdale in the 1770s, and an even longer gap exists

---

[78] Pinchbeck, *Women Workers*, p.59.
[79] Pinchbeck, *Women Workers*, p.63.
[80] Pinchbeck, *Women Workers*, pp.65, 92. Contemporaries likened the bondage system to West Indian slavery. The dependence, work intensity and moral decline it was seen to precipitate was regarded in the same way as factory labour elsewhere.

between the demise of the Wealden cloth industry and the establishment elsewhere of the steam-powered textile factories.[81]
Other explanations for the decline of the Weald must be sought. First, the Weald, despite its national importance as an industrial centre in the seventeenth century, was an 'underdeveloped' region because it had been continuously subordinated to political, economic and social decisions made outside its borders. London was the source of much of the Weald's investment capital and credit, while the centres of manorial power around the edges of the region had milked its natural reserves of timber, raw materials and grazing without investing much in agricultural improvement. Loose controls over land use and transmission had resulted in a great deal of partible inheritance and therefore inmigration, a falling marriage age, population pressure and poverty.

Secondly, Wealden entrepreneurs (clothiers, ironmasters, timber merchants and glassmakers) were merchants whose interests were guided by national and international forces: 'the social structures, processes and landscapes which they did so much to create were in tune with national and international forces and not with the long term development needs of the Wealden region'.[82] Glass, cloth, ordnance and timber products were sent to metropolitan and foreign destinations and were controlled largely by monopolistic merchants in the capital. The weaknesses of monopoly pricing were clearly exposed in the eighteenth century when suppliers of Wealden ordnance found competition difficult in the bidding for naval and army contracts. Furthermore, the expertise upon which the three main industries of glass, cloth and iron were based was international and mobile. Technological expertise had come from Lorraine and Normandy to the glass industry, from northern France to the iron works, and from the Low Countries to textile manufacture. Although some indigenous expertise developed from these migrant skills, entrepreneurs may have felt less of a connection with their region and certainly many were quick to move elsewhere as the Wealden industries began to falter. For example, all but one of the French glass makers had moved to Stourbridge or Newcastle upon Tyne by the mid seventeenth century.

Thirdly, partly because of their very separate markets and mercantile arrangements, there was little overlap in terms of capital and entrepreneurship between the Wealden industries. Interdependent diversity was missing. Even the spatial overlaps tended to retreat as the

[81] B. M. Short, 'The De-industrialisation Process: A Case Study of the Weald 1600–1850', in Hudson, *Regions*. The survey of Wealden decline presented here is heavily dependent on this source which summarises much of the rest of the available literature. For a more detailed account see, P. F. Brandon and B. M. Short, *The South-East from AD 1000* (London, 1989), and B. M. Short, 'The South East: Kent, Surrey and Sussex', in J. Thirsk, ed., *The Agrarian History of England and Wales* v, i: *1640–1750. Regional Farming Systems* (Cambridge, 1984).
[82] Thirsk, *The Agrarian History of England and Wales*, p.162.

industries declined. There were thus no external scale economies which might have benefited all the industries. And, when decline came, 'each could be picked off separately, for it could not rely on security within an industrial complex'.[83]

Wealden industries retreated because of their own internal and external problems and not because of the comparative advantage offered by agriculture. Although the region was well supplied with transport links to London, production of foodstuffs for the metropolitan market mainly came much later than the decline of industry. Competition for woodland, to provide hop poles, did not reach a peak until the second quarter of the nineteenth century, and cattle breeding, poultry production and dairying expanded mainly from the later eighteenth century. The primacy of Wealden industry had dampened the process of agricultural change in the seventeenth century. Some Wealden land was treated with marl from iron ore bell pits, and with ashes from iron works, but for the most part industry had competed with agriculture for land, labour and capital to the long-term detriment of the latter. Furthermore, failing industrialists did not invest in Wealden farming: some speculative landlords sold timber and underwood recklessly to recoup their investments, thus contributing to deforestation of the area; some looked to closer links with London finance and Jamaican and other plantations. Because there was little identity of interest between merchant and industrial capital in the Weald in the seventeenth century, metropolitan mercantile capital switched to government stocks and foreign investment rather than bolster the industrial structure from which they had made major gains. Only where government or landed capital continued to supply finance, as with the Fullers or Ashburnhams, was Wealden manufacturing prolonged after 1750.

When industrial capital did flow into the Weald again in the Victorian period it was to invest in the recreational and landscape qualities of the area and to build rural retreats from urban and northern industrialism. Earlier industrial decline had left hammer ponds, fine Jacobean houses and fascinating ruins half hidden in the reclaiming woodland. Cultural attitudes to industrialism are thus important in the continuing deindustrialisation of south-east England in the nineteenth century. Changing patterns of national and international finance and cultural change are the keys to understanding deindustrialisation in the Weald (and elsewhere) rather than explanations which rely solely on factors within the region itself.

Cumbria: a case of contrasts
Cumbria was a major seat of cloth making from medieval times and was an early user of water power for the fulling process. Rural industries (iron, paper, gunpowder, cotton) became more varied and

[83] Thirsk, *The Agrarian History of England and Wales*, p.174.

widespread throughout the region between the Tudor period and the end of the eighteenth century, but none was powerful enough radically to alter demographic behaviour or to stimulate major social transformation. The different industries were not significantly linked together in terms of capital or entrepreneurship, and seasonalities of labour were disparate and even clashing. The eighteenth century also saw the development, under the Lowther family, of the coal industry of the Cumberland coast. There was no agrarian 'revolution', although rural industries and the cattle trade led to an accumulation of savings among the peasantry. Agrarian feudal tenures were weakened partly because the peasantry resisted them and the Common Law and the courts upheld peasant rights where the integrity of tenants' customs could be proved. Population increased throughout the region and market towns expanded in size and function during the eighteenth and early nineteenth centuries.

But the industrial revolution which occurred in Cumbria during the classic period and beyond was confined to the north and west coastal areas. Its leading sectors (coal, iron, steel, shipbuilding and cotton) bore little organic or locational relationship to the earlier widely diffused and largely domestic industries inland. And as coal-based industrialisation gathered pace it was accompanied by selective and later wholesale deindustrialisation of the Cumbrian land mass, so that more than 100,000 people left the region during the middle and late nineteenth century. The Carlisle cotton industry, isolated from its competitors, began to decline in the 1860s. By 1900 even the industries of west Cumberland were less buoyant as the basic process of steel making destroyed the former near monopoly of non-phosphoric ore and 'Bessemer iron'. By the late Victorian period only one important and enduring 'industry' burgeoned: that of Lake District tourism.[84]

Thus, in the case of Cumbria, a form of proto-industrialisation occurred at a time when regional society as a whole was still dominated by feudal structures. The region had all the staples of the industrial revolution in coal, iron, steel and cotton but it never achieved a stage of mature industrialisation in a Rostovian sense and substantial deindustrialisation was the twentieth-century fate even of the west coast. The long-term vitality of the region was weakened by an early lack of integration in terms of entrepreneurship, capital and labour supplies between the coal and iron industries of the coast and manufacturing in inland Cumbria. There was diversity but limited interdependence, and few external economies in terms of infrastructure, transport, and tertiary development accrued to the whole region.

---

[84] These remarks about Cumbrian development are derived from J. D. Marshall, 'Stages of Industrialisation in Cumbria', in Hudson, *Regions*. This distils and discusses much of the secondary literature on the region.

Conclusion

The industrial revolution saw a marked acceleration in the regional relocation of industry and the creation of specialised, internally cohesive industrial regions linked to national and international markets. Through the build up of transport, commercial and financial infrastructures and external economies, the industrialising regions created a dynamic which reached out to affect the whole country. They experienced significant shifts in the nature of industry and trade, in the deployment of men, women and children and in the way of life of all social classes. They experienced industrial revolution (generally without the rise to dominance of the factory system) while other regions deindustrialised as a consequence and/or moved away from manufacturing towards agricultural or service employments. It is erroneous to suppose that because no revolution in technology had occurred in many sectors and regions – and only limited changes in economic organisation – that these were left unaffected by transformations elsewhere: all industries, occupations and lives were profoundly affected in such a small country by its industrialising regions. By the mid nineteenth century, those working in the so-called 'traditional' sector (small-scale, hand technology and serving local rather than distant markets) and those in agrarian and service occupations, all felt the effect of more regular working, closer links with urban markets, gadgets which eased and speeded up work, gas lighting, water pipes, cheap printing and advertising, lowering prices of raw materials, low-cost food, more credit, stiffer competition and unprecedentedly high bankruptcy rates arising from periodic booms and slumps. All these rose directly from the expansion of manufacturing and trade and from structural shifts which characterised the economy as a whole.

5 DEMOGRAPHY AND LABOUR

In the 600 years from the time of the Domesday Book to the end of the seventeenth century the population of England and Wales increased around five-fold and it did this in a succession of great cycles of growth followed by stagnation or decline. In the nineteenth century, by contrast, the population almost quadrupled before the appearance of a more stable balance between fertility and mortality based on birth control and lower death rates.[1] Thus the industrial revolution was accompanied by an historically unique period of rapid demographic increase, and population growth was thereafter sustained. Peak rates of growth were reached in the 1800s, a decade which saw for the first time a decline in the association between population expansion and rising food prices.[2] These facts not only highlight the radical impact of the industrial revolution but also prompt questions about the connections between demography and economic change. Did population growth stimulate an industrial revolution? Did it merely coincide with economic change or was it the result of economic development? What was the nature and direction of causal connection between the two?

To answer these questions information about the timing of population increase in the eighteenth century and its chronological link with economic change is needed. It is also necessary to ask to what extent demographic increase was a result of rising birth rates or declining death rates, as each has a different set of possible connections with economic change. In gaining this knowledge historians are dogged from the outset by the difficulties and omissions of surviving source materials. The first Census was not conducted until 1801 and there is little reliable census information on age, marital status, occupations or place of birth before 1851. Civil Registration began only in 1837: before this reliance has to be placed largely on parish registers, which present major difficulties when used for population estimation. Their survival and quality is variable and there are large discrepancies

---

[1] The 'demographic transition' from relatively high birth and death rates to a regime based on birth control and low mortality is a characteristic of industrialised societies. In England it appears largely to have occurred in the third quarter of the nineteenth century. Most often rapid population growth accompanies a lagged transition where improvements in mortality precede the compensating fall in fertility.

[2] Population could from then on apparently rise without economic penalty. For a recent concise but comprehensive account of this transition see R. Woods, 'Population Growth and Economic Change in the Eighteenth and Nineteenth Centuries', in P. Mathias and J.A. Davis, eds., *The First Industrial Revolutions* (Oxford, 1989), pp.127-53.

between baptisms and births and between burials and deaths. Nonconformity and religious indifference were significant and varied over time and space. Despite the survival of some nonconformist registers we know little about the demographic experience of those who did not associate with the Anglican church, and migratory populations are similarly very difficult to document. Estimating the chronology of eighteenth-century population growth in a precise way is thus full of pitfalls.[3]

Population change

An early indication of the chronology of population change was gained by John Rickman, who was in charge of the first census of 1801. He asked parish priests and overseers for decadal statistics for the

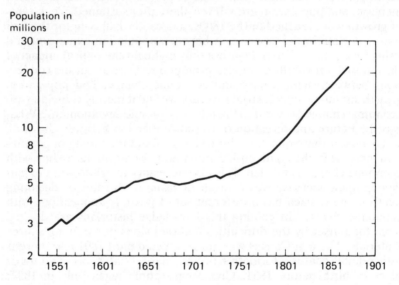

Figure 5.1: English population totals 1541-1871

Source: Back projection estimates from E.A.Wrigley and R.S.Schofield, *The Population History of England 1541-1871: A Reconstruction* (London, 1981), p.207, and table A3.1, pp.527-35.

[3] Tax returns are another source. Gregory King used the Hearth Tax returns to calculate the population of England and Wales in 1695 at 5.5 million but his choice of a multiplier to convert households to population was crucial and the scope for error great. Despite this, Wrigley and Schofield's more sophisticated calculations suggest that King's figure was fairly accurate. For full discussion of the problems see E.A. Wrigley and R.S. Schofield, *The Population History of England 1541-1871* (London, 1981); E.A. Wrigley, ed., *An Introduction to English Historical Demography* (London, 1966); M. Drake, ed., *Population Studies from Parish Registers* (Matlock, 1982).

previous century. These suggested that the acceleration of population growth dated from about 1740 and that the earlier decades of the century had seen only very modest increase. Since the publication of Wrigley and Schofield's *Population History of England, 1541-1871* in 1981 we know a great deal more about the nature of demographic increase in the eighteenth century and Rickman's rough chronology has been confirmed.

Wrigley and Schofield's study is based on a sample of 404 parish registers and uses a technique called back projection which enables mid-nineteenth-century census returns to be used to estimate the level of omission from the earlier sources. They find that average life expectancy at birth rose from about 32.4 to 38.7 years between the 1680s and 1820s, with most change occurring from the early 1730s. However, reproduction rates were increasing markedly in the second half of the eighteenth century and they estimate that rising fertility contributed two and a half times more to the population boom than did mortality improvement. They find no sustained evidence of change in marital fertility but nuptiality varied considerably over time: the great acceleration of population growth in the later eighteenth century is thus attributed largely to earlier and more universal marriage. The mean age of first marriage fell from about 26 to 23 years and the proportion of women never marrying fell from 15% to no more than 7.5%. These two developments appear to account for the bulk of the observed increase in eighteenth-century reproduction rates and the rest was caused by a significant increase in illegitimacy. Illegitimacy accounted for about 2% of all births at the beginning of the eighteenth century and 6% at the end. At the beginning of the century less than one-tenth of all first births were illegitimate. By 1800 half of all first conceptions were occurring outside marriage: one quarter illegitimate, one quarter pre-nuptial.[4]

Wrigley and Schofield's analysis

Because of the primacy that Wrigley and Schofield attach to nuptiality change, recent causal explanations of population growth and the search for links between economic and demographic change during the industrial revolution have concentrated on the factors governing marriage. Wrigley and Schofield themselves argue that, as household size remained stable during both the population stagnation of the seventeenth century and the rise in the eighteenth century, population growth through rising nuptiality must have been a function of the ability to set up new households. As real-wage movements may be seen as an indication of this ability, Wrigley and Schofield proceed to demonstrate a significant correlation between real wages and nup-tiality *if* a lag of about 30 years is introduced into the marriage rate

4 Wrigley and Schofield, *Population History*; E.A. Wrigley, 'The Growth of Population in Eighteenth Century England: A Conundrum Resolved', *Past and Present* 98 (1983).

series. In other words, higher or lower real wages were followed 30 years or so later by a rise or fall in nuptiality. The correlation remains good for the whole period 1541-1841. Thus it is argued that a relationship between living standards and fertility was well established from at least the sixteenth century, before proto-industrialisation, before the accelerated growth of the urban proletariat and before significant change in the social relations of production traditionally associated with the industrial revolution. Population growth in England from the mid eighteenth century was a delayed response to earlier rises in real wages. The relationship between real wages and nuptiality also survived the industrial revolution and continued to the 1840s or so. This, Wrigley and Schofield argue, came out of a distinctive cultural norm which demanded economic independence for the newly married. English society had a capacity for demographic self-control via the notion of a basic living standard below which people would not marry or form a new household. This acted as a preventive check on population growth after periods of economic depression and was more important than the positive check or mortality crisis which occurred when population growth outstripped the resources available and famine resulted. In Wrigley and Schofield's words, English demography exhibited 'dilatory homeostasis'. England had a low-pressure demographic regime where preventive rather than positive checks, prudence rather than pestilence, acted to keep population growth in line with economic conditions (after a delay – hence the term dilatory). By assigning the major role in population growth to nuptiality rather than mortality, Wrigley and Schofield placed new emphasis on the active role of the population in demographic change. Figure 5.2 shows the lines of causation in a pre-industrial demographic system embodying both positive and preventive checks. These connections were first suggested and elaborated by Malthus in his essays of 1798 (which stressed the positive check) and 1803 (which stressed the preventive check).[5]

Problems with the preventive check

Although quite properly regarded as a major breakthrough in demographic study, Wrigley and Schofield's work, especially their causal analysis, has met with some criticism. Setting aside the issue of whether or not back projection and allowances for omissions and biases in the parish register sample have yielded an accurate picture, at the aggregate level, of the timing and magnitude of changes in vital

[5] Wrigley, 'The Growth of Population'. For a survey of this analysis and some of the difficulties and alternatives see R.M. Smith, 'Fertility, Economy and Household Formation in England Over Three Centuries', *Population and Development Review* 7 (1981); D.R. Weir, 'Life Under Pressure: France and England 1670-1870', *Journal of Economic History* XLIV (1984). For discussion of the back projection technique see R.D. Lee, 'Inverse Projection and Back Projection: A Critical Appraisal and Comparative Results for England', *Population Studies* 39 (1985).

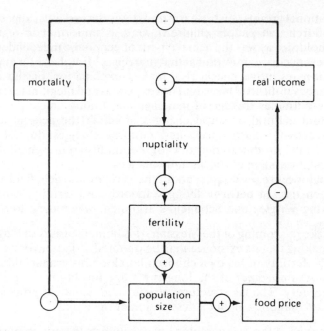

Outer ring: Positive check
Inner ring: Preventive check

Figure 5.2: The positive and preventive checks

Source: E.A.Wrigley and R.S.Schofield, *The Population History of England 1541-1871: A Reconstruction* (London, 1981), p.458.

rates, and also assuming that the Phelps Brown and Hopkins wage index which they use, and their price deflator, are a reasonable basis for assessing the movement of real incomes or living standards at the aggregate level, difficulties remain.[6]

An initial problem arises in considering whether the constancy of household size actually tells us as much about the general acceptance of the need for economic independence of the newly married as historians suggest. It may well be that kinship and neighbourhood networks of material support, migration, early death and remarriage, and customs regarding the living arrangements of different social or

---

[6] It remains the case that compensating for errors, omissions and biases in their Parish register sample (which includes no London parishes) is a difficult task and one reviewer of their work pointed out that the entire birth rate boom of the late eighteenth century only appears after underregistration and other allowances have been added to the series (P.H. Lindert, 'English Living Standards, Population Growth', and Wrigley and Schofield, *Explorations in Economic History* 20 (1983)). Their chronology of real wage movement is also questionable, dependent as it is on southern craft wages and limited price series.

occupational groups (such as farm and domestic servants, apprentices, stepchildren and pauper children) were as important in regulating household size as was the achievement of economic independence for each new nuclear family unit at first marriage.[7] Emphasis on nuptiality and the preventive check also makes explanation of the rise in illegitimacy difficult. One would not expect to find illegitimacy rising at the same time as the age of marriage was falling unless there were important cultural or social changes affecting the general level of sexual activity. Such social and cultural changes do not figure prominently in the framework of continuity represented by the homeostatic system of checks and balances.

A major cause for disquiet about the Wrigley and Schofield analysis has been the lag between living standards and fertility. Mokyr, in reviewing Wrigley and Schofield's argument was moved to remark:

> Like the coming of the Messiah, this homeostasis is so long in the making that its existence may be doubted…since no one controls the fertility of his own children let alone his grandchildren, the *modus operandi* of the long-run wage-fertility nexus remains a mystery. The lag structure Wrigley and Schofield propose is no explanation at all but a description of the data.[8]

In fact none of the demographic series supports the notion of stability or equilibrating adjustment. Fertility, mortality and nuptiality fluctuate wildly in the short run and the long run. The only sense in which equilibrium can be said to have existed is in the relative absence of catastrophic preventive checks. Furthermore, the variability of birth rates and death rates declined during the eighteenth century whereas, at least according to the Phelps Brown and Hopkins index, the variability of real wages remained quite high. This may be taken to imply either that the causes of demographic variability were not necessarily embedded in changes in the standard of living *or* that the causal relation changed structurally at some point after 1700. Either way, it points to the possibility of a different material connection between population increase and economic change coming into being in the eighteenth century.[9] Anderson has also shown that there are alternative explanations compatible with the aggregate series and

[7] See M. Chaytor, 'Household and Kinship: Ryton in the Late Sixteenth and Early Seventeenth Centuries', *History Workshop Journal* 10 (1980) and reply by K. Wrightson, 'Household and Kinship in Sixteenth Century England', *History Workshop Journal* 12 (1981); J. Hajnal, 'Two Kinds of Preindustrial Household Formation System', *Population and Development Review* 8 (1982). M. Anderson has argued that if the desired living arrangement was the extended family, low life expectancy alone in the preindustrial period would ensure that this was only possible in around one third of households, *Approaches to the History of the Western Family* (London, 1980), pp.31-2.
[8] J. Mokyr, 'Three Centuries of Population Change', *Economic Development and Cultural Change* 32 (1983), p.190.
[9] Mokyr, 'Three Centuries', pp.183-92.

correlations. For example, the link between living standards and nuptiality/fertility could be spurious if it arose from simultaneous association with a third variable such as expanding job opportunities.[10] The main difficulty with the Wrigley and Schofield approach is the problem of lumping the whole population together and then using aggregate results to analyse patterns of individual motivation. Eighteenth-century English society comprised a mass of loosely linked local and regional economies at very different levels of development and with widely different social, agrarian and industrial profiles. Furthermore, markedly different experiences were apparent between different classes and occupational groups within regions. There is a strong likelihood that national series of demographic statistics conflate opposing tendencies in different sectors, regions and social groups. The aggregate picture is valid as a statistical exercise, but it provides limited clues for detailed causal analysis.[11] What is needed is data by region, sector and class: different sorts of workers or social groups in different areas probably had different demographic regimes to start with and are likely to have reacted to different developments or to have varied in their reaction to the same economic changes. 'If labourers acted in response to different stimuli from those that prompted craftsmen, miners or textile workers, this response is lost in the process of aggregation', argues Levine.[12] The multi-class and mixed region totals inevitably mask structural variation. The result is an excessive preoccupation with national comparisons and an assumption that lower classes and backward regions lag behind but eventually conform to a national pattern.[13]

Parish reconstitution studies suggest that changes at parish level were influenced most by factors in the *local* economic and social setting. These included varying cultural assumptions and traditions, shifts in gender-specific employment patterns, migration, economic insecurity, and the attitudes of parish élites in their control and administration of poor relief and settlement.[14] Influences such as these are certainly mentioned in the Wrigley and Schofield account but,

[10] A point made strongly by M. Anderson in, 'Historical Demography after The Population History of England', *Journal of Interdisciplinary History* xv (1985).
[11] For an excellent discussion of the explanatory problems of demographic work, see M. Anderson, *Approaches to the History of the Western Family* (London, 1980), pp.30–6. Anderson argues that we need more sociological sensitivity to context to offset and enrich the rigours of demometric and econometric analysis; see 'Historical Demography'.
[12] D. Levine, 'The Population History of England 1541–1871: A Review Symposium', *Social History* 8 (1983), p.155.
[13] See W. Seccombe, 'Marxism and Demography', *New Left Review* 137 (1983), p.35.
[14] D. Levine, *Family Formation in an Age of Nascent Capitalism* (New York, 1977); K. Wrightson and D. Levine, *Poverty and Piety in an English Village: Terling 1525-1700* (New York, 1979); Levine, *The Making of an Industrial Society: Whickham 1560-1765* (Oxford, 1991). Economic security in these studies is not just a question of real income but of seasonality and variability of work.

because their causal analysis focuses on manipulation of the aggregate statistics, economic determinants are necessarily reduced to the manageable aggregate variable of real-wage change.

Regional and occupational studies show that fertility and migration patterns varied a great deal between textile and mining areas, for example, and that migration between areas and between country and towns was important in spreading the repercussions of economic factors within distinct regions.[15] As de Vries has said: 'The "national" demographic pattern projected in the work of Wrigley and Schofield may obscure a series of distinctive regional demographic processes that were linked together by migration'.[16]

A wider range of influences and of local and regional factors attract attention in two other, overlapping, approaches to understanding the cause of demographic increase in the period, centred on proto-industrialisation and proletarianisation.

Proto-industrialisation and demography
Most of the writing linking demographic change to proto-industrialisation has deliberately attempted to avoid approaches that treat the demographic regime in isolation from the immediate social, institutional and economic context. Unlike the Wrigley and Schofield approach, the focus of proto-industrialisation theory is the region, and the aim is to relate the expansion of population directly to major change in the mode of production and in the social relations and institutions of production at regional level. Proto-industrial analysis directly addresses the demographic impact of social and cultural changes, such as shifts in intra-family relationships, the definition and redefinition of gender, and changes in emotional and sexual attitudes. The theory emerged from European research which indicated that major population change in the eighteenth and early nineteenth centuries came from areas of expanding manufacturing in the countryside. These areas were growing more rapidly than peasant (largely subsistence) regions and more rapidly (in terms of natural increase) than most towns.[17]

[15] For an important regional discussion see S. Jackson, 'Population Change in the Somerset–Wiltshire Border Area 1701-1800: A Regional Demographic Study', *Southern History* 7 (1985), pp.119-44.
[16] De Vries' work on Holland suggests that the model of negative and positive feedback loops is impossible to apply in the Dutch case because of the importance of external influences, particularly migration. He suggests the usefulness of a more open economy model also in the English case: J. de Vries, 'The Population and Economy of the Pre-industrial Netherlands', *Journal of Interdisciplinary History* xv (1985), p.682.
[17] See F.F. Mendels, 'Proto-industrialization: The First Phase of the Industrialization Process', *Journal of Economic History* xxxii (1972); P. Kreidte, H. Medick and J. Schlumbohm, *Industrialisation Before Industrialisation* (Cambridge, 1981), which includes F.F. Mendels, 'Agriculture and Peasant Industry in Eighteenth-century Flanders', first published in W.N. Parker and E.L. Jones, eds., *European Peasants and Their Markets* (Princeton, 1975).

Most proponents of the proto-industrial approach suggest that extra-agricultural earnings allowed the positive checks keeping population growth in line with locally available resources to be broken. The same land area could now support a larger population, with manufacturing incomes purchasing food from other regions specialising in agriculture. Average real incomes are only part of the issue here: as important was the effect of proto-industry on the growth of the market and the monetisation of the economy which allowed the extension of inter-regional trade. Specifically, proto-industrialisation affected fertility. The age of marriage tended to decline because proto-industry gave a source of independent income early in life: new households could be established without having to await the inheritance of land. Marriage rates also tended to be higher because they were unconstrained by the availability of inheritable land. Mendels found that in eighteenth-century Flanders the rate of marriage (the proportion of the population marrying) correlated directly with movement in the relative price of linen goods (an index of the prosperity of the linen industry compared with agriculture). Levine found a similar relationship in the hosiery-making village of Shepshed in Leicestershire.[18]

The proto-industrialisation literature suggests other links between manufacturing earnings and fertility. Higher illegitimacy levels are said to have occurred because of a loosening of the parental controls over courtship and marriage that were characteristic of landholding peasant societies. It is argued that manufacturing earnings from an early age promoted intergenerational independence and greater isolation of the nuclear from the extended family. Selection of a spouse became a more individual matter and affective individualism became the hallmark of relationships. Proto-industrial employment may also have encouraged premarital sex in the knowledge that marriage could follow more easily. The 'transformation of eroticism' first suggested by Shorter with respect to the nineteenth century has, with proto-industrialisation theory, been pushed back in time over the preceding century.[19]

It is perhaps surprising that little attention has been paid thus far to the impact on breast feeding practices of increasing proto-industrial work for women. Research has suggested that breast-feeding habits are crucially important in birth spacing and infant health. Manufacturing in the home under competitive conditions is not likely to have been compatible with prolonged breast feeding and if busy mothers forced

[18] See references in fn.17, esp. Mendels, 'Proto-industrialization'; D. Levine, 'The Demographic Implications of Rural Industrialisation: A Family Reconstitution Study of Shepshed, Leicestershire 1600-1851', *Social History* 2 (1976); also Levine, *Family Formation*.
[19] H. Medick, 'The Proto-industrial Family Economy: The Structural Function of Household and Family During the Transition from Peasant to Industrial Capitalism', *Social History* 1 (1976); E. Shorter, *The Making of the Modern Family* (London, 1976), esp. ch.3.

early weaning, or substituted the bottle for the breast, conceptions would recur more readily.[20] Medick and others have argued that higher fertility within marriage was also encouraged because children were such an important earning asset in proto-industrial households. It may be that a 'demographic hot house' was created in expanding proto-industrial regions because the organisation of industry and income earning encouraged population growth to occur even during prolonged periods of depression in manufacturing earnings. The proto-industrial family adhered to peasant norms of sufficiency, independence and task-orientated self-exploitation. The reaction of most working families to periods of low piece rates was to work longer hours and to increase family size in order to increase production. The result was demographic destabilisation and increasing poverty rather than any kind of equilibrium or stasis in line with income levels – often aggravated in proto-industrial regions by the inmigration of landless poor, particularly in the nubile and child-bearing age ranges.[21] Figure 5.3 is an attempt to set out these links between external demand for manufactures, proto-industrialisation, proletarianisation and demographic increase.

Despite the logic of the links posited between proto-industrialisation and demography, empirical work has exposed a large gap between theory and the reality of demographic increase in proto-industrial areas, particularly in England.[22] It is certainly the case that most areas of expanding proto-industry were densely populated but the effects of commercial manufacturing on the age of marriage and fertility are difficult to separate from the initial conditions found in regions where much proto-industry took root. In England especially, proto-industry was often found in areas of partible inheritance which already contained large numbers of landless cottagers not bounded by the ideal typical preventive checks of late marriage and patriarchal control that are argued to have governed peasant landholding societies.[23] In addition, proto-industrialisation theory places major emphasis on putting-out systems. Although these were the most

[20] See D. McClaren, 'Fertility, Infant Mortality and Breast Feeding in the Seventeenth Century', *Medical History* XXII (1978), pp.378-96. Research on the relationship between breast feeding practices and gender specific labour demands in central Europe is further advanced. See J. Knodel, 'Breast Feeding and Population Growth', *Science* CXCVII (1977), pp.1111-115; W.R. Lee, 'Women's Work, and the Family: Some Demographic Implications of Gender Specific Rural Work Patterns in Nineteenth Century Germany', in P. Hudson and W.R. Lee, eds., *Women's Work and the Family Economy in Historical Perspective* (Manchester, 1990), pp.50-75.
[21] Medick, Kreidte and Schlumbohm, *Industrialization Before Industrialization*, ch.3, esp. pp.76-7. Levine, *Family Formation*.
[22] See R. Houston and K.D.M. Snell, 'Proto-industrialization?: Cottage Industry, Social Change and Industrial Revolution', *Historical Journal* 27 (1984).
[23] J. Thirsk, 'Industries in the Countryside', in F.J. Fisher, ed., *Essays in the Economic History of Tudor and Stuart England* (London, 1961); A. Macfarlane, *The Origins of English Individualism*, ch.1.

widespread organisational form of domestic manufacture, the small master/artisan workshop structure was also common, in the West Yorkshire woollen industry, for example, and in some of the metalwares trades of South Yorkshire and Birmingham. These structures are likely to have had very different demographic implications because conditions of landholding and inheritance of the family business, the length of apprenticeship in the home and the controlling role of the male household head are likely to have resulted in a late marriage/low fertility regime.[24]

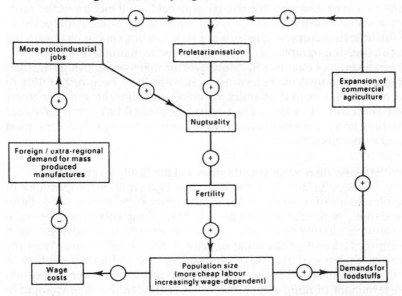

Figure 5.3: Proto-industrialisation and demographic change (ignoring urban sector links)

Although, in some trades, ancillary tasks for children and youths proliferated, children were not everywhere prized as an earning asset, especially when childbearing reduced the earnings of the wife for lengthy periods. The work process in different sectors and regions and their gender and age-specific labour demands varied enormously, modifying the potential impact of earnings on family size and age of marriage. Social and cultural attitudes within the family, social norms and collective discipline in village life also interfered with the relationship between the earning capacity of young people and their sexual or social independence. For example, young people often

24 P. Hudson, 'Proto-industrialisation: The Case of the West Riding Wool Textile Industry in the Eighteenth and Early Nineteenth Centuries', *History Workshop Journal* 12 (1981); for a European example see M.P. Gutman and R. Leboutte, 'Rethinking Protoindustrialization and the Family', *Journal of Interdisciplinary History* XIV (1984).

thought of their earnings as essential to their families rather than as a route to individual freedoms. Others had little choice because earnings accrued or were paid to the household head and not to individual workers. Wall found that the age of leaving home (and, by implication, of marriage) could be high amongst female lace-makers because their earnings were so important to the family unit.[25]

Clearly the links between proto-industry and demographic behaviour were complex and varied; but, even if they do emerge as important in the light of future research on England, it is unlikely that this model of demographic change will yield a full picture of the roots of population growth in the eighteenth century. Some rural parishes with little or no proto-industry were experiencing similar change in the age of marriage and in fertility to that found in manufacturing districts. Urbanising regions also had low ages of marriage and high fertility rates.[26] Demographic behaviour is likely to have been responding to economic and social changes common in different ways to many different sorts of region. The overriding general link between higher fertility and economic change is likely to have been proletarianisation and work opportunities.

Proletarianisation, work opportunities and the family wage economy
Even in demographic analysis at the aggregate level the importance of proletarianisation and work opportunities is now becoming more apparent. A re-examination by Schofield of the correlation between real-wage change and nuptiality in the seventeenth and eighteenth centuries taken separately has begun to direct attention away from the causal primacy of real-wage changes for the eighteenth century at least. It appears that the rate of marriage was a more important determinant of nuptiality in the seventeenth century than changes in the age of marriage and it was highly responsive to real-wage shifts. But after 1700 the mean age of marriage appears to have been more important in determining nuptiality and this exhibited little or no relationship to real wages, especially in the period of the industrial revolution itself.[27] Schofield himself has pointed out the need to explain the 'unusually large' change in age of marriage during the

[25] R. Wall, 'Age at Leaving Home', *Journal of Family History* 3 (1978), pp.182-201.
[26] Houston and Snell, 'Protoindustrialization?'. It might of course be argued that the impetus for urbanisation and for commercial agricultural development came initially from the expansion of rural industry and that high death rates in towns focus attention on rural population increases which fed urban growth. Certainly the interaction between towns and the countryside must be a major concern in the demographic and economic history of the eighteenth century. See G. Hoppe and J. Langton, *Town and Country in the Development of Early Modern Western Europe* (Norwich, 1983).
[27] R.S. Schofield, 'English Marriage Patterns Revisited', *Journal of Family History* 10 (1985). This was written in response to D.R. Weir, 'Rather Never than Late: Celibacy and Age at Marriage in English Cohort Fertility 1541-1871', *Journal of Family History* 9 (1984), who suggested that spinsterhood was the key to fertility regulation before 1700.

industrial revolution. He emphasises economic opportunities following on changes in economic structure as crucially important. The decline of live-in apprenticeships and of residential farm service (especially in the agrarian south and east) continued to remove some older institutional restrictions on age of marriage. But population mobility and urbanisation must also have been important, as well as the expansion of manufacturing and service employments, and shifts in local customs and community pressures.[28]

Goldstone has also reworked the Wrigley and Schofield aggregate figures to show that their homeostatic equilibrium was broken around 1750 by the emergence of a group of young marriers in the population who continued to marry young despite the pressures of population growth on income levels. This group was responding not to real-wage improvements but more likely to the increasing availability of employment for proletarianised workers in the industrial revolution. This reasoning fits much better with the evidence we have about the stagnation (or worse) of real-income levels for the mass of the population in the later decades of the eighteenth century; it also fits better with Lindert's regression work on the Wrigley and Schofield data, which indicates that in the period 1760-1815 the wage rate had a declining and insignificant effect on the birth rate. Thus sharp change in the determinants of nuptiality and fertility in England around the 1750s or 60s is as compatible with the aggregate figures as the notion of continuation of the same demographic regime.[29]

Clearly this is important if we are trying to establish the extent to which the period of the industrial revolution witnessed radical change or any sort of watershed in economic and social life. But there is a difficulty in deciding to what extent apparently quite radical changes in behaviour (at aggregate level) disguise shifts in practice *within* value systems of greater historical duration. How do we distinguish between continuity (involving the adaptation of behaviour) and radical reorientation of attitudes and actions? Demographic change that appears to be of fundamental structural significance may indicate instead the existence of 'multiple routing': that is, variation in choice amongst several accepted avenues to desired ends. Greater clarity of the

---

[28] But because nuptiality ebbed in the nineteenth century when proletarianisation was still increasing, the mechanism linking the two must have been complex and may have changed again in line with private and public attitudes to marriage and the disincentive effects of the 1834 Poor Law. Schofield, 'English Marriage Patterns Revisited', see also Wrigley, 'Growth of Population', p.144. On the importance of considering the marriage age of women, what constituted marriage in the eighteenth century and what motivated *women* to marry see B. Hill, 'The Marriage Age of Women and the Demographers', *History Workshop Journal* 28 (1989).

[29] J.A. Goldstone, 'The Demographic Revolution in England: A Re-examination', *Population Studies* XLV (1986); Lindert, 'English Living Standards'.

concept of 'demographic regime' is obviously required if we are to talk about moving from one to another.[30]

Identifying the timing of transition from one economic and socio-demographic regime to another is made difficult by the fact that radical structural change would necessarily give rise to various demographic responses concerning marriage and new household formation because of the combined and uneven nature of the transition in production methods and social relations between sectors and regions. Seccombe argues that the eighteenth century and the industrial revolution period exhibited at least three types of household-formation system in different mixes over time and across space – the peasant, the proto-industrial and the proletarian.[31] Levine has addressed this question in a similar way to Seccombe but he offers a reconciliation between the Wrigley and Schofield approach and the idea of significant shifts in demographic behaviour. He accepts that the English demographic regime continued in the industrial revolution period as before to be marriage-driven and to manifest a well-established cultural heritage based on a triadic axiom of economic independence before marriage, nuclear family households and (other things being equal) a late age of first marriage for women. However, his main point is that different social classes and occupational groups could interpret this same cultural heritage in different ways. He stresses in particular the difference between peasant and proletarian interpretations. Thus for Levine the significant change during industrialisation was the unprecedented and irreversible shift in the social composition of the population arising from proto-industrialisation on one hand and commercialising agriculture on the other. Both increased the proletarianised proportion of the population living in households with a family wage economy rather than one which co-ordinated the labour of all household members. The latter had embodied a peasant family strategy of marriage restraint in line with property and inheritance imperatives, whereas the former embodied the proletarian model of reproduction marked by earlier marriage and by higher rates of both marriage and illegitimacy. Increasing illegitimacy arose not because of any revolution in sexual habits but largely because increasing dependence on the fluctuating fortunes of wage labour did much to frustrate marriage plans.[32]

---

30 This is discussed by P. Kreager, 'Demographic Regimes as Cultural Systems', in D. Coleman and R. Schofield, eds., *The State of Population Theory: Forward from Malthus* (Oxford, 1986). See also D. Levine, 'Industrialisation and the Proletarian Family in England', *Past and Present* 107 (1985).
31 Seccombe, 'Marxism and Demography'.
32 Levine, 'Industrialisation and the Proletarian Family', p.185. On this point Levine agrees with the critique of Shorter found in J.W. Scott and L.A. Tilly, 'Women's Work and Family in Nineteenth Century Europe', *Comparative Studies in Society and History* 17 (1985), pp.36-64.

...ases in infant and maternal mortality.[41] Better nutrition and diet ...lting from more efficient production, distribution and marketing ...oodstuffs, fuel and other necessaries, particularly in urban areas, ...her than medical care or public health measures may be a better ...us in examining declining mortality. Research suggests that the ...uses of death that were linked to diet led the decline in mortality in ...e nineteenth century and that they were particularly important in ...ducing infant mortality.[42]

Urbanisation

English urbanisation in the early modern period was more rapid than elsewhere in Europe and, aside from Holland, England was a significantly more urbanised economy by the seventeenth century than its contemporaries. (See tables 5.1 and 5.2.) In the two centuries after 1600 the percentage of the total population living in towns quadrupled in England, scarcely changed in the rest of north-west Europe and advanced only modestly on the continent as a whole. The proportion of total European urban growth occurring in England was one-third in the seventeenth century rising to 70% in the second half of the eighteenth century. Given that England contained only 5.8% of the European population in 1600 and only 7.7% in 1800, it is clear that the level and the pace of urban growth in England in particular was remarkable.[43] At roughly the same per capita income, by 1840 England had a much higher urban share (48%) than did the rest of

Table 5.1: Urbanisation in England and on the Continent: percentage of total population in towns of 10,000 or more people (revised estimates)

	1600	1700	1750	1800
England	6.1	13.4	17.5	24.0
North and west Europe minus England	9.2	12.8	12.1	10.0
Europe minus England	8.1	9.2	9.4	9.5

Source: E.A. Wrigley, 'Urban Growth and Agricultural Change: England and the Continent in the Early Modern Period', *Journal of Interdisciplinary History* xv (1985), pp.683-728, esp. table 6.

[41] McKeown and Brown, 'Medical Evidence'; Branstrom and Tedebrand, *Society, Health*; A. Rubenstein, 'Subtle Poison: The Puerperal Fever Controversy in Victorian Britain', *Historical Studies* 20 (1983).
[42] Kearns, 'Urban Penalty'; M.K. Matossian, 'Death in London 1750-1990', *Journal of Interdisciplinary History* xvi (1985). P. Laxton and N. Williams, 'Urbanisation and Infant Mortality in England: A Long Term Perspective and Review', in M.C. Nelson and J. Rogers, eds., *Urbanisation and the Epidemiological Transition* (Uppsala, 1985).
[43] J.G. Williamson, *Coping with City Growth During the British Industrial Revolution* (Cambridge, 1990), pp.4-5.

Recomposition of the agrarian and industrial populations had a dramatic effect on the rate of population growth: whereas a peasant population had taken two hundred years to double itself, a proletarian population could do so in a quarter of the time. Like Wrigley and Schofield, Levine argues that Malthus comprehended the full implications of the decline of the prudential check just as it was disappearing: just as the more homeostatic relation between population and economy was breaking down. The identifying feature of the industrial revolution period, just when Malthus was writing, is that population growth could, for the first time, accelerate *without penalty* either in terms of massively higher death rates or of restricted fertility.[33]

The interesting thing about Levine's contribution is his assumption of the close interconnectedness of production and reproduction and the fact that both witnessed fundamental change in the period of the industrial revolution. His interpretation also rejects the idea that the family is a passive adapter to changing economic circumstances. In fact he argues that even in the strained decades of the industrial revolution the family was never simply the object of change. The proletariat had a pro-active reproductive response which profoundly affected subsequent developments.[34]

Mortality

Until Wrigley and Schofield published their results, improvements in death rates had been given primacy in explanations of demographic change in the eighteenth century.[35] But the current stress on fertility via changes in nuptiality and on the relatively closed nature of the homeostatic system may have unjustifiably diverted attention away from the mortality side of the demographic equation. Waves of epidemic disease or warfare could increase mortality irrespective of the state of the economy. The homeostatic system would predict that reductions in food prices, rising real wages and hence a compensating upward movement in nuptiality would follow waves of mortality increase until the system regained equilibrium. Fertility might also respond directly after periods of bubonic plague, smallpox or other

[33] For a much expanded version of David Levine's ideas see *Reproducing Families: The Political Economy of English Population History* (Cambridge, 1988); for discussion of Malthus and the close of his system see E.A. Wrigley, 'Elegance and Experience: Malthus at the Bar of History', in Coleman and Schofield, *State of Population Theory*.
[34] Levine argues that the mass of population never reverted to an anomic or irrational culture of poverty, *Reproducing Families*, ch.3.
[35] T. McKeown and R.G. Brown, 'Medical Evidence Related to English Population Change in the Eighteenth Century', *Population Studies* 9 (1955), pp.119-41; McKeown and Brown, 'Reasons for the Decline in Mortality in England and Wales During the Nineteenth Century', *Population Studies* 16 (1962), pp.94-122; T. McKeown, 'Food, Infection and Population', *Journal of Interdisciplinary History* xiv (1983). P.E. Razzell, 'Population Growth and Economic Change in Eighteenth and Early Nineteenth Century England', in E.L. Jones and G.E. Mingay, eds., *Land, Labour and Population in the Industrial Revolution* (London, 1967), pp.260-81.

epidemics because of the pressures to replace lost family members and to reassert the viability of the family as an economic unit. It may be that the population upturn of the 1730s was initiated by such a normal compensating swing (following high death rates from epidemics and harvest failures in the late 1720s). Thus the moment requiring more unusual explanation may be when this compensating swing became sustained and accelerated towards the end of the eighteenth century. It is, however, impossible to assign a reliable causal weight to mortality as an independent variable because it is difficult to separate out from the Malthusian positive check itself. Famine, as a symptom of overpopulation, was often accompanied by increases in epidemic diseases because of the lowered resistance of the population. Wrigley and Schofield's findings suggest that, although there were periods of dearth, epidemics and high death rates (especially around 1600 and in the early eighteenth century), England did not suffer any national subsistence crises after the mid sixteenth century and the Malthusian positive check in any extreme form appears to have been less important throughout Europe in the early modern period than was once thought. The significant mortality shift which occurred in the eighteenth and nineteenth centuries concerned death rates that were not just a direct result of a changing balance between population and resources. Mortality improvement was not just a question of escape from Malthusian constraint or crisis.[36]

Wrigley and Schofield's assessment of the significance of improvement in background mortality rates in the eighteenth and early nineteenth centuries is probably unduly low. Woods has suggested that lack of significant improvement in life expectancy in the Wrigley and Schofield account for the period 1750-1850 may be an artefact of the averaging together of very different regional and local mortality patterns. The redistribution of the population in favour of towns makes it particularly difficult to interpret the national figures.[37] Through the period, urban death rates were significantly higher than rural death rates. In 1801, for example, people in towns over 10,000 had an average life expectancy at birth of 31, people in rural areas of 41. Urbanisation was marked and continuous so that there was a significant shift in the proportion of the population living within the high-mortality regime. In 1670 13.5% of the population lived in towns over 5,000 compared with 21% in 1770 and 27.5% by 1801.[38] If

[36] Wrigley and Schofield, *Population History*, pp.412-17, 645-85. R. Woods, 'Population Growth and Economic Change in the Eighteenth and Nineteenth Centuries', in P. Mathias and J.A. Davis, eds., *The First Industrial Revolutions* (Oxford, 1989), pp.127-53.
[37] R. Woods, 'The Effects of Population Redistribution on the Level of Mortality in Nineteenth-century England and Wales', *Journal of Economic History* XLV (1985).
[38] E.A. Wrigley, 'Urban Growth and Agricultural Change: England and the Continent in the Early Modern Period', *Journal of Interdisciplinary History* xv (1985), pp.683-728, 688.

urbanisation was associated with no change i[n] the urban penalty, one would expect (othe[r] aggregate mortality rates to rise. The fact that [n]and that life expectancy at the aggregate level i[n] years during the period c.1680-c.1820 suggests mortality was falling rapidly enough to compensate proportion of the population at risk in the towns, o penalty was decreasing in intensity. The answer proba combination of both but Woods has suggested that the d mortality was particularly significant in the first half of t[he] century.

Between 1811 and 1861 national life expectancy at birth [in] and Wales was extended from 38 to 41 years. In London it ro[se] to 37, large towns (over 100,000) saw a change from 30 to 3 other towns (10,000 to 100,000 population) the figures were 3[2] The rural/residual areas reflect the more sluggish national figur[e] concern during the last two decades has been to investiga[te] working of the preventive check and of nuptiality more generally the importance of improvements in life expectancy (especiall[y] towns) in fuelling population growth is perfectly compatible w[ith] significant contemporary shifts in fertility and even with such shif[ts] being *apparently more significant* at the national level.[39]

Earlier studies linked improvements in mortality to more efficient food and coal distribution, the availability of cheaper more easily washable textiles and soap, better medical services and smallpox innoculation. Developments in public health and sanitation have also been stressed.[40] The impact of improvements in hygiene, medicine and public health appears to have been exaggerated in some earlier accounts and their effect remains the subject of debate. Smallpox innoculation was too restricted to have had a major effect and action in the sphere of public health was minimal before mid century. It has been argued that not until the later nineteenth century were hospital patients more likely to die of the disease for which they were admitted than from other unconnected contamination, but this harsh judgement of medical facilities is probably only applicable to surgical cases. Greater intervention by male physicians in pregnancy and childbirth in the nineteenth century certainly appears to have been accompanied by

[39] G. Kearns, 'The Urban Penalty and the Population History of England', in A. Branstrom and L. Tedebrand, eds., *Society, Health and Population During the Demographic Transition* (Stockholm, 1988), pp.213-36; Woods 'Population Redistribution'.
[40] T.S. Ashton, *An Economic History of England: The Eighteenth Century* (London, 1955); McKeown and Brown, 'Medical Evidence'; Razell, 'Population Growth and Economic Change'.

Table 5.2: Percentages of urban (U), rural agricultural (RA) and rural non-agricultural (RNA) populations in England, Holland and France 1500-1800

	England			Holland			France		
	U	RA	RNA	U	RA	RNA	U	RA	RNA
1500							9.1	72.7	18.2
1520	5.5	76.0	18.5						
1550				20.8	59.6	19.6			
1600	8.0	70.0	22.0	29.0	50.0	21.0	8.7	68.9	22.3
1650				37.1	41.6	21.3			
1670	13.5	60.5	26.0						
1700	17.0	55.0	28.0	38.9	40.3	20.8	10.9	63.3	25.8
1750	21.0	46.0	33.0	35.1	42.9	22.1	10.3	61.4	28.2
1800	27.5	36.3	36.3	38.6	44.3	22.6	11.1	58.7	30.2

Sources: R. Woods, 'Population Growth and Economic Change in the Eighteenth and Nineteenth Centuries', in P. Mathias and J.A. Davis, eds., *The First Industrial Nation* (Oxford, 1989), p.149. Figures derived from E.A. Wrigley, 'Urban Growth and Agricultural Change: England and the Continent in the Early Modern Period', *Journal of Interdisciplinary History* xv (1985), pp.683-728.

Europe in the mid to late nineteenth century. It is this high urban share rather than the speed of growth of towns during industrialisation which set the English experience aside and made it unique.[44]

In the sixteenth century urban growth relative to the rising national population trend was largely confined to London. In the following century national population growth slowed and was falling gently during the third quarter. On the continent the stagnation or decline of European populations was even more marked. Yet urbanisation continued and was most prominent in England in both absolute and percentage terms. London continued to dominate the picture, but unlike the continental experience in this century, growth also occurred in smaller centres, especially after 1670 when their rate of growth was four times faster than that of the national aggregate. Several major provincial centres – notably Norwich, Bristol, Newcastle and Exeter – increased by between 50% and 100% during the century. There was also significant growth in newer towns which reached the 5,000 population mark by 1670 – Birmingham, Manchester and Leeds – whilst Liverpool also exceeded 5,000 by 1700.

In the eighteenth century the long-established hierarchy in the size of English towns was radically overturned by the rapid growth of towns in industrial areas and ports. Many older centres such as Norwich, York and Exeter declined in relative terms whilst Manchester, Liverpool and Birmingham rose to stand second, third and fourth respectively after London in the size hierarchy shown in table 5.3.

[44] Material here and in the next two paragraphs relies heavily on Wrigley, 'Urban Growth'.

Other centres of newly expanding industry also began to figure in the list of largest towns: Leeds, Sheffield, Bolton, Stockport, Wolverhampton and Stoke. Ports such as Portsmouth, Plymouth, Hull and Sunderland also grew strongly. London, though still much greater

Table 5.3: Urban populations (thousands), and the urban size hierarchy

c.1520	c.1600	c.1670	c.1700	c.1750	1801
London 55	London 200	London 475	London 575	London 675	London 959
Norwich 12	Norwich 15	Norwich 20	Norwich 30	Bristol 50	Manchester 89
Bristol 10	York 12	Bristol 20	Bristol 21	Norwich 36	Liverpool 83
York 8	Bristol 12	York 12	Newcastle 16	Newcastle 29	Birmingham 74
Salisbury 8	Newcastle 10	Newcastle 12	Exeter 14	Birmingham 24	Bristol 60
Exeter 8	Exeter 9	Colchester 9	York 12	Liverpool 22	Leeds 53
Colchester 7	Plymouth 8	Exeter 9	Gt Yarmouth 10	Manchester 18	Sheffield 46
Coventry 7	Salisbury 6	Chester 8	Birmingham ⎫	Leeds 16	Plymouth 43
Newcastle 5	King's Lynn 6	Ipswich 8	Chester	Exeter 16	Newcastle 42
Canterbury 5	Gloucester 6	Gt Yarmouth 8	Colchester	Plymouth 15	Norwich 36
	Chester 6	Plymouth 8	Ipswich } 8-9	Chester 13	Portsmouth 33
	Coventry 6	Worcester 8	Manchester	Coventry 13	Bath 33
	Hull 6	Coventry 7	Plymouth	Nottingham 12	Hull 30
	Gt Yarmouth 5	King's Lynn 7	Worcester	Sheffield 12	Nottingham 29
	Ipswich 5	Manchester 6	Bury St	York 11	Sunderland 26
	Cambridge 5	Canterbury 6	Edmunds	Chatham 10	Stoke 23
	Worcester 5	Leeds 6	Cambridge	Gt Yarmouth 10	Chatham 23
	Canterbury 5	Birmingham 6	Canterbury	Portsmouth 10	Wolverhampton 21
	Oxford 5	Cambridge 6	Chatham	Sunderland 10	Bolton 17
	Colchester 5	Hull 6	Coventry	Worcester 10	Exeter 17
		Salisbury 6	Gloucester		Leicester 17
		Bury St Edmunds 5	Hull		Gt Yarmouth 17
		Leicester 5	King's Lynn		Stockport 17
		Oxford 5	Leeds } 5-7		York 16
		Shrewsbury	Leicester		Coventry 16
		Gloucester 5	Liverpool		Chester 16
			Nottingham		Shrewsbury 15
			Oxford		
			Portsmouth		
			Salisbury		
			Shrewsbury		
			Sunderland		
			Tiverton		

Source: E.A. Wrigley, 'Urban Growth and Agricultural Change: England and the Continent in the Early Modern Period', *Journal of Interdisciplinary History* xv (1985), pp.683-728, table 1.

than any other city and containing about 11% of the national population throughout the century, no longer stood out as the major source of national urban growth.[45] The share of the other towns larger than 5,000 in population increased dramatically, rising from 6% to 17% of the national total and for the first time surpassing London's share.[46]

[45] P. Corfield, *The Impact of English Towns 1700-1800* (Oxford, 1982), *passim*.
[46] Tables 5.1 to 5.3 do incorporate wide measures of uncertainty as discussed by Wrigley, 'Urban Growth'. In particular it should be considered whether it is wise to take an arbitrary dividing line of 5000 to categorise 'urban' and whether the dividing line should be redefined over time with the growth of population so that the urban figures would genuinely reflect structural shifts in the economy.

Theories of urban growth

It is possible in theory to link urbanisation with rising real incomes, as does Wrigley. In a simple model of a closed economy one would expect that rising real incomes would stimulate the demand for secondary and tertiary products (manufactures and services) rather than for primary products (agricultural goods) and thus promote expansion of employment mainly in towns rather than in the countryside. This would result in a tendency for urban populations to rise more than rural through natural increase and through increased migration from the countryside, whether because of push factors (linked to rural poverty and hence to migration in search of subsistence) or pull factors (linked to the desire for betterment). But neither the rapid growth of London in the sixteenth century nor the growth of the new manufacturing towns of the late eighteenth century (as opposed to the stagnation of some older regional centres) can be explained by this model.[47]

Another model used to explain the swings between urban and rural growth in pre-industrial Europe is that developed by Hohenberg. Again, a closed economy is assumed but this time the fortunes of towns are seen as dependent upon the demands for luxury manufactures and on urban and rural rents, whilst the economic buoyancy of the countryside is determined by real incomes which affect the demand for foodstuffs and the low-priced mass manufactures of rural industry. The long economic cycles of the pre-industrial period can be seen as representing swings in comparative advantage between town and countryside. When population rises and food prices rise in the wake, then property incomes rise and towns are more buoyant than the countryside. This would characterise the period from the late fifteenth to the late sixteenth century. However, when population grows more slowly or stagnates, food prices remain stable or decline and real incomes rise to give an advantage to proto-industrial trading and to internal demand for a greater variety of foodstuffs, including meat. Thus the late fourteenth/fifteenth and the late seventeenth/early eighteenth centuries can be seen as 'rural phases'. Both proto-industrialisation based on inter-regional trading and the idea of the fifteenth century as the 'century of the common man' are given a fresh perspective in the light of this model.[48] But closed-economy models necessarily ignore the impact of external trade. For the eighteenth century, the expansion of international trade and the ending of the great population cycles suggest the need for different ways of conceptualising urbanisation as we move to the period of the industrial revolution.

One model of European urbanisation which links preindustrial patterns to the experiences of the late eighteenth century is that

---

[47] Wrigley, 'Urban Growth'; Wrigley and Schofield, *Population History*, pp.463-4.
[48] P. Hohenberg and L.H. Lees, *The Making of Urban Europe 1000-1850* (Harvard, 1985), ch.4.

developed by de Vries. He suggests that the seventeenth century can be seen as a turning point in the creation of a European urban system. In the sixteenth century urban mini-systems existed associated with state-building and the setting up of privileged towns and administrative centres. Most urban centres were in the Mediterranean region but there were others of importance in central and north-west Europe. In the seventeenth century a much sharper differentiation between towns was occurring against the backcloth of slow population growth and the deceleration of extra-European expansion. There was a rapid growth of capital cities (stimulated by the administrative needs of absolutist and constitutional states), of Atlantic port cities and of the largest commercial centres of north-west Europe: Paris, Amsterdam, Rotterdam and London. Thus by the end of the seventeenth century a hierarchy of European cities had emerged with a single core in north-west Europe, as distinct from the earlier polycentric development. The growth and functions of specialised commercial centres of north-west Europe integrated the continent in an urban system such that it is impossible after 1700, argues de Vries, to make sense of urban growth in any one European country without looking across the borders at inter-urban links. After 1750 a new period of more rapid urban growth in Europe began, but unlike the previous centuries it was no longer largely confined to big centres: a large addition to the number of cities with populations over 10,000 occurred. Urban growth in this period came 'from below', nurtured by population growth, industrial expansion, and inter-regional and international trade in manufactures and primary products. According to de Vries, then, it was this new context of European urbanisation which set the scene for the industrialisation of western Europe.[49]

De Vries places particular emphasis on the absence of growth in smaller towns in the period 1600-1750. He argues that expansion of secondary employments in the countryside was responsible, in this 'age of the rural proletariat'. Smaller towns stagnated, lost political autonomy and lost the balance of advantage for the location of labour-absorbing industries. This may be a useful way of understanding European urbanisation as a whole, but the English case stands out as different because the paralysis which affected all but the largest towns on the continent was absent in England. Towns with between 5,000 and 10,000 inhabitants doubled in number from 15 to 31, while in the same period in Europe (minus England) they fell from 372 to 331. And the major eighteenth-century change in the urban hierarchy in England had no counterpart on the continent. The expansion of proto-industry and of the rural non-agricultural population in England was not at the expense of widespread urban growth (see table 5.2).[50]

[49] J. de Vries, *European Urbanisation 1500-1800*, esp. chs.10 and 11.
[50] This point is made very strongly by Wrigley in 'Urban Growth'.

Williamson's recent study of city growth during the industrial revolution also suggests that urbanisation did not occur to the detriment of industrial accumulation. He argues that the demand for labour in cities was very buoyant in the crucial decades 1821-61, when problems of urban growth may have reached a peak, and that immigrants were absorbed into urban labour markets quite easily. If anything, argues Williamson, British cities were starved of labour (and capital) and their growth was too slow. From the point of view of the economy as a whole, Britain may have underinvested in her cities.[51]

The impact of urbanisation

The regional 'redistribution' of the urban population and the growth of very large and smaller urban centres had a major impact on national rates of population growth in England and on economic, social and cultural change more generally. The greatest demographic impact of towns was excess urban mortality: until at least the later eighteenth century urban death rates considerably exceeded urban birth rates, especially in the larger centres, and towns could only grow by sucking in population from outside. Towns continued to have higher mortality rates, particularly infant mortality rates, than the countryside until the later nineteenth century: their rapid growth was thus dependent upon inmigration.[52] This in turn prevented national mortality levels from falling more substantially. It could also be argued that agricultural productivity stimulated growth in towns and that it was this coupled with high urban mortality that stimulated high rates of rural fertility.

It has been shown that migration into London in bad years resulted in very high mortality. Death rates were high to start with in bad years because of high food prices but they were aggravated by the deaths of rural migrants and their infants, exposed to urban diseases for the first time.[53] Thus English towns in general and London in particular (where mortality levels were actually increasing around 1800) can be seen to have acted as safety valves preventing too rapid an increase in population which might have led to a major fall in real incomes and an aborting of economic growth.[54]

The impact of growing towns in the eighteenth century was of course not solely demographic but also economic, social and cultural. Historians stress the growth and innovations in the tertiary sector to

[51] Williamson, *Coping with City Growth*, ch.10.
[52] The level and rate of urbanisation, and migration from the countryside to towns, was a crucial demographic variable which probably set England apart from her neighbours more obviously than the operation of a distinctively English preventive check.
[53] J. Landers, 'Mortality, Weather and Prices in London 1675-1825: A Study of Short Term Fluctuations', *Journal of Historical Geography* 12 (1986); P.R. Galloway, 'Annual Variations in Deaths by Age, Deaths by Cause, Prices, and Weather in London 1670-1830', *Population Studies* 39 (1985).
[54] Woods, 'Population Growth'; M.J. Daunton, 'Towns and Economic Growth in Eighteenth Century England', in P. Abrams and E.A. Wrigley, eds., *Towns in Societies: Essays in Economic History and Historical Sociology* (Cambridge, 1978), pp.245-77.

which urbanisation gave rise; the boom in public and private building (with its effects on the construction industry); the agrarian specialisation of rural hinterlands; the spread of literacy and skills; a renaissance of urban culture; the establishment of a more modern social structure, with power concentrated in upper- and middle-class groups (who acted together in defence of urban order against the threat of disturbance from below); and the growth of new attitudes to both wage earning and consumption.[55]

Migration

We know that the balance of net migration from England was outward through the period from the sixteenth to the nineteenth centuries but it was always small, averaging just over 1 per 1,000 with slightly lower rates in the period c.1770s – c.1830s. Peak rates were reached in the mid-seventeenth century, when poor economic conditions at home and a desire for religious and political toleration combined to produce rates of transatlantic emigration not approached again until the later nineteenth century.[56] Net migration figures (subject to severe errors of estimation) are all we have and we do not know to what extent net rates were actually a result of more significant emigration (to the American colonies in particular) accompanied by less immigration (largely Irish, Dutch and Jewish). The economic impact of changing sex and ethnic ratios and changing skill supplies is therefore difficult to quantify. The links between migration of foreign craftsmen and innovations in technology in a range of industries from textiles to glass and metalwares in the seventeenth and eighteenth centuries is well established.[57] Furthermore, although the net rates of migration were small, their cumulative demographic effect over three centuries was substantial and must be included in any model of the demographic system. We can see it as an important restraint on population increase particularly before 1750 and the male bias in emigration increased the proportion of females in the population, which may have affected labour supply and employment. The slowing down of emigration which seems to have occurred in the late eighteenth century was partly responsible for a resumption of more even sex ratios, which may well

[55] P. Clark, ed., *The Transformation of English Towns* (London, 1984), esp. ch.1; P. Borsay, 'The English Urban Renaissance: The Development of English Urban Culture 1680-1750', *Social History* 3 (1977). The impact of London alone under all these headings was massive, see E.A. Wrigley, 'A Simple Model of London's Importance in the Changing English Society and Economy 1650-1750', *Past and Present* 37 (1967), pp.44-70.
[56] Wrigley and Schofield, *Population History*, pp.219-28, 531-5.
[57] D.C. Coleman, 'An Innovation and its Diffusion: The "New Draperies"', *Economic History Review* xxii (1969); W. Cunningham, *Alien Immigrants to England* (1897); W.C. Scoville, 'Minority Migrations and the Diffusion of Technology', *Journal of Economic Histoy* xi (1951); B. Short, 'Deindustrialisation: A Case Study of the Weald', in P. Hudson, ed., *Regions and Industries: A Perspective on the Industrial Revolution in Britain* (Cambridge, 1989).

have influenced the marriage market and hence fertility during the peak of population expansion.[58]

The stream of international migration most associated with the industrial revolution in England was Irish, particularly following the potato famine of the 1840s. Irish immigration was significant during the whole period of the industrial revolution but until the 1840s it was well below the rate to compensate for emigration.[59] Recent thinking on the subject suggests that the Irish migration neither hindered nor significantly promoted industrialisation. Williamson argues that the elasticity of demand for unskilled labour was high enough to absorb much of the influx and that the impact of Irish immigrants in lowering wages was therefore not of major significance. Landlords and capitalists gained significantly from the labour influx but Williamson argues that the Irish did not directly foster industrialisation both because they mainly entered the unskilled and labour-intensive sectors and, more importantly, because they concentrated in cities. This tended to discourage the migration of English farm labour from country to town.[60]

There is still much to learn about the pattern and impact of population redistribution and internal migration in the eighteenth and early nineteenth centuries. Souden and Clark have emphasised the expansion of social migration: the attraction of the town as a place to shop, frequent coffee houses, gamble, parade at assemblies, and otherwise display fashion, wealth and political patronage. As the social life of the landed classes centred more and more on the towns in this way, an important geographical transfer of wealth occurred. There also appears to have been a significant decline in longer-distance migration in the period 1650-1750 and a greater degree of permanency of residence, especially in the industrial areas. Several reasons are suggested for this: slower population growth led to a decline in migration induced by severe hardship (there were lower food prices and fewer subsistence crises in upland areas); the growth of new industries in new locations; the increasing sophistication and diversity of northern towns; and improvements in poor relief.[61] The operation of the Settlement Laws, once seen as an obstacle to migration, are now

---

[58] Wrigley and Schofield, *Population History*, pp.219-28. D. Souden, "East, West-Home's Best"? Regional Patterns in Migration in Early Modern England', in P. Clark and D. Souden, eds., *Migration and Society in Early Modern England* (London, 1987).

[59] Wrigley and Schofield, *Population History*, pp.129, 596.

[60] J.G. Williamson, 'The Impact of Irish on British Labour Markets During the Industrial Revolution', *Journal of Economic History* XLVI (1986). The impact on England as opposed to Britain is likely to have been much greater, even using Williamson's methods.

[61] Clark and Souden, *Migration and Society*, pp.11-48, 293-332. See also D. Souden, 'Movers and Stayers in Family Reconstitution Populations', in *Local Population Studies* 33 (1984).

viewed as having only a modest regulative effect on population movement (especially the movement of young people to farm service and apprenticeships and the seasonal migration of agricultural workers). In areas of expanding industry and employment the Settlement Laws were seldom strongly applied except in times of crisis. But it has been suggested that the poor-relief system in England was important in *facilitating* migration because the local community accepted the responsibility of supporting older people whose kin had migrated from the area. This general acceptance, so much more prevalent than it would perhaps have been in an environment where the extended family was a more dominant residential group, may have encouraged migration in the knowledge that the poor-relief system would support any dependents left behind.[62]

In the study of internal migration 'one of the great mysteries still is what happened in the later eighteenth century'.[63] Hunt's discovery of a shift in regional wage differentials in the period 1760s – 1790s, with wages becoming higher in the north compared with the south (excluding London and its environs), suggests a less than fluid labour market at the national level and it appears that the bulk of movement continued to be short distance.[64] Deane and Cole, working before Wrigley and Schofield's data was available, made some interesting observations about the relationship at county level between rates of natural increase, urbanisation and migration. They found that inter-county migration increased over the eighteenth century but more slowly than one might expect (given population increase and the pace of urbanisation), such that by the early nineteenth century it was only double that of one hundred years earlier. After 1750, migration into the London area declined relative to the total volume of migration and, with the gradual disappearance of excess deaths over births, as a factor in the growth of the population of the area itself. The provincial towns became more important magnets. But what is surprising is the limited role that migration appears to have played in the development of the main industrial areas. All industrial areas grew largely through natural increase although the extent of inmigration varied: Staffordshire and the West Riding for example had little net migration whereas Lancashire and Warwickshire had lower rates of natural increase and relied more heavily on inmigration. Deane and Cole attribute this contrast to the nature and degree of urban concentration. In Lancashire and Warwickshire industrial development was accompanied by greater urbanisation in large towns so that there was only a

---

62 R.M. Smith, 'Transfer Incomes, Risk and Security: The Roles of the Family and the Collectivity in Recent Theories of Fertility Change', in Coleman and Schofield, *State of Population Theory*.
63 Clark and Souden, *Migration and Society*, p.38.
64 E.H. Hunt 'Industrialisation and Regional Inequality: Wages in Britain 1760-1914', *Journal of Economic History* 46 (1986).

relatively small surplus of baptisms over burials and more migrant labour was needed.[65] Regionally specific migration patterns became endorsed by habit and custom and by kinship links and information networks and so they are only partly understood in terms of the demand for and supply of labour. But these migration patterns and their link with the urban mortality penalty and with the differential sex ratios thrown up by sex-specific movement are fundamental to our understanding of demography and labour supply in the industrial revolution.

Population growth and economic growth

During the industrial revolution an older, more balanced demographic regime (in aggregate and over the long term) was in retreat and the seven decades or so after 1780 were unique in witnessing accelerated growth, a *marked* decline in the age of marriage, increased illegitimacy, and sustained improvements in mortality rates. All of these factors can be seen to have been closely related to economic change: the expansion of the economy and of income-earning opportunities, proletarianisation, migration and improvements in food production and distribution. Once this expansive demographic regime had been initiated it in turn influenced economic change which affected later demographic increase.

Of course the relationship between demographic growth and economic development is not always a positive one as experience in many countries of the contemporary Third World has shown. It can result in declining per capita incomes and the basic needs of a growing population can compete with the capital accumulation necessary for economic growth. It can also retard the adoption of labour-saving technology because labour is cheap. For population growth to be a positive stimulus in the industrialisation process it must not be too rapid. And other factors in the economic environment must be favourable: availability of resources, a high rate of savings, an efficient agricultural sector and/or a cheap supply of food from outside, and expanding employment.

Given a favourable environment, population increase may provide a stimulus to industrialisation through the supply of labour and through the demand it creates for food and manufactured goods. If we take the demand side first, it is worth speculating whether the industrial revolution required as a vital precondition not accelerated growth of population but the *control* of population growth so that per capita incomes could rise well beyond the level necessary for subsistence. If so, both the preventive check and the urban mortality penalty can be seen as important regulators in the English case. It may be that this regulation was much more important than any stimulus

65 P. Deane and W.A. Cole, *British Economic Growth 1688-1959* (London, 2nd edn, 1969), pp.106-22.

from the rapid expansion of population in the late eighteenth century –
indeed that expansion may have been, if anything, a hindrance to the
industrialisation process.[66] Demographic expansion was accompanied
by a marked rise in the dependency ratio (the ratio of those
economically dependent to those economically active), by increasing
poverty, by rising food prices and depressed real incomes. On the
positive side, there were certainly more mouths to feed and the
expansion of the urban and rural proletariat increased the size of the
market for basic food, fuel, clothing, housing and other needs.
Agricultural development was no doubt stimulated by this, although,
as we have seen, it was slow to respond and imports, particularly from
Ireland, rose. Improvements in coal mining and transport can be
attributed in part to population growth – one third of coal mined was
for domestic fires as late as 1840 – but housing was slow to respond as
evidenced by rising rents and overcrowding, especially in towns.
Further, it is impossible to assess the impact of population growth on
the internal demand for textiles and other manufactured products
without firm evidence of the substitutability and potential expansive-
ness (elasticity) of export demand. Mokyr has estimated that population growth *alone* may have increased demand by less than 10% of the
growth in total output in the first half of the nineteenth century and
probably by even less in the preceding 50 years. So even if it is assumed
that population growth was fully exogenous, its significance in
generating demand for increased industrial production was probably
marginal.[67]

Demand in the economy arose not so much because there were
more mouths to feed and bodies to clothe but because certain groups in
the population enjoyed buoyant incomes and because needs and
market involvement altered in line with a decline in the subsistence
sector, growing proletarianisation and wage dependency and the
growth of new consumption patterns and horizons. In other words,
changes in consumption (demand) were linked to prior changes in
production (supply). The concentration of the population into towns
and the growth of London and other major cities was also important in
changing consumption and spending habits. But urban growth was not
a simple function of population expansion. It arose from major
reorganisation of the agrarian social structure, from the process of
regional specialisation, from the growth of specific employment
opportunities and from the changing role of England in international
trade and finance.

If population growth in itself had a major causal effect on
industrialisation in England it may have been through the creation of a

[66] P. O'Brien, 'Agriculture and the Home Market for English Industry 1660-1820',
English Historical Review CCCXCIV (1985), p.786.
[67] J. Mokyr, 'Demand vs Supply in the Industrial Revolution', in J. Mokyr, ed., *The
Economics of the Industrial Revolution* (London, 1985), p.101.

cheap labour supply. Labour was by far the largest element in production costs in all industries throughout the period, so cheap labour was important for the expansion of markets, through more 'affordable' prices, for profitability and thus for re-investment and capital accumulation. But there are problems in identifying a straightforwardly positive relationship between labour supply and economic growth. First, as we have seen, industrial expansion mostly occurred in regions far removed from those experiencing labour surplus and industrial employers were often dogged by problems of recruitment and retention of labour. Second, an increasing labour supply is not a major stimulus if it lacks the necessary skills and habits of industrial employment. Third, as Habakkuk most forcefully argued, technological change in the English industrial revolution was slower than it need have been and was often biased against those innovations that substituted capital for labour because labour was so plentiful and relatively cheap.[68] Finally, the effects of rapid population growth in increasing both family size and the number of dependants ensured that much of the cheap labour available in the economy was that of women and children. (See figure 5.4.) It was the employment of women and

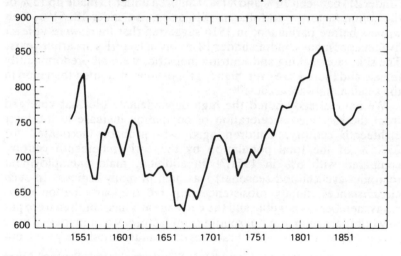

Figure 5.4: The dependency ratio 1541-1871

Source: E.A. Wrigley and R.S. Schofield, *The Population History of England 1541-1871: A Reconstruction* (London, 1981), p.444. The dependency ratio is taken as the number of those aged 0-14 and 60 or over per 1000 persons aged 15-59.

[68] H.J. Habakkuk, 'The Economic Effect of Labour Scarcity', in S.B. Saul, *Technological Change: The United States and Britain in the Nineteenth Century* (London, 1970), pp.23-76, extracted from H.J. Habakkuk, *American and British Technology in the Nineteenth Century* (Cambridge, 1962).

children alongside and as a substitute for men in many 'less-skilled' tasks and processes that really cheapened the labour supply during the industrial revolution.

The family and labour supply

The extent of incorporation of female and child labour into the most rapidly expanding commercial manufacturing sectors (in households, workshops and factories) and its association with increased intensification and labour discipline was unprecedented. Yet in most historical work only male labour is studied.[69] It is of course difficult to quantify the extent of female and child labour as both were largely excluded from official statistics and even from wage books (where often only payments to male-headed family groups or gangs were documented). But analyses based only on adult male labour forces are clearly inadequate and peculiarly distorting for this period. In the West Country woollen industry, women's and children's labour accounted for 75% of the workforce and child labour exceeded that of women and of men. In Bradford and Halifax worsted mills in 1835, females formed over 60% of the labour force and male and female juveniles together (under 21) between 70% and 80%. Children under 13 made up 13% of the cotton factory workforce in 1816 and those under 18, 51%. One witness before parliament in 1816 suggested that there were at least five times as many children under 10 in cotton factories in earlier years. The silk, lace-making and knitting industries were all predominantly female and there were even higher proportions of women than men in the small metalware trades.[70]

We have already noted the high dependency ratio that emerged from the sustained acceleration of population increase in the later eighteenth century. Children aged 5-14 probably accounted for 23-25% of the total population by the early nineteenth century compared with 6% in 1951.[71] In addition, male unemployment (chronic, cyclical and seasonal) was high in many regions. In such circumstances, family subsistence required the participation of as many members as possible and the early age at which children were put to work, particularly in household manufacture, was a matter of note to contemporaries: 'in some branches of the button trade they were put

[69] See for example, P.H. Lindert and J.G. Williamson, 'English Workers' Living Standards in the Industrial Revolution: A New Look', *Economic History Review* xxxvi (1983), pp.1-25; P.H. Lindert, 'English Occupations 1670-1811', *Journal of Economic History* xl (1980), pp.685-712.

[70] N.F.R. Crafts, *British Economic Growth During the Industrial Revolution* (Oxford, 1985), pp.4-5; M. Berg and P. Hudson, 'Rehabilitating the Industrial Revolution', *Economic History Review* xlv (1992); C. Nardinelli, 'Child Labour and the Factory Acts', *Journal of Economic History* xl (1980), pp.739-55; I. Pinchbeck, *Women Workers During the Industrial Revolution 1750-1850* (London, 1981); M.Berg, 'Women's Work, Mechanisation and the Early Phases of Industrialisation in England', in P. Joyce, ed., *The Historical Meanings of Work* (Cambridge, 1987), pp.64-98.

[71] Wrigley and Schofield, *Population History*, pp.528-9.

"as soon as they were in any way tall enough to reach the lathe"...around Wolverhampton children began "hard work regularly at nine", and in chain-making districts from eight to nine. Pin makers...frequently began at five years of age, since it was asserted, pin heading "can be done by a child as soon as it acquires the use of its arms and legs"; and when one of the factory commissioners visited a pin manufactory in 1833, he declared in astonishment that it "reminded him more of an infant school than anything else."'[72]

On the demand side the need for hand skills, dexterity and work discipline encouraged the absorption of female and juvenile labour into commercial production. This was encouraged by sex differentials in wages which may have been increasing under the impact of demographic pressure in these years. In the context of household income for a wage-dependent family, an increase in fertility, a deterioration of the breadwinner's wages (as may have occurred in the context of male labour oversupply), or a combination of both, could put strong pressure on women and children to take paid employment whenever possible and under whatever conditions. For very poor families there was in any case no choice in the matter but for all hands, where possible, to enter the labour market.[73] More female and child labour thus became available for employers and this drove down the levels of acceptable piece-rate and wage payments for such workers. And the extent of child labour in the textile trades in particular was a major force in keeping female wages low.[74] The attraction of both low wages and long hours was very important to employers at a time when no attention was yet paid to the incentive effects of payment by results or shorter hours.

The high proportions of female and child workers in the industrial revolution influenced and was influenced by innovation. New work disciplines, new forms of subcontracting and putting-out networks, factory organisation and even new technologies were tried out initially on a female and child workforce.[75] The system of adult worker with child assistants was massively expanded in the industrial revolution to workshops and sweatshops and to factories employing family work groups. And for decades child labour was seen as integral to the design of textile and other machinery. The original spinning jenny had a horizontal wheel requiring a posture most comfortable for children of nine to twelve.[76] And there was a parallel association between child and female labour and mechanisation in the north-east United States, where women as a proportion of the manufacturing labour force rose

[72] Pinchbeck, *Women Workers*, p.273. see also pp.120-2, 160-8, 205, 231-5.
[73] O. Saito, 'Labour Supply Behaviour of the Poor in the English Industrial Revolution', *Journal of European Economic History* 10 (1981).
[74] Pinchbeck, *Women Workers*, p.190.
[75] M. Berg, *The Age of Manufactures* (London, 1984); Berg, 'Women's Work'.
[76] Berg and Hudson, 'Rehabilitating'.

from 10 to 40% between 1812 and the 1830s. In the States this was linked to the innovation of large-scale technologies specifically designed to dispense with more expensive and restrictive adult male labour.[77] This was an important factor in the English case, too, but the increase in women's employment was also a product of the ready reserves of cheap and skilled female labour which had long been a feature of domestic and workshop production. In addition in England many agricultural regions shed female workers first during the process of agricultural change and much migration within rural areas and from rural to urban areas consisted of young women in search of work.[78]

By the mid-nineteenth century the uniquely important role of female and child labour was beginning to decline through a mixture of legislation, the activities of male trade unionists and the increasingly pervasive ideology of the male breadwinner and of 'fit and proper' female activities. A patriarchal stance was by this time also compatible with the economic aims of a broad spectrum of employers. According to Hobsbawm, larger employers as well as male labour were learning the 'rules of the game' in which higher payments (by results), shorter working hours and a negotiated terrain of common interests could be substituted for extensive low-wage exploitation, with beneficial effects on productivity.[79] It is the earlier phase of extensive low-wage exploitation of the female and child members of the family in particular that was unique to the industrial revolution. If we reclaim for women and children their rightful and critical place in the economic history of the period it will require major rethinking not just of the links between demography and labour supply but also of the timing and magnitude of shifts in employment from the primary to the secondary and tertiary sectors, the growth of productivity, the place of labour-intensive innovation and the movement of average earnings and family living standards.

Conclusion

What emerges from this study of demography, urbanisation and labour supply is the close link between production and reproduction, between the external functioning of the local, national and international economy and the internal world of the family and household;

[77] C. Goldin and K. Sokoloff, 'Women, Children and Industrialisation in the Early Republic: Evidence from the Manufacturing Censuses', *Journal of Economic History* XLII (1982), pp.721-74.
[78] K.D.M. Snell, *Annals of the Labouring Poor: Social Change and Agrarian England 1660-1900* (Cambridge, 1985), chs 1, 4; Clark and Souden, *Migration and Society*, p.35; Williamson, *City Growth*, pp.70-1. The role of women in urban-bound migration was first stressed by E.G. Ravenstein, 'The Laws of Migration', *Journal of the [Royal] Statistical Society* 48 (1885), 52 (1889).
[79] E.J. Hobsbawm, 'Custom, Wages and Workload', in Hobsbawm, ed., *Labouring Men: Studies in the History of Labour* (London, 1964), pp.344-70 esp. 353, 355.

between the way in which goods and services were produced and exchanged and the regional redistribution of the population with its economic, social and cultural repercussions. Unless we place these connections at the heart of our analyses, elements of change that were uniquely important in the industrial revolution will remain hidden and undervalued.

6 Consumption and Commerce

Malthus recognised that 'demand is quite as necessary to the increase of capital as the increase of capital is to demand.'[1] Yet supply-side analysis has always occupied the high ground in discussion of industrialisation. In 1932 Gilboy broke with tradition by suggesting that the factory and mass production could not become typical until demand had been extended throughout the population to consume the products of large-scale industry.[2] More recently, demand has assumed a central role in some interpretations: a consumer revolution has been identified as 'the necessary convulsion on the demand side of the equation to match the convulsion on the supply side.'[3] Consumption has even been seen as precipitating industrialisation, becoming 'an engine of growth'[4] and 'the ultimate economic key to the industrial revolution'.[5] This stress on the central role of changes in internal demand has occurred alongside a tendency to place much less emphasis than formerly on the dynamic force of overseas trade in the late eighteenth and early nineteenth centuries.[6] This chapter attempts to assess the competing claims of demand- and supply-side changes and of domestic and foreign markets in underpinning economic change. A strong argument for the integrated study of supply and demand emerges and the stimulus from foreign trade is seen to be both wider and more profound than recent interpretations suggest.

The sources of demand

There has been much debate about whether it is correct to consider demand as an independent variable in the growth process or whether (in long-term as opposed to short-term analysis) it must be regarded as

[1] T.R. Malthus, *Principles* quoted in P. Sraffa, ed., *Works and Correspondence of Ricardo* II, pp.349–50.
[2] E. W. Gilboy, 'Demand as a Factor in the Industrial Revolution', in A. H. Cole *et al.*, eds., *Facts and Factors in Economic History* (Cambridge, Mass., 1932), reprinted in R. M. Hartwell, ed., *The Causes of the Industrial Revolution in England* (London, 1967), pp.121–38.
[3] N. McKendrick, 'The Consumer Revolution in Eighteenth-Century England', in N. McKendrick, J. Brewer and J. H. Plumb, eds., *The Birth of a Consumer Society: The Commercialisation of Eighteenth-Century England.* (London, 1982), p.9.
[4] McKendrick, 'Consumer Revolution', p.66.
[5] H. Perkin, *The Origins of Modern English Society 1780–1880*, (London, 1969), p.91.
[6] R. Davis, *The Industrial Revolution and British Overseas Trade* (Leicester, 1979), ch.5.

166

arising from increasing incomes or prior growth itself. McCloskey, for example, has argued that although it may be proper to treat demand symmetrically with supply when explaining the growth of iron, cotton or wheat production or of a single firm, it is improper to do so in considering the economy as a whole.[7] But there are some circumstances where it is possible to conceive an autonomous role for demand in industrialisation; where it can be seen to arise independently of increasing industrial output itself.

The most obvious possibility is export demand. But it can be argued that export growth was not an autonomous stimulus: exports in this period were largely driven by needs and demands for imports which gave trading partners the purchasing power to buy British goods. And from the 1820s, or earlier, a major factor driving exports was the decline in prices arising from innovation, and from the lower transaction costs characteristic of a more developed industrial and commercial economy.[8] We thus return to the supply side again but questions of state policy, militarism, power and coercion, together with political and economic changes in other parts of the globe, were important in gaining a growing share of world trade and in doing so on particular terms. These issues are dealt with in the second half of this chapter.

Agricultural improvement can reduce the relative cost of foodstuffs, leaving more income to be spent on manufactures. But, as seen earlier, the relative prices of agricultural and industrial products were moving *in favour of agriculture* and not industry during much of the period of greatest expansion of industrial output from the late eighteenth century.[9] In any case, even if demand for industrial goods did increase as a result of agricultural improvement, it would be dependent upon innovation and structural change in agriculture, which would themselves require explanation.

A third possible source of autonomous demand has already been discussed: population expansion which increases the numbers of consumers. However, demographic growth appears to have been largely conditional on prior economic growth. Furthermore, *by itself*

[7] D. N. McCloskey, 'The Industrial Revolution 1780–1860: A Survey', in R. Floud and D. N. McCloskey, eds., *The Economic History of Britain* I (Cambridge, 1981), p.120. McCloskey argues that the biggest impact of demand is on the *composition* of output but he dismisses the importance of autonomous causes of demand. For other negative discussions of the role of demand see J. Mokyr, 'Demand vs Supply in the Industrial Revolution', in J. Mokyr, ed., *The Economics of the Industrial Revolution*, (London, 1985), pp.97–118; J. F. Gaski, 'The Cause of the Industrial Revolution: A Brief "Single Factor" Argument', *Journal of European Economic History* 11 (1982) pp.227–34.
[8] R. P. Thomas and D. N. McCloskey, 'Overseas Trade and Empire 1700–1860', in Floud and McCloskey, *Economic History of Britain*. Cf. F. Crouzet, 'Towards an Export Economy: British Exports during the Industrial Revolution', *Explorations in Economic History* 17 (1980), pp.65, 69, 81.
[9] See ch.3 and P. O'Brien, 'Agriculture and the Home Market for English Industry 1660–1820', *English Historical Review* CCCXCIV (1985), p.776.

population growth might decrease per capita real incomes as it drives up the price of food and other necessities. There is some dispute about whether this happened in the British case or whether population growth had a less negative effect because of the economies of scale that it enabled in the economy.[10] The balance of opinion is that population growth *alone* had only a modest effect on output growth.[11]

A change in the distribution of income in society in favour of those with a larger propensity to consume the products of manufacturing industry is a fourth, potentially important, source of demand stimulus.[12] But this presupposes that income is spent on a range of goods wider than luxury crafted products and it also assumes a relatively closed economy where the impact of income redistribution is not concentrated (as it may well have been to a great extent in the British case) on the purchase of imported goods. The relative movement of agricultural and industrial prices and rising rents may have shifted income from the industrial sector to landowners and farmers in the later eighteenth century. In addition, industrial and commercial profits and the flexible supply of low-cost labour may have led to income shifts favouring the employing middle class. The system of regressive national taxation and the popularity of investment in the national debt also shifted income, in the form of interest payments, from the mass of the tax-paying population to those willing and able to invest in government stocks. Thus spending at the upper end of the market was probably bolstered by a significant shift in income redistribution in the period of the industrial revolution, and this may have been accompanied by a decline of hoarding in favour of spending on the wider range of manufactured goods becoming available.

Williamson, following Kuznets, has argued that the early stages of industrialisation are likely to see growing income inequality.[13] In the British case, he argues that there was great pressure on certain skill

[10] See ch.5 and P. Lindert, 'English Living Standards, Population Growth and Wrigley and Schofield', *Explorations in Economic History* 20 (1983); J. Mokyr, 'Three Centuries of Population Change', *Economic Development and Cultural Change* 32, (1983), p.191.

[11] Mokyr, 'Demand vs Supply', p.101 and see ch.6 in this volume.

[12] We know that the per capita consumption of manufactures and imported groceries was increasing in the late eighteenth century despite stagnant or falling real-wage levels and mass poverty. This indicates the need to look at the distribution of income as a source of the demand. By encouraging imports demand from this source would also have resulted in more exports.

[13] This feature was first identified by Kuznets and thus is called the Kuznets curve: P. H. Lindert and J. G. Williamson, 'Growth, Equality and History', *Explorations in Economic History* 22 (1985). Eversley also stresses that increasing differentials between skilled and unskilled wages did much to underpin the maintenance of consumption levels in the third quarter of the eighteenth century: D. E. C. Eversley, 'The Home Market and Economic Growth in England 1750–1780', in E. L. Jones and G. E. Mingay, eds., *Land, Labour and Population in the Industrial Revolution* (London, 1966); O. Saito, 'The Other Faces of the Industrial Revolution', *Keio Economic Review* 39 (1988); R. V. Jackson, 'The Structure of Pay in Nineteenth-Century Britain', *Economic History Review* XL (1988).

supplies in the early nineteenth century which forced up the remuneration of many workers. Technological change tended to be laboursaving in the short run and occurred at the expense of unskilled labour which was, in any case, in good supply. The earnings evidence which Williamson cites to support his theory has been disputed by Feinstein, so the existence of a Kuznets curve (of rising inequality during industrialisation) remains in dispute.[14] However, geographical as well as social shifts in the distribution of income add weight to the argument that the industrial revolution was accompanied by significant growth in incomes for *certain* groups and in *particular* regions, which is likely to have had an impact on consumer demand. Conversely, amongst the mass of the wage-earning population, whose skills were not at a premium and whose mobility was restricted, evidence for the possibility of a consumer revolution arising from buoyant incomes is negligible. The growing opportunities for women and children to earn incomes in domestic, workshop and factory employments possibly bolstered family incomes and purchasing power for those lower down the social scale but it must be remembered that such opportunities were geographically concentrated and that women's wages tended to be low. Furthermore, women usually worked because of the dire necessity of sustaining larger families and as a response to more uncertain and irregular earnings of male household members.[15]

A further possibility of an independent role for demand would arise if there was an increased desire for income at the expense of leisure. Greater labour input may have helped to push up per capita and family incomes despite static or falling piece rates. This may have been caused by the breakdown of traditional attitudes to work and leisure, sufficiency and needs. When life was short, disease rife and there were few consumer goods easily available it is likely that the mass of the population worked as long and as much as necessary to cover basic subsistence after which leisure was preferred even where paid work was available. This lifestyle was exaggerated in a contemporary rhyme:

You know that Munday is Sundayes brother;
Tuesday is such another;
Wednesday you must go to Church and pray;
Thursday is half-holiday;

[14] C. H. Feinstein, 'The Rise and Fall of the Williamson Curve', *Journal of Economic History* 48 (1988).
[15] N. F. R. Crafts, *British Economic Growth During the Industrial Revolution* (Oxford, 1985), p.132. Crafts here estimates that workers' consumption of gross domestic output fell from around 20% in 1760 to around 10% in 1831. See also O. Saito, 'Labour Supply Behaviour of the Poor in the English Industrial Revolution', *Journal of European Economic History* 10 (1981); M. Berg, *The Age of Manufactures 1700–1820*, (London, 1985), ch.6; I. Pinchbeck, *Women Workers and the Industrial Revolution 1750–1850* (repr. London, 1981), *passim*.

On Friday it is too late to begin to spin;
the Saturday is half-holiday agen.[16]

It is quite possible that the ideal of sufficiency (which can be visualised as a backward sloping supply curve for labour: as wages rise the labour supply diminishes) was disappearing before and during the industrial revolution. People began to work longer hours and more days of the week, preferring increasing consumption to leisure. But there are problems in conceptualising shifts in work intensity in terms of an indifference curve. In the pre-industrial period work and leisure were not clearly separated, particularly for those who produced for subsistence need rather than the market, especially women involved in the tasks of household subsistence, including spinning, weaving, making clothes, rush lights and other personal and household necessities. Their shift into paid or market production could have a dynamic effect on demand without reflecting a decline in leisure preference. Greater dependency on the market for the purchase of goods previously produced at home is likely to have been a more crucial variable for the mass of the population than any choice between work and leisure. Work outside the home or even proto-industrial production within it meant greater regimentation and regularity of hours of work and less flexibility. Thus it is likely that any increase in income earning or consumption at the expense of 'leisure' arose from supply-side changes: from competition and from coercion by employers seeking to lengthen the working day to minimise costs, to fulfil production schedules, or to keep fixed capital continuously employed. Finally, a reduction in leisure preference, if it occured in the absence of increased job opportunities, would merely have created unemployment or greater under-employment elsewhere and the effect on industrial demand would therefore have been limited.[17]

The independent role for demand from any of the sources discussed would only be fully realised if the economy had significant underemployed resources and mass unemployment: that is, if the situation was akin to a modern economy in depression arising from demand deficiency. Without unemployed reserves of factors of production (land, labour and capital), economic expansion initiated by demand would run into difficulties. Mokyr and McCloskey deny that there were involuntarily unemployed resources in the pre-industrial economy in the modern sense and attribute chronic under-utilisation of labour and other factors to poor communications, primitive technology and high disease and death rates that ensured massive 'frictional' unemployment, particularly on a seasonal basis.[18] But perhaps these

[16] Quoted in E. P. Thompson, 'Time, Work Discipline and Industrial Capitalism', *Past and Present* 38 (1967).
[17] S. Marglin 'What Do Bosses Do?', in A. Gorz, ed., *The Division of Labour* (Brighton, 1976), p.34.
[18] McCloskey, 'Industrial Revolution', p.122; Mokyr, 'Demand vs Supply', pp.107-9.

historians underplay the extent to which the pre-industrial characteristics of endemic unemployment were changing by the early nineteenth century in favour of a larger degree of involuntary underactivity and unemployment precipitated by technological change and the trade cycle. Certainly, many contemporary mercantilist writers thought unemployment could only be remedied by the expansion of effective demand.[19]

Demand and innovation

Discussion of the sources of changing demand is important because it may be argued that demand pressure is the major stimulus to both technological and organisational innovation: that innovation occurs when demand is buoyant and when attention is drawn to bottlenecks in the production process. But bottlenecks are as easily solved by shifting resources between processes as by innovation.[20] In addition, it is difficult to prove the connection between demand pressure and technological or organisational change, and it is certainly possible to find examples of a connection between slumps in demand and innovation on the part of manufacturers eager to maintain market share in depression and (with capital-intensive innovation) to take advantage of low interest rates. The pressure of competition at different points of the trade cycle may be a more important variable in provoking innovation than demand in itself.[21] Debate rages about the degree of independence technological change has as a variable in the growth process. Gaski argues that decisions to innovate do not face a demand constraint: they create demand and thus technological change is the *only* exogenous variable in industrialisation.[22] However, incremental technological improvements of the 'learning by doing' sort (introduced piecemeal by craftsmen and workers with on-the-spot experience and so common in the industrial revolution) are likely to

[19] William Potter, James Stewart, William Petty, George Berkeley and Nicholas Barbon quoted in Mokyr, 'Demand vs Supply'.
[20] Mokyr, 'Demand vs Supply', p.104.
[21] These factors are discussed in J. Schumpeter, *The Theory of Economic Development: An Enquiry into Profits, Capital, Credit, Interest, and the Business Cycle* (Cambridge, Mass., 1949). See also N. Rosenberg, 'Factors Affecting the Diffusion of Technology', *Explorations in Economic History* x (1972).
[22] Gaski, 'Single Factor'. Much of the debate concerns analysis of long- and short-term change. Say's Law (the idea that supply creates its own demand) is the dominant long-run thesis but individual firms are more often concerned in innovation decisions with short-term effective demand. See K. Bruland, 'Say's Law and the Single Factor Explanation of British Industrialisation: A Comment', *Journal of European Economic History* 14 (1985); I. Inkster, 'Technology as the Cause of the Industrial Revolution: Some Comments', *Journal of European Economic History* xii (1983); B. Fine and E. Leopold, 'Consumerism and the Industrial Revolution', *Social History* 15 (1990), pp.158–62; Mokyr, 'Demand vs Supply', pp.103–6; N. Rosenberg, 'Science, Invention and Economic Growth', *Economic Journal* lxxxiv (1974).

have been more forthcoming when the pressure of demand was favourable and sustained.[23]

Greater demand can potentially help any firm or industry, but whether this leads to cushioning or to innovation is conditioned by factors on the supply side such as the availability of finance. The idea of firms straining to revolutionise supply but held back by deficient demand presupposes either a monopoly having mopped up the available markets, or a fragmented industrial structure operating in the absence of competition.[24] Otherwise firms would compete with each other for the available demand and rationalise or innovate where economies of scale warranted it. In other words, in the absence of monopoly, individual firms are always faced by elastic demand in terms of their innovating potential and in the industrial revolution large numbers of small firms in competition with each other were the major characteristic in most sectors.[25]

The role of demand in technological change becomes potentially more important if we consider new technologies that embody economies of scale: those that reduce average costs of production at a given level of output. But there is some dispute about the existence of increasing returns to large scale in manufacturing before the 1870s at the level of individual firms (or potential scale economies unrealised because of inadequate demand). Even for the cotton sector it has been said that 'size in itself guaranteed neither efficiency in good times nor viability in bad.'[26] The most important economies of scale initiated by increases in demand during the industrial revolution were probably economies not for a single firm but for a whole sector: the ability of a sector to train a highly differentiated and specialised workforce, to support specialised subcontracting and specialist suppliers of machinery, marketing or financial services.[27] Regional concentration and specialisation helped in the process of accumulating both scale economies and the cheapening of input and service costs for entire sectors, as we have seen. The development of transportation, particularly canals and railways, is likely to have gained most from economies of scale. In the absence of a high level of demand, large fixed costs are likely to have kept the costs of transport high. In transport and some other sectors larger markets were certainly important in innovation decisions.

[23] Mokyr, 'Demand vs Supply', p.106.
[24] Fine and Leopold, 'Consumerism', pp.159–60.
[25] Bruland, 'Say's Law'.
[26] V. A. C. Gattrell, 'Labour, Power and the Size of Firms in Lancashire Cotton in the Second Quarter of the Nineteenth Century', *Economic History Review* xxx (1977), pp. 95–139. Chapman attributes the small size of cotton firms to financial constraints and implies that opportunities for increasing returns to scale were held back: S. D. Chapman, 'Financial Constraints in the Growth of Firms in the Cotton Industry 1790–1850', *Economic History Review* xxxii (1979).
[27] McCloskey, 'Industrial Revolution', pp.122–3.

The discussion so far has suggested that the sources and role of demand in the economy can only be fully understood by integrating the analysis of demand with what we know about shifts in supply. It is now an appropriate point to consider recent work on the nature and determinants of internal and external demand for British manufactured goods. In doing so the need for an integrated study of structural change and of the agency of consumers again becomes apparent as does a need to link these to the changing balance of political and economic power both internally and internationally.

Internal demand

A consumer revolution

According to McKendrick, the third quarter of the eighteenth century marked a watershed in the consumption of manufactured goods: a conjunction of rising incomes and rising desires. 'Men and in particular women bought as never before'.[28] Perkin had earlier stressed the social snobbery endemic in the finely graded social structure and 'the compulsive urge for imitating the spending habits of one's betters which sprang from an open aristocracy in which each member from top to bottom of society trod closely on the heels of the next above'.[29] The rich indulged in an orgy of spending on houses, furniture, porcelain and silver as well as clothing and draperies. 'On such luxuries industrial revolutions are based', suggested Perkin[30]. McKendrick followed his lead:

> In imitation of the rich the middle ranks spent more frenziedly than ever before, and in imitation of them the rest of society joined in as best they might ... Spurred on by social emulation and class competition men and women surrendered eagerly to the pursuit of novelty, the hypnotic effects of fashion, and the enticements of commercial propaganda ... The closely stratified nature of English society, the striving for vertical social mobility, the emulative spending bred by social emulation, the compulsive power of fashion begotten by social competition – combined with the widespread ability to spend (offered by novel levels of prosperity) to produce an unprecedented propensity to consume: unprecedented in the extent to which it penetrated the lower

[28] McKendrick, 'Consumer Revolution', p.9.
[29] H. Perkin, 'The Social Causes of the Industrial Revolution', in Perkin, *The Structured Crowd: Essays in Social History* (Brighton, 1981). For discussion of the limits of this openness ascribed to English society see R. Porter, *English Society in the Eighteenth Century* (Harmondsworth, 1982), p.65 and for a contrary perspective addressed to a different theme (of class relations) see E. P. Thompson 'Patrician Society, Plebeian Culture', *Journal of Social History* 7 (1974).
[30] Perkin, *Origins*, p.93.

reaches of society and unprecedented in its impact on the economy.[31]

McKendrick places stress on several elements in the consumer revolution aside from the finely graded social structure which he sees as so important for the transmission of new wants and for the working of social emulation. The role of domestic servants in mimicking the household and personal spending of their masters and mistresses is stressed as a vital link in the chain of emulation, especially as servants tended to be a mobile group capable of spreading new ideas through their own family and kinship networks and between towns and their hinterlands. Second, there was the size and role of London: the social composition and functions of the capital as well as its retail outlets, its shops, lifestyles and prevailing fashions were an important influence in forming new consumption habits which then extended throughout the country. 'Without the existence of London it would have been much more difficult for commercial manipulation to achieve the ephemeral conformity of taste which so suited the standardised production of the new factory system.'[32]

Third, McKendrick places emphasis on the force of new marketing and commercial skills, deployed to capture and *expand* the market for consumer goods.[33] In his detailed studies of Wedgwood and his surveys of the activities of some other entrepreneurs McKendrick illustrates the importance of advertising, the use of salesmen and warehouse displays, exhibitions and special publicised sales to 'taste makers who led the fashion' and who gave to goods their snob appeal. John Foster used the Countess of Bective to give appeal to his carpets and Wedgwood sold or gave away sets of fine china to the Duchess of Devonshire, the Tsar of Russia and others. Cheaper pottery versions were then sold to a mass market. Setting styles and changing fashions became more important than ever before in continuously enlivening the market. Styles and the colour and pattern of materials were altered

---

[31] McKendrick, 'Consumer Revolution', p.11.
[32] See McKendrick et al., eds., *Consumer Society*, introduction and part 1.
[33] N. McKendrick, 'Josiah Wedgwood: an Eighteenth Century Entrepreneur in Salesmanship and Marketing Techniques', *Economic History Review* XII (1959/60) and McKendrick et al., eds., *Consumer Society*. There is an important difference between McKendrick's argument of 1960 and that of 1982; earlier he argued that the entrepreneurial talents of Wedgwood gave him a competitive edge over his rivals from which he gained market share at their expense; in 1982 it is suggested that Wedgwood's activities were typical of entrepreneurs who were creating additional demand and hence providing an active motive force in industrialisation. On this see E. Jones, 'The Fashion Manipulators: Consumer Tastes and British Industries, 1660–1800', in L. Cain and P. Uselding, eds., *Business Enterprise and Economic Change: Essays in Honour of Harold F. Williamson* (Kent State, 1973).

frequently, especially in clothing: shoes for example went from sharp-to round- to square-toed as remorselessly as in the twentieth century.[34] Even lesser men of business in more mundane fields were active in new advertising and commercialising activities. In George Packard's campaign to promote his razor strops and proprietory shaving paste in the mid-1790s at least 60 different advertisements appeared in 26 newspapers, illustrating a range of techniques of salesmanship. Some advertisements used dialogues between friends or with servants, others consisted of fables and some used congratulatory messages from satisfied customers. Even ladies were targeted, with assurances about the benefits of a smooth cheek in a lover and the advantage of a smooth shave on the temper of a husband. Newspaper advertising such as this was facilitated by the growth of the provincial press and by the relatively high literacy levels in the general population.[35]

Finally, the 'consumer revolution' thesis places emphasis on the new importance of women and children as consumers in the period.[36] Most indicators, as we have seen, suggest that real wages were falling in the late eighteenth century under the impact of population pressure and rising agricultural prices. But McKendrick stresses that family earnings may well have been boosted to unprecedented levels because of the wider income-earning opportunities for women and children. He argues that female and child wages gave families the ability to buy more whilst their own wages gave women more power in household consumption decisions. This resulted in the sale of more goods attuned to female and child preferences and tastes, such as clothes, curtains, linens, pottery, cutlery, furniture, brass, copper, buttons and fashion accessories and toys.

A consumer revolution?

The major criticisms of McKendrick's thesis have centred on his view that the consumer revolution occurred specifically in the later eighteenth century; that it was gentry-led through a social emulation in which London and the domestic servant class played key roles; and that Wedgwood can be taken as an exemplar of general sales expertise (with the ability to *create* mass demand).

The work of Thirsk, Spufford and Weatherill has indicated a great spread of spending on manufactures from the later seventeenth

[34] McKendrick, 'Commercialisation of Fashion', in McKendrick *et al.*, eds., *Consumer Society*.
[35] McKendrick, *et al.*, eds., *Consumer Society*, ch.4; R. Houston, 'Literacy and Society in the West 1500–1850', *Social History* 8 (1983).
[36] N. McKendrick, 'Home Demand and Economic Growth: A New View of the Role of Women and Children in the Industrial Revolution', in N. McKendrick, ed., *Historical perspectives: Studies in English Thought and Society in Honour of J. H. Plumb*, (London, 1974).

century, accompanied by innovations in the design and production of consumer goods such as knitted stockings, knitted caps, cheap earthenware, nails, tobacco pipes, lace and ribbon, processed foods and drinks. Thirsk and Spufford suggest that this spread of spending extended down to the ranks of husbandmen, smallholders, cottagers and labourers and that there was a perpetual restructuring of the consumer industries forced by 'fickle' demands of consumers. The sources indicating the downward extension of demand are, however, sparse and difficult to interpret even though the later seventeenth century is likely to have witnessed a general buoyancy of real wages. Upper-class commentary is an untrustworthy source as it usually takes the form of condemnation of the lower orders for their profligacy and clearly exaggerates to make a case. Weatherill's detailed study of nearly 3,000 probate inventories covering various areas of the country and different (though not all) social classes, questions the idea of the emergence of a 'humble consumer society' by the early eighteenth century and suggests that there was a social cut-off point in the demand for non-essential consumer goods which left the bulk of the population (below and including many small farmers and craftsmen) outside the rise in consumption.[37]

The evidence of change in real incomes for the masses, of poverty levels in the later eighteenth century and of the redistribution of income in society in favour of rent and profit receivers makes it likely that the mass of the population remained below the level at which they could participate in revolutionary fashion-orientated consumption of either domestic manufactures or imported commodities in the period of the industrial revolution itself. However, structural changes in supply, particularly the greater use of wage-dependent, proletarianised labour and of women and children, did mean that more household essentials (such as clothes, beer, butter, candles and crockery) had to be bought, given that women had less time for the production of subsistence items. Beyond the increased purchase of processed food and drink, household and personal essentials previously made by women, there is little evidence of women being at the forefront of spending, particularly of competitive or emulative spending in any social class. The domestic diaries and accounts of middle- and upper-class women show that they valued their chattels more consistently for practical and sentimental reasons than for social effect

[37] J. Thirsk, *Economic Policy and Projects: the Development of a Consumer Society in Early Modern England* (Oxford, 1978); M. Spufford, *The Great Reclothing of Rural England: Petty Chapmen and Their Wares in the Seventeenth Century* (London, 1984); L. Weatherill, 'Consumer Behaviour and Social Status in England 1650–1750', *Continuity and Change* 1 (1986); Weatherill, *Consumer Behaviour and Material Culture in Britain 1660–1760,* (London, 1988).

or conspicuous display – but clearly much work remains to be done, particularly on the role of middle-class women as consumers.[38]

We must also be wary of accepting the notion of gentry-led emulation as the engine that drove the expansion of demand. Probate inventories for the late seventeenth and early eighteenth centuries show no simple association between socio-economic status and ownership of material goods, especially items like china, window curtains, books and pictures. Tradesmen and professional people appear to have been the most innovative consumers, whilst relatively high-status yeomen owned fewer manufactured consumer goods than craftsmen. And the regional distributions of such goods do not support the notion that London played *the* key role in promoting the spread of tastes and fashions. Urban culture both in the provinces and in the metropolis was important in promoting specific changes in demand and in aspirations to ownership of material goods.[39]

Campbell has argued that the spread of new consumption habits and tastes was not a question of social emulation but of wider change affecting values and attitudes amongst the middle class, who were the major source of the expansion in demand for mass manufactures. He links these changing values to the growing influence of protestantism, arguing that there were two cultural traditions in the protestant ethic. Alongside thrift, hard work and self-denial, there was also an ethic of individualism, romanticism and hedonism which gave legitimacy to the search for pleasure as a good in itself and included pleasure in self-expression through ownership of material goods.[40] The need to look closely at change in middle-class attitudes to spending and leisure in studying the industrial revolution is also highlighted by Plumb who has shown that the expanding demand for theatre, music, dancing, sport and cultural pastimes was very much a middle-class phenomenon; and the rise of the romantic novel and the spread of the fiction-reading public provides similar evidence of a possible change in the desires and

---

[38] A. Vickery, 'Elite Women's Consumption and Material Culture in Eighteenth-Century Lancashire', in P. Hudson and P. Laxton, eds., *Economic History for the 1990s* (summaries of papers presented at the Economic History Society Conference, 1990; University of Liverpool mimeo).
[39] Weatherill, 'Consumer Behaviour'. Unfortunately probate inventories become uncommon after the 1760s and we cannot easily gather similar evidence of the dissemination of consumer tastes geographically or socially for the industrial revolution period itself. There are problems in using probate records for these purposes even for the earlier period because they list only goods at death and are socially selective. On urban culture and consumption see P. Borsay, 'The English Urban Renaissance: The Development of Provincial Urban Culture c. 1680–c. 1760', *Social History* 5 (1977); and E. A. Wrigley,' A Simple Model of London's Importance in the Changing English Economy and Society', *Past and Present* 37 (1966); P. Corfield, *The Impact of English Towns 1700–1800* (Oxford, 1982).
[40] C. Campbell, *The Romantic Ethic and the Spirit of Modern Consumerism* (Oxford, 1987).

emotional attitudes of the middle class.[41] However, Campbell's grand theory of a new hedonistic ethic underlying modern consumerism from the eighteenth century onwards needs to be considered alongside much contradictory evidence. The protestant ethic in dress, usually emphasising modesty and conformity in place of showiness, indisputably arose in the middle classes and extended into the growing class of professionals: doctors, lawyers and clergymen all turned to wearing unadorned black. The impractical finery of court dress became reserved for rare ceremonial occasions. The protestant ethic may thus have resulted in greater mass demand for regular items of clothing and of cloths but it hardly sprang from hedonistic tendencies.[42]

The role in a consumer revolution of domestic servants emulating their superiors seems less likely to have been important if it is remembered that their conditions were generally unpromising: they were almost invariably low paid or worked largely for payment in kind or for their board and training. The dampening effect of a large servant class largely cut off from the market for consumer goods rather than participating in it must be considered. (In 1806 there were about 800,000 female and 110,000 male servants; about 1 in 11 of the entire population.) Furthermore, servants often had clothes bought for them to emphasise the status of their employer and their scope for exercising choice was further limited by loans of clothing, hand-me-downs and bequests.[43]

Much of the non-probate evidence for spreading consumption habits low down the income scale throughout the eighteenth century is derived from contemporary comment and writing about fashion in the clothing trades. But it may be unwise to generalise about changing consumption habits for all household and domestic goods from the example of clothing and, in any case, some of the evidence on clothing is itself easy to misinterpret. For example, much of the trickle-down effect of demand assumed by historians from descriptions of what the poor were wearing ignores the major trade in cast-offs, which created only limited stimulus in the manufacturing sector. Innovation occurred more in the accessories used in remakes; braids, ribbons, buckles, buttons. Clothes and the textiles from which they were made were seen as consumer durables by the mass of the population; they were handed

---

[41] J. H. Plumb, 'The Commercialisation of Leisure', in McKendrick et al., eds., Consumer Society.
[42] Fine and Leopold, 'Consumerism', p.172, critical discussion of the McKendrick thesis in this chapter draws heavily on the arguments raised by Fine and Leopold. A. Rebeiro, Dress in Eighteenth-Century Europe 1715–1789 (London, 1984).
[43] Rebeiro, Dress in Eighteenth-Century Europe, p.169, quoting figures from J. Hecht, The Domestic Servant Class in Eighteenth Century England (London 1956), p.34.

riving force behind eighteenth-century exports. By the second
ter of the nineteenth century, the declining prices (arising largely
innovations) of exported manufactures, especially textiles, and
need to import more foodstuffs under worsening terms of trade,
pressure on policy-makers to adopt new strategies of expansion.
us 'free trade' was promoted *alongside* imperialism in both old and
w markets. Domestic conditions were vital causal factors in the
pansion of trade and in influencing the nature of trading relation-
ips with other parts of the globe.

But to analyse the evolution of an increasingly anglocentric world
rading system only as a response to conditions in the major metropole
underemphasises the extent to which European rivals and more
dependent trading partners could shape the trajectory of world trading
development or the terms of dependency. It also understates the effect
that unforeseen events in the outside world could have on trade, such
as the rapidity of the independence of Latin America arising from
Napoleonic policy and Spanish incompetence. The role of foreign
trade as an exogenous stimulus must not be neglected.

The pattern of overseas trade

External trade accounted for about 10-12% of GNP in the mid
eighteenth century, 18% by 1800. After this it appears to have fallen
back to 14% by 1851. But this modest contribution had a potentially
large effect on industry because exports consisted overwhelmingly of
manufactures, many of them with the potential for being mass
produced. In no other European economy were manufactures such an
important proportion of exports so early and at such a low export level.
At times during the late eighteenth and early nineteenth centuries, as
much as 35% of industrial output was exported.[52] Export markets
were also important to manufacturing expansion because they grew
faster than domestic demand and their growth was concentrated in
particular surges whose impact on innovation may well have been
greater than slowly moving domestic demand. In addition, the export
of manufactured goods was highly concentrated in textiles, iron and
metalwares, which all exported high proportions of their output. The
Yorkshire wool textile industry for example exported about 70% of its
production in the 1770s, as did the Birmingham and Wolverhampton
hardware trades. Forty-two per cent of wrought iron was exported in
this period and about 40% of the output of the copper and brass
industries.[53] Thus exports were a vital component of concentrated
demand felt by particular industrial regions. (See table 6.1)

[52] Crafts, *British Economic Growth*, ch.7. Davis, *Industrial Revolution*.
[53] J. M. Price 'What Did Merchants Do? Reflections on British Overseas Trade 1660–
1790', *Journal of Economic History* XLIX (1989), p.283.

down in wills and they were frequently taken apart to be remade or
restyled.[44]

Neither is the spread of particular garments and styles through the
ranks of society necessarily evidence of fashion being led by changing
tastes in the upper classes. Some foreign visitors noted that servants
and labourers in England wore the paniers and sacks, the knee
breeches and occasionally even the perukes of their betters.[45] But the
lower classes most often demonstrated their independent tastes in
clothing, which included considerable innovation, especially as cheap
printed calicos like ginghams became available. This presaged an
increasing differentiation of manual occupations by dress in the
nineteenth century: navvies, for instance, had a 'uniform' of fustians,
miners wore red kerchiefs. And some lower-class fashions were copied
higher up the social scale (rather in the manner of denim jeans in the
twentieth century). For example, the workman's frock coat was worn
by people across a wide social spectrum. By the mid-eighteenth
century 'gentlemen' had taken it up as a comfortable alternative to the
stiff heavy coat and, with its reputation as a more 'democratic' form of
dress, it became increasingly popular during the French Revolution as
a symbol of opposition to the *ancien régime*.[46] These and other shifts in
dress may signify a decline in the aristocracy's role as the arbiter of
taste, the rising importance of middle-class and independently evolving working-class tastes. The dissemination of fashion was certainly
not a simple matter of top-down emulation.

In stressing the role of creative salesmanship in expanding the
market for consumer goods, the example of Wedgwood is perhaps
over-used: he was not a typical entrepreneur and not even the leading
manufacturer in pottery. Furthermore, it is very plausible to see the
luxury tableware market of the eighteenth century as an *obstacle* to the
development of mass production. The same principle applies to the
clothing industry. Here was a major sector where conspicuous
consumption and popular wear alike depended (with the exception of
fashion accessories) on the provision of goods by labour-intensive
methods in short runs, if not individually tailored. It can be argued that
the marked development of fashion changes and demand in clothing
impeded the growth of mass production by extending handicraft
techniques in both the new and second-hand trades.[47] The slow

[44] B. Lemire, 'Developing Consumerism and the Ready-Made Clothing Trade in
Britain 1750–1800', *Textile History* XV (1984); Fine and Leopold, 'Consumerism', pp.
173–5.
[45] Perkin, *Origins*, p.94
[46] Fine and Leopold, 'Consumerism', p.172.
[47] Fine and Leopold, 'Consumerism'. Demand for mass-produced cloth as opposed to
clothing was obviously stimulated by the expanding market for new as opposed to
second-hand clothes. But off-the-peg mass production in clothing awaited the
innovation of the sewing machine in the later nineteenth century and the growth of real
incomes for wage earners in that period, especially in the northern industrial areas.

development of mechanised manufacturing techniques in general in the nineteenth century has been attributed to mid-Victorian bourgeois taste, obsessed with securing household products that expressed individuality and luxury. Such consumers constituted the bulk of effective demand for many objects and this reinforced the role of speciality in design and production. Entrepreneurs such as Wedgwood were creating differentiated demand by stressing enhancement of status: demand was being fragmented as a marketing strategy. With the technology then prevailing, mass production is likely to have been obstructed.[48]

The integration of supply and demand

The 'consumer revolution' thesis must be assessed in the light of two separate causal factors which act together. First, there is a rising *ability* to consume (at least amongst certain groups in the population), which is a function of income earning, income levels and income distribution. Second, an increased *desire* to consume domestically produced manufactures rather than to save money, to spend it on more or better food or to buy luxury craft goods or imported commodities such as wines, silks or colonial groceries. The decline of the subsistence sector and increased income-earning opportunities, coupled with some change in the distribution of income, appear potentially more important than buoyant family incomes in raising the ability to consume manufactured goods. But all these factors are closely linked to structural change in the economy; proletarianisation, urbanisation and industrialisation. This suggests the need for an integrated approach so that both demand and supply can be seen as inter-related developments in the overall process of change. An increased *desire* to consume provoked by shifts in cultural attitudes, emulation, salesmanship or whatever, can be seen as an autonomous dynamic emanating from the demand side; and clearly there were important changes here that accelerated during the industrial revolution and that add to the distinctiveness of the period. However, it must be remembered that much of the evidence of new fashion consumption amongst the masses is drawn from contemporary middle-class and upper-class commentary voiced at a time when profligacy and high wages were seen as a source of national economic weakness. Desire to consume can of course only be translated into something more tangible if resources permit and it seems likely that income levels would have limited the dynamic of consumption (outside of household necessities) to the upper end of the social structure and to very limited groups below that level. Upper- and middle-class consumerism, whilst adding to effective demand, may have been disproportionately directed at imports and

[48] R. Samuel, 'Workshop of the World: Steam Power and Hand Technology in Mid-Victorian Britain', *History Workshop Journal* 3 (1977).

may have slowed down mass production bec… fashion and individualism.

The current emphasis on consumption as a ke… industrial revolution has highlighted the narrow… side interpretations and the need to incorporate d… long-run change. But both supply and demand cu… the product of an evolving structure of economic… which must be the real subject of research. Laying s… emulation rather than upon income, its distributio… relations involved in changing methods of production… proletariat had no independent material culture or s… artifacts to give a sense of community or solidarity.[49] A… layered consensus and social harmony implied by emulat… fits ill with the polarised picture of patricians and p… eighteenth-century society, painted by Thompson and o… short, the causes and course of shifts in demand have to be re… dynamic explanation of the industrial revolution as a whole. C… consumption patterns and habits may indeed have been revolu… but they need to be seen as both effect and cause of changes in… the family, social life, geographical horizons, the developme… transport and communications and the changing political and s… identities of men, women and children.

External commerce, colonies and markets

The rest of this chapter concerns the relationship between the expansion of external trade and empire and the nature and growth of the domestic economy. Here again shifts in demand can be fully understood only as part of the dynamic of the industrial revolution as a whole.

The uneven growth of manufacturing industry, the enduring power of the landed interest and the growing influence of industrial, commercial and financial lobbies in policy-making probably contributed as much as the working of comparative advantage to shape the direction and nature of overseas trade and investment.[51] Growing internal demand for tea, coffee, sugar, raw cotton, spices and other consumer goods and raw materials gave trading partners the purchasing power to buy English manufactures, which some historians see as

[49] Fine and Leopold, p.176. They argue that accepting that emulation may be a two-way process deprives luxury spending of its progressive attributes.
[50] Thompson, 'Patrician Society'; D. Hay, P. Linebough, J. Rule, E. P. Thompson, C. Winslow, eds., *Albion's Fatal Tree: Crime and Society in Eighteenth Century England* (Harmondsworth, 1975); A. J. Randall, *Before the Luddites*, (Cambridge, 1990).
[51] For an analysis of these internal determinants see P. J. Cain and A. J. Hopkins, 'Gentlemanly Capitalism and British Expansion Overseas: 1: The Old Colonial System 1688–1850', *Economic History Review* xxxix (1986).

Table 6.1: The composition of British overseas trade 1700-1851 (%)

	Manufactures	Raw Materials	Foodstuffs
(i) Exports			
1700	80.8	8.2	11.0
1750	75.4	16.8	7.8
1801	88.1	5.0	6.9
1831	91.1	5.5	3.4
1851	81.1	13.3	5.6
(ii) Retained Imports			
1700	28.4	45.0	26.6
1750	14.4	54.5	31.1
1801	4.9	56.2	38.6
1831	2.2	70.4	27.4
1851	4.9	58.2	36.9

Source: N.F.R. Crafts, *British Economic Growth during the Industrial Revolution* (Oxford, 1985), p.143. Figures largely derived from R. Davis, *The Industrial Revolution and British Overseas Trade* (Leicester, 1979).

Table 6.2: Shares of major exports in total merchandise exports (%)

	Cottons	Woollens	Iron and Steel
1700	0.5	68.7	
1750	1.0	46.7	
1801	39.6	16.5	9.3
1831	50.8	12.7	10.2
1851	39.6	14.1	12.3

Proportions of gross output sold abroad (%)

	Cotton	Wool	Iron
1760	50	46	
1801	62	35	24
1831	56	19	23
1851	61	25	39

Source: N.F.R. Crafts, *British Economic Growth during the Industrial Revolution* (Oxford, 1985), p.143.

The eighteenth century saw significant growth and shifts in the pattern of external trade. Exports as a proportion of gross industrial output may have risen from a quarter to more than one third during the course of the eighteenth century.[54] Imports and exports both expanded more than five-fold, whilst re-exports increased nine-fold and accounted for around one third of the total value of exports at their peak of influence

[54] Crafts, *British Economic Growth*, p.132. Cole places the 1700 figure at one fifth; Cole, 'Factors in Demand', p.40.

in the third quarter of the eighteenth century. Re-exports consisted mainly of colonial consumer goods, such as sugar, tobacco, tea, coffee, rum and spices. These were shipped to Europe, enabling England to continue to buy linen, timber, naval supplies and other products from the continent. The high level of trade in re-exportables together with growing domestic demand for colonial groceries and for raw cotton sustained purchasing power in North America and the West Indies for English manufactured goods and gave the trans-Atlantic economy a key role in the early industrial revolution. English combined exports to the North American colonies and the West Indies expanded by an amazing 2,300% in the eighteenth century. North America and the West Indies contributed 42% and 18% respectively of the increase in value of British exports in the first three quarters of the eighteenth century and the proportion of exports taken to North America alone rose from 10% to 37% of the total. Protectionism in Europe and Britain put severe limits on the expansion of trade with long-standing European partners and it was the colonies, largely the West Indies and North America, that sustained the expansion of exports through the eighteenth century.[55]

Early in the century differences in technologies then prevailing between Britain and her rivals were slight and comparative advantage accrued largely from geographical position and the market catchment gained from state policy, militarism, colonial expansion and diplomacy. By these means Britain after 1707 came to be part of a 'quasi-common market' with Ireland, and the British colonies in the Americas. The dependencies were discriminated against in this market: colonial iron and Irish woollens faced tariffs and colonial wheat and some Irish agricultural products faced prohibition, particularly before 1760. For British exporters, however, it was a free-trade area, the largest in the world and the fastest growing. Between 1670 and 1770 it grew in population by 70% and per capita consumption remained stable (at worst).[56]

Prising open Asian markets was more difficult because British goods were at first unable to dislodge local manufacturers and commercial expansion depended on import-led demand in Europe for Indian textiles, China tea and culinary spices. By contrast, the Atlantic colonies had no well-established industries of their own; they were relatively prosperous and for an important period they were required to buy most of their manufactured goods from Britain. The growing trade with colonies of European settlement was very important in stimulating demand for manufactured goods that could be mass-produced: printed textiles, blankets, nails, ropes, cordage, buckets,

[55] Estimates of overseas trade vary considerably. For the most reliable see Davis, *Industrial Revolution;* Thomas and McCloskey, 'Overseas Trade'; and Crouzet 'Towards an Export Economy'.
[56] Price, 'What Did Merchants Do?', pp.270-1.

hand tools, copper and wrought-iron products, beaver hats, linens and sails. But demand was not confined to necessities. Especially in North America, prosperous farmers were straining to buy a wide variety of more 'fashionable' products: earthenware of all kinds, buckles, buttons, silks, pewter, and fancy cloths.[57] The extremely rapid growth of the relatively egalitarian white northern market, to say nothing of the homogeneity of demand for slave chains and coarse blankets, is likely to have been disproportionately significant in the development of mass production in England. It was certainly behind the rise of the Yorkshire blanket trade, Manchester piece goods, and some of the Black Country hardwares.

From the 1780s the situation changed somewhat with the loss of the North American colonies and the rapid expansion of cotton exports. The ratio of exports to national income doubled between 1783 and 1801 and cotton was largely responsible (see table 6.2). The principal markets were found in Western Europe, the United States and (after 1806-7, when the European markets were closed to British exports) Latin America. The expanding cotton industry needed more and more raw cotton and its needs were eventually met by the development of cosmopolitan trading links outside the empire. But in other trades colonial ties were strengthened, the occupation of India continued and trade was extended with New South Wales and the Cape. Efforts were made to create sources of raw-material supply in the dependencies, and cotton supplies from the West Indies became crucial for a time in the 1780s and 1790s.

After 1815 cotton exports to Europe declined in relative terms because European countries developed their own textile industries as a conscious policy of import substitution aided by protective tariffs. This aggravated the problems of an industry suffering from excess capacity and pushed down prices and profit margins. The tendency thereafter was for Britain to become a supplier of semi-finished manufactures (such as yarn) to her industrial rivals, especially in Europe, thus aiding their industrialisation. The effect was aggravated by the lack of any effective prohibition of migration of skilled labour and by the lack of controls on the export of machinery. The search for new markets aided by 'free trade' and imperialism were amongst the consequences.[58]

In some cases the growth of trade with new areas could be accommodated without force, in others the use of power, especially naval power, was blatant. Depressions led to more frequent use of the political and military arm of expansionism. The China war of 1839-41 can be seen in this light and the 1837-42 depression, when Chartism

---

[57] This has rightly been termed 'an empire of goods': T. Breen, 'An Empire of Goods: the Anglicization of Colonial America 1690–1776', *Journal of British Studies* xxv (1986), pp.467–99.
[58] D. A. Farnie, *The English Cotton Industry and the World Market 1815–1896* (Oxford, 1979).

was at its climax, resulted in aggressive expansionism. Free-trade treaties were pressed on North West frontier provinces in the 1830s, Turkey in 1838, Egypt and Persia in 1841, and Aden was occupied in 1839. There was also intervention in central and South America, as with the extension of trade in the River Plate (explicitly seen as preparing a market which might substitute for declining prospects in Europe) and the support for the liberal Rivera against Rosas in Uruguay in the 1840s. Control of India made the sub-continent the most successful linch-pin of overseas expansion from the 1830s and provided compensation for the decline of the West Indies.[59]

Thus from the second quarter of the nineteenth century Britain was able to develop international trade to an abnormal extent. Her level of mechanisation in textiles in particular maintained a competitive edge and bolstered European demand despite increasing competition and protectionism.[60] Furthermore, she succeeded in extending and endorsing the dominant relationship with the underdeveloped world (Africa, the Near East, Asia, Australia and Latin America) that she had pursued from the early eighteenth century and especially after 1780. (See table 6.3.)

Table 6.3: Geographical distribution of manufactured exports (%)

	Europe	USA, Canada, West Indies	Africa, Near East, Asia, Australia, Latin America
(i) All Manufactures			
1699/1701	83.6	13.3	3.1
1772/4	45.0	46.9	8.1
1804/6	37.3	49.4	13.3
1834/6	36.3	34.7	29.0
1854/6	28.9	28.1	43.0
(ii) Cottons			
1699/1701	20.0	80.0	0.0
1772/4	20.4	79.6	0.0
1804/6	47.1	45.1	7.8
1834/6	47.4	19.8	32.8
1854/6	29.4	16.3	54.3

Source: N.F.R. Crafts, *British Economic Growth during The Industrial Revolution* (Oxford, 1985), p.145.

[59] Cain and Hopkins, 'Gentlemanly Capitalism'; Cain and Hopkins, 'The Political Economy of British Expansion Overseas 1750–1914', *Economic History Review* xxxiii (1980); J. Gallagher and R. Robinson, 'The Imperialism of Free Trade 1815–1914', *Economic History Review* iv (1953–4); P. J. Cain, *Economic Foundations of British Overseas Expansion 1815–1914* (London, 1980).

[60] Crafts argues that comparative advantage was maintained by Britain in a limited range of commodioties, especially textiles and iron goods and that comparative advantage lay in the use of low-paid, relatively unskilled labour and coal-powered processes. Crafts, *British Economic Growth*, pp.142–47.

The impact of overseas trade

Historians used to emphasise the export-led nature of growth in the industrial revolution. But the role of imports in creating overseas demand for exports, and, later the increase in exports by volume, fuelled by the declining prices of manufactured goods, especially textiles, have made this argument difficult to sustain at the macro-economic level for any prolonged period between the mid-eighteenth and the mid-nineteenth century. Certainly, the 35% expansion of imports in the period 1745-60 must have been a crucial force underlying export demand and the fastest rate of growth of exports in the nineteenth century (1830s-50s) coincided with the greatest decline in the relative prices of British and overseas tradeables. These facts both suggest that export demand had little independent role to play.[61] Thus the dominant interpretation currently is that foreign trade was of little importance to British growth. Davis, for example, sees it as less important in the industrial revolution itself than in the decades immediately before or after.[62]

But the causal links running from imports to exports may have been less significant than is generally assumed. A study by Hatton, Lyons and Satchell suggests that before 1745 exports were not causally linked to imports and that imports appear on the contrary to have fluctuated in response to prior charges in the re-export trade. After 1745 the statistical series show that export variation systematically preceded import variation, suggesting that imports were themselves a function of the export of home-produced goods and not the reverse. This opens up the possibility of a much more significant and independent role for exports in the economy.[63]

In addition, perhaps imports should themselves be seen as a stimulus to expansion and growth. Between the sixteenth and eighteenth centuries the search for cheaper essential imports was met by suppliers in the Far East, the Baltic and elsewhere who did not demand manufactures in return. This resulted in deficit trading and in various forms of forced exchange and other measures to provide suitable currencies – such as the East India Company's collecting of local taxes in Bengal in the 1760s and the later development of the opium trade. Furthermore, by the eighteenth century thousands of vessels that brought sugar, tobacco, rice, and coffee from the Americas to England carried less bulky cargoes as their outward cargo.

---

61 Thomas and McCloskey, 'Overseas Trade', pp.101–2.
62 Davis, *Industrial Revolution*, p.61.
63 T. J. Hatton, J. S. Lyons and S. E. Satchell, 'Eighteenth-Century British Trade: Homespun or Empire-made?', *Explorations in Economic History*, 20 (1983). Crafts also argues that exports underpinned by rising incomes abroad were important in supporting real-income growth in the period 1820–1870 despite declining terms of trade: Crafts, *British Economic Growth*, pp.148–51.

This and the competition for outward cargoes kept freight rates low and encouraged exports.[64]

A much more positive view of the role of trade through the whole period from the mid-eighteenth to the mid-nineteenth century is also supported if we move away from the narrow concern of examining the chicken-and-egg sort of argument concerning imports and exports and if we take a broader view of the gains from trade than that provided simply by an assessment of the contribution to GNP. As Lee has suggested, without trade the cotton industry would never have existed, the iron industry would have been much smaller, the expansion of the woollen industry would have been curbed and agriculture would have developed more slowly, especially in the first half of the eighteenth century: 'A hypothetical British economy cut off from imports of food, timber, luxury products like tobacco and sugar, as well as industrial raw materials such as cotton and iron would surely have been much diminished in income and economic activity'.[65] It is impossible to understand the evolution of the domestic economy, and particularly of those sectors and regions which spearheaded industrial change, without considering the direct and indirect impact of external trade. Indirect gains occurred in the growing sophistication and importance of the transport, financial and service sectors of the economy which were vitally linked to external commerce. Export merchants gave long credits to their overseas customers and received long credit in turn from their wholesale suppliers. And because the big wholesalers and other vendors gave long credit to exporters they found it difficult to resist giving credit almost as long to the internal trade. Import merchants and dealers in domestic raw materials such as wool staplers were forced by competition to give their customers long credits also. Thus the internal credit system was influenced by the extent of foreign trade and the commercial practices evolved in it. This oiled the wheels of internal and external commerce alike. But the chief beneficiaries were manufacturers: in some trades the credit extended on their raw-material supplies virtually covered the period of production and realisation. Only very large and atypical manufacturers were moving by the late eighteenth century to cut out middlemen and sell direct to exporters or foreign customers on credit. Most manufacturers were net receivers of credit.[66]

Since they were used to dealing with credit, foreign trade merchants of London and the outports moved into a variety of other new

[64] Price, 'What Did Merchants Do?', pp.272–3.
[65] C. H. Lee, *The British Economy since 1700: A Macroeconomic Perspective* (Cambridge, 1986), p.116. Thomas and McCloskey would object to this way of looking at it because of their assumption that resources would have been allocated to other activities but there is no strong reason to believe that this would have happened.
[66] Price, 'What Did Merchants Do?', pp.278–284; P. Hudson, *The Genesis of Industrial Capital* (Cambridge, 1986), chs.5–8.

commercial and financial ventures such as joint-stock insurance companies, insurance underwriting and private banking. They invested in canal building, road and river improvement, dock development, mineral extraction and industry (even if few actually became industrialists). Thus an important legacy of eighteenth-century foreign trade was a commercial infrastructure of benefit to the wider economy: insurance companies, banks, the stock exchange and even the improved postal service owed their existence largely to the demands of foreign trading.[67] And without the demand for government revenues to finance costly trade wars, the internal financial system and the national debt would not have developed in the revolutionary way it did.[68]

The monopolisation by Britain of much of the world's shipping services by the late eighteenth century and improvements in marine insurance, trade institutions, multi-national and multilateral credit and bill networks, established an efficient flow of foreign trade and investment across the globe. Overseas investment was stimulated greatly by the extension of trading links, and investment in turn bolstered the purchase of British manufactures. By 1850 around £200 million of foreign securities may have been held by British subjects, principally in the United States and the colonies.[69] London replaced Amsterdam as the major international capital market and its role in financial and investment services was underpinned by the development of cosmopolitan trade. Contemporaries recognised this indirect gain from trade: the commercial reforms of the 1820s were expected to increase invisible income and re-exports more than commodity exports.[70] Furthermore, returns on mercantile services (shipping, insurance, bill discounting) together with the returns on overseas loans were vital to balance-of-payments stability by the second quarter of the nineteenth century, a stability that was instrumental in maintaining the imports necessary for domestic employment.

Only if we focus narrowly on the direct impact of trade on manufacturing industry nationally is there scope for the view that overseas expansion had a minor effect on industrialisation. If we look at particular industries and regions and at the important effects of foreign trade on shipping, insurance, discounting and on the commercial and financial infrastructure, a different picture emerges. And, as we have seen, there were important elements of the expansion of

[67] Price, 'What Did Merchants Do?'; S. D. Chapman, *The Rise of Merchant Banking* (London 1984), ch.1. See also discussion of the impact of the slave trade below.
[68] Chapman, *Rise of Merchant Banking*; P. G. M. Dickson, *The Financial Revolution in England (London, 1967)*; J. Brewer, *The Sinews of Power: War, Money and the English State 1688–1783* (London, 1989).
[69] L. H. Jenks, *The Migration of British Capital to 1875* (London, 1963), p.1. See discussion of the accuracy of this figure in D. C. M. Platt, 'British Portfolio Investment Overseas before 1870', *Economic History Review* xxxiii (1980).
[70] Cain and Hopkins, 'Political Economy', p.478.

world trade and of world demand for manufactured goods that were independent of internal economic conditions in England and thus provided an exogenous dynamic force. European demands for re-exports were a key to the success of England's trade before the 1780s; the protectionism and growing competition of European countries forced a radical reorientation of English trade in favour of more distant areas and put a premium upon government and military support for such expansion; American and later South American independence radically affected trade; and the use of slavery in the plantation economies, for a crucial period, underpinned a most profitable multilateral and extensive trading and credit network.[71]

Gentlemanly capitalism and overseas expansion

In recent years it has been suggested that too little attention has been paid to non-industrial forms of capitalism in analysing British overseas expansion. Cain and Hopkins argue that between 1688 and 1850 the dominant influence on overseas policy was the landed interest but that in the eighteenth century an alliance was necessarily forged between the landed élite, the City and southern investors that played a major role in overseas expansion. This perspective fits well with recent interpretations of the industrial revolution which stress that the triumph of industry was not characteristic of the period, that the manufacturing interest did not enjoy a steady or complete rise either to economic or political supremacy and that the industrial revolution ushered in a gentlemanly form of capitalism.[72]

The 'gentlemenly capitalism' thesis rejects the idea that overseas trade and colonial policy followed from any insatiable search for raw materials and markets in response to the rise of industrial capitalism. It also rejects the notion of an industrial bourgeiosie capturing production abroad to offload surplus capital and to supplement declining manufacturing profit at home (as a crude theory of capitalist imperialism might suggest). Traders in the eighteenth century were not the advanced guard of a new industrial order. Investment in Indian cotton, for example, was made to find a means of buying tea from China. The financial and mercantile interests were the main beneficiaries of overseas trade.[73]

Cain and Hopkins see the policy of promoting the growth of Britain's foreign trade outside the empire after the 1780s as a response to the need to maintain the raw materials for domestic employment

---

[71] J. E. Inikori, 'Slavery and the Development of Industrial Capitalism in England', in B. L. Solow and S. L. Engerman, eds., *British Capitalism and Caribbean Slavery: The Legacy of Eric Williams* (Cambridge, 1989), pp.51–134; see also pp.1–24.
[72] Cain and Hopkins, 'Gentlemanly Capitalism'. Cain and Hopkins argue that after 1850 the landed interest was succeeded as the dominant group by the financial and commercial magnates of the City and the wealthiest and most influential elements arising from the growth of services in the south and east.
[73] Cain and Hopkins, 'Political Economy', p.471.

and to nourish state revenues. The more open the system became, the more threat there was to agricultural self-sufficiency which underpinned some of the power of the landed interest. Not surprisingly, therefore, the loss of the American colonies in 1783 was followed by attempts to reinforce the empire. Recognition of the impossibility of agricultural self-sufficiency, the ability of the industrial and financial sectors to compete abroad without state aid and the dangers of social unrest lay behind the Tory government's modification of the Corn Laws, tariff schedules and Navigation Laws in the 1820s. These signified a shift to a more liberal trading policy and towards incorporating (in a subordinate role) the provincial manufacturing interest into national political life. But the shift was not the reflection of a self-confident industrial power or a conversion to *laissez-faire* ideology. It indicated a continued change in attitude within the landed class. Many had business and financial interests which gave them sympathy for free trade and, importantly, the liberation of trade received powerful support from the moneyed interests of southern England, which gained considerably from the widening circle of world trade. Thus it is argued that England's role as a clearing house of the world preceded its role as workshop of the world and continued to predominate.[74]

Interesting though these arguments of Cain and Hopkins are, their views have by no means gained common currency. They claim to confront a whole tradition in historiography from Harlow to Wallerstein (from the right and the left of the political spectrum respectively) and stretching back to Marx and the classical economists, that suggests 1763 was a watershed between a 'mercantilist' empire and the start of a new type of imperialism owing its character to the development of industrial capitalism. However, in laying down the challenge in this manner, Cain and Hopkins to a large extent create a straw man: they exaggerate the place given to a narrowly defined 'industrial capitalism' in the writing of both liberal and Marxist historians. Most earlier writers have in fact given good weight to the role of the landed élite, the *rentier* and mercantile interests in analysing overseas expansion and the nature of British capitalism in this period.[75]

The 'gentlemanly capitalist' thesis has also been shown to have underemphasised the role of cosmopolitan capitalists in English overseas expansion and to have overemphasised the separation of interests and cultures between the landed, financial and mercantile

[74] Cain and Hopkins, 'Political Economy'. For Tory policy making in the period see B. Hilton, *Corn, Cash and Commerce: The Economic Policies of the Tory Governments 1815–30* (Oxford, 1977).
[75] V. T. Harlow, *The Founding of the Second British Empire 1763–1793* I (London, 1952); I. Wallerstein, *The Modern World System* II (New York, 1980); D. K. Fieldhouse, *The Theory of Capitalist Imperialism* (London, 1967). A. N. Porter, 'Gentlemanly Capitalism and Empire: The British Experience since 1750', *Journal of Imperial and Commonwealth History* 18 (1990), highlights the 'straw man' nature of the Cain and Hopkins argument.

groups on the one hand and industrialists on the other. Each had complex portfolios of mixed investments, intermarriage was common and these were by no means internally homogeneous or cohesive groupings.[76] There were close links and complementarity of interests between City financiers and northern industrial interests: the existence of the bill discount market is a major example of this. And there are many instances of direct trade and investment links between industrial provinces and overseas partners (including colonies) which contributed to regional growth and were carried on relatively independently of London's mediation. Much of the trading and *rentier* wealth of Liverpool and Glasgow, for example, was built on such direct connections.[77]

It has been necessary to look closely at Cain and Hopkins's thesis because of its central position in current debates about the industrial revolution and the nature of British capitalism. However, 'gentlemanly capitalism seems too Anglocentric, too essentially metropolitan, too committed to the idea that the economics of the colonising power's capitalism offers the key to the politics of empire'.[78] In the context of the industrial revolution we must also suspect that it underplays the radical nature of political and economic change (within as well as between social classes), and the direct relationship between overseas trade and rapidly growing provincial industrial regions.

The slave trade

It is appropriate at this point to turn to the long-standing debate about the contribution of slavery and the slave trade to British industrialisation, not just because it is currently being recontested but also because it provides a good case study and illustration of most of the factors raised in the preceding discussion of the nature and role of overseas expansion. It highlights the links between foreign trade, colonisation and the development of the British economy; it illustrates the need to take a broad and multilateral perspective in assessing the gains from trade; it demonstrates the independent role of West Africa, the

[76] M. J. Daunton, 'Gentlemanly Capitalism and British Industry 1820–1914', *Past and Present* 122 (1989); S. D. Chapman, 'The International Houses: the Continental Contribution to Britain's Economic Development', *Journal of European Economic History* 6 (1977); C. A. Jones, *International Business in the Nineteenth Century: The Rise and Fall of a Cosmopolitan Bourgeoisie* (Brighton, 1987).
[77] Porter, 'Capitalism and Empire', pp.277–9. Daunton, 'Gentlemanly Capitalism'; D. Richardson, 'The Slave Trade, Sugar, and British Economic Growth 1748–1776', in Solow and Engerman, *British Capitalism*, p. 133. Cain and Hopkins's insistence on the unity of the period 1688–1850 in terms of imperial policy is also weakened by studies such as: P. Marshall, *'A Free though Conquering People': Britain and Asia in the Eighteenth Century*, (London, 1981); C. A. Bayly, *Imperial Meridian: The British Empire and the World 1780–1830* (London, 1989), p.15. See also B. Stanley, 'Commerce and Christianity: Providence Theory, the Missionary Movement and the Imperialism of Free Trade 1842–60', *Historical Journal* 26 (1983); R. Mukherjee, 'Trade and Empire in Awadh 1765–1804', *Past and Present* 94 (1982).
[78] Porter, 'Capitalism and Empire', pp.18–19.

Caribbean, North and South America in determining England's trading patterns and policy; and it shows the complexity and close nature of links between provincial industrialists and merchants and London financiers. Quantifying the slave trade in a precise way is impossible but it appears that between 1700 and 1810 6.4 million Africans were transported as slaves to the Americas. The trade reached its peak in the 1780s, when more than 88,000 slaves were involved per annum. British slave traders were responsible for almost half of these. By the mid eighteenth century the slave supply to the North American colonies was sustained by natural increase and a limited internal trading system. Slave shipments thereafter were directed at the Caribbean and Brazil. England dominated this trade, dealing largely with the West Indies from the ports of London, Bristol and increasingly, Liverpool. The latter became the premier slave-trading port from the 1740s and by the end of the century was responsible for between 70% and 85% of the English trade.[79]

Liverpool traders proved efficient at assembling the varied and changing cargoes of manufactures in demand on the West African coast. Insofar as these consisted of South Lancashire textiles, Midlands metalwares and American re-exports such as rum and tobacco, Liverpool traders were at an advantage in having the necessary contacts. But Liverpool merchants also proved efficient at assembling those exports to West Africa (about one third and rising to a half after the 1790s) that consisted of Indian cottons, European products (such as Swedish bar iron, Italian beads, German linens, firearms and gunpowder) and Asian items such as cowry shells. West Africa's share of total English exports was about 4% in the late eighteenth century. Some of the foreign goods were obtained through Dutch middle-men but that route became less important than supplies obtained directly once Liverpool became dominant in the trade in the second half of the eighteenth century.[80]

Satisfying West African demands for manufactures was a vital element in the trade. This demand varied by region and shifted over

[79] P. D. Curtin, *The Atlantic Slave Trade: A Census* (Madison, 1969), pp. 135, 212, 216, 268. Curtin suggests that England maintained a 50% share of the total slave trade 1768–98. S. Drescher, *Econocide: British Slavery in the Era of Abolition* (Pittsburgh, 1977), pp.28, 205–13; R. Anstey and P. E. H. Hair, *Liverpool, the African Slave Trade and Abolition* (Liverpool, 1976), p.78; P. E. Lovejoy, 'The Volume of the Atlantic Slave Trade: A Synthesis', *Journal of African History* xxiii (1982).

[80] D. Richardson, 'West African Consumption Patterns and their Influence on the Eighteenth-Century English Slave Trade', in H. A. Gemery and J. S. Hogendorn, eds., *The Uncommon Market: Essays in the Economic History of the Atlantic Slave Trade.* (New York, 1979); B. K. Drake, 'The Liverpool–African Voyage c.1790–1807: Commercial Problems' and D. Richardson, 'Profits of the Slave Trade: The Accounts of Richard Davenport 1757–1784', both in Anstey and Hair, *Liverpool.*

the course of the century as English traders moved east and south-wards on the West African coast to avoid competition and to exploit new sources of slave supply at the Bight of Biafra, Old Calabar and, particularly, in Cameroon and Gabon. Beads were favoured in the Cameroons together with brass pans, iron bars and basins; in Old Calabar cotton textiles and copper rods were more important. Items like pots and pans were cheap and traded at low profit illustrating the influence West African demand had on the commodity mix. West African trading partners were by no means fickle or passive in their acceptance of goods.[81]

In the West Indies slaves were sold and return cargoes purchased. It seems that return shipments of sugar on slave ships declined and had become unimportant by the later eighteenth century. The development of the guarantee system from 1750 meant that slave ships found it more difficult to obtain return cargoes and they thus made a much smaller contribution to the transport of West Indies plantation products than separate bilateral shippers and commission agents trading direct from England to the islands. Slave ships came back carrying bills of exchange, African timber, furs, ivory, South American goods like logwood, dyes and cacao, and low value ballast goods to avoid waiting for cargoes.[82]

Slavery and the industrial revolution

In 1944 Eric Williams's book *Capitalism and Slavery* broke new ground in sustaining an analysis of the use of slave labour in terms of its profitability and in attributing to the slave system and slave trade a leading role in financing the industrial revolution in Britain:

> The West Indian islands became the hub of the British Empire, of immense importance to the grandeur and prosperity of England. It was the Negro slaves who made these sugar colonies the most precious colonies ever recorded in the whole annals of imperialism ... the profits obtained provided one of the main streams of that accumulation of capital in England which financed the industrial revolution.[83]

Williams stressed the importance of investment of plantation and slave-trade profits in shipping, banking, insurance and in industry. Although some subsequent work has supported the view that substantial profits were made on West Indian investments, other historians have highlighted the high cost of defence and administration of the

[81] Richardson, 'West African Consumption'; Drake, 'Liverpool–African Voyage'.
[82] W. E. Minchinton, 'The Triangular Trade Revisited', in Gemery and Hogendorn, *The Uncommon Market;* F. E. Hyde, B. B. Parkinson and S. Marriner, 'The Nature and Profitability of the Liverpool Slave Trade', *Economic History Review* v (1952–3).
[83] E. Williams, *Capitalism and Slavery* (first pub. London, 1944; New York, 1966 edn.), p.52.

colonies and have calculated that Britain would have been better off without them.[84] But this argument misses the point: so long as high *private* returns were made the potential was there for investment in industrialisation regardless of the *social* costs. The main burden of these in any case fell on those with little propensity to invest in industry. The 'cost' of colonial defence was, furthermore, often a stimulus to the economy, especially the demand for munitions, ships, provisions and uniforms.

Numerous investigations into the profitability of the slave trade itself have shown that average rates were modest and only just comparable with other sorts of more secure investment at around 8% per annum. But the major feature of slave trade profitability was variability. Substantial profits, over 25% per year, are recorded, with some much higher rates for short periods of years.[85] This was particularly the case where Letters of Marque had been obtained and where slave traders engaged simultaneously in the opportunities their trade routes brought them for privateering. This was a common practice amongst Liverpool merchants and the prize money was often substantial. In the course of the second voyage of the Liverpool slave ship *Hawke* in 1781 she seized the *Jeune Emilia* and netted profit of 147%.[86] A key question must remain: where did the profits of this trade (and of plantations) go?

Social commentaries and novels of the early nineteenth century are replete with examples of West Indian planters and investors buying land and building fine houses in England and there is no doubt that much capital was directed into land ownership and conspicuous consumption. Bristol merchants who had moved into plantation finance (often involuntarily, where slaves had been exchanged for plantation mortgages) commonly moved into landowning on retirement or on withdrawal from West Indian involvements. It is likely that

---

[84] J. R. Ward, 'The Profitability of Sugar Planting in the British West Indies 1650–1834', *Economic History Review* XXXI (1978); P. R. P. Coelho, 'The Profitability of Imperialism: The British Experience in the West Indies 1768–72', *Explorations in Economic History* 10 (1973); R. P. Thomas, 'Sugar Colonies of the Old Empire: Profit or Loss for Great Britain?' *Economic History Review*, XXI (1968); cf. R. B. Sheriden, 'The Wealth of Jamaica in the Eighteenth Century', *Economic History Review* XVIII (1965), where he estimates that 8–10% of the income of Britain came from the West Indies in the late eighteenth century and probably more before the War of Independence. Much of this debate rests on assumptions about the extent to which there was full employment in the economy, ie whether the opportunity-costs of employment within the slave system were low.

[85] Richardson, 'Profits'.

[86] Richardson, 'Profits', p.79; B. L. Anderson, 'The Lancashire Bill System and Its Liverpool Practitioners: The Case of a Slave Merchant', in W. H. Chaloner, ed., *Trade and Transport: Essays in Economic History in Honour of T. S. Willan* (Manchester, 1977). Gomer Williams, *History of the Liverpool Privateers and Letters of Marque with an Account of the Liverpool Slave Trade* (Liverpool, 1897; repr. Liverpool, 1966).

more Fonthills than factories were built with slave profits.[87] But Liverpool slave traders dealt largely with the factoring agents of London houses in the West Indies rather than direct with planters and rarely got involved in plantation finance or ownership. The basis of Liverpool's success compared with Bristol or with French and Dutch rivals was the ability to realise profits quickly by receiving their proceeds in bills and promptly rediscounting them.[88] The Liverpool traders included few nabob types (although the Tarleton family is a major exception) and, although evidence is far from systematic, they appear to have invested as much in coal mining and slate extraction, canal companies, marine insurance, miscellaneous manufacturing and especially in founding banks, as in ostentatious land ownership. The Heywoods, for example, invested in sugar-refining and banking in Liverpool as well as in woollen manufacture in Wakefield.[89]

But the role of slavery in industrialisation involves a much wider remit than the level and direction of investment of slave-trade or plantation profits. It involves consideration of the role of the Atlantic economy in which slavery and the West Indies were for a time the crucial linchpins. We must also consider the ways in which the slave trade contributed to external demand for British manufactured goods in West Africa, the Americas and Europe.[90] Finally, it is important to examine the contribution this trade made to the build-up of an efficient commercial, financial and credit infrastructure in Britain. Fixed capital investment (in plant and machinery) in industry rarely exceeded circulating capital requirements (for wage payments, raw-material purchase etc.), even in the cotton sector, before 1850. Thus more important than the flow of slave profits into fixed industrial invest-ment, was the extent to which the bill system and bank finance, in south Lancashire, the West Riding, the West Midlands and elsewhere, was underpinned by trans-Atlantic remittances.

Slavery: an assessment

Slavery was a vital factor in the dynamic growth of the whole Atlantic economy in the eighteenth century. Slave labour was the key to exploiting the resources of thinly populated colonial conquests

[87] R. Pares (source uncited), quoted by F. Crouzet, 'Capital Formation in Great Britain during the Industrial Revolution,' in Crouzet, ed., *Capital Formation in the Industrial Revolution*, p.176.

[88] The London houses were accommodating the growing indebtedness of the planters: Anderson, 'Lancashire Bill System', p.61.

[89] Thomas Leyland associated with the Clarkes and Roscoes to found a bank in 1802; Jonathan Blundell was involved in coal mining; Joseph Brookes owned a brewery; the Penryns were involved in Welsh slate mining; several slavers owned roperies and most slave-traders were involved in general merchanting and manufacturing alongside foreign trade. Prize money was an important source of set up capital in several Liverpool private banks of the period. Anderson, 'Lancashire Bill System', p.94.

[90] It must also not be forgotten that English re-exports of sugar, tobacco and rum from the Americas were important in enabling the purchase of vital European supplies.

quickly.[91] England gained greater investment opportunities, furthered her commercial institutions and set up factor, commodity and capital flows that were important for economic growth. The sugar and tobacco trades made Britain the entrepôt for Europe's supply of these and they formed the important pillars of the re-export trade. Before 1783 North America, particularly New England and Newfoundland, traded agricultural products, horses, timber and fish to the West Indies and used the proceeds to buy British manufactures. And most of the Anglo-West Indian commerce, as we have seen, took the form of bilateral exchange, mainly of English manufactures for sugar. But the importance of slavery and the slave trade in underpinning this direct source of Caribbean demand for English manufactures is seldom included in assessments of the impact of slavery. Yet practically all slave-traders had direct links with the American mainland and many were also involved in the re-export trade between the West Indian islands and with South America.[92] These wider links are what Wadsworth and Mann clearly had in mind in saying that the slave trade was an important *route* along which British, and especially Lancashire, manufacturers tested their competitive strength in the expanding markets served by the Atlantic trades.[93] Furthermore, the stimulus to certain sectors of English manufacturing from demand along the West African coast was far from negligible. Africa was second only to the American colonies as a market for wrought-iron exports in the mid-eighteenth century and both the Carron and Coalbrookdale companies had warehouses in Liverpool, largely to supply the slave trade. Similarly, in the peak year of 1792 Africa took nearly one quarter of British cotton exports.[94] Development of the trade in Asian and European goods to satisfy the African market was also considerable, 'Wherever sugar and slavery went, a web of international trading flows in capital, merchandise, labour supply and shipping was woven.'[95]

Richardson has pinpointed the third quarter of the eighteenth century as seeing perhaps the most dynamic impact of the slave system on the British economy. The slave trade to the Caribbean expanded fastest in these years and he attributes this to the expansion of domestic

[91] B. L. Solow, 'Capitalism and Slavery in the Exceedingly Long Run', in Solow and Engerman, *Caribbean Slavery*.
[92] Anderson, 'Lancashire Bill System', p.71. Surpluses on Caribbean trade were vital to the mainland colonies, allowing them to pay for almost 18% of their recorded imports from Britain around 1770: Richardson, 'Slaves, Sugar and Growth', pp.129–30.
[93] A. P. Wadsworth and J. de L. Mann, *The Cotton Trade and Industrial Lancashire 1600–1780* (Manchester, 1931), p.227.
[94] Wadsworth and Mann, *Cotton Trade*, p.118; Anderson, 'Lancashire Bill System', p.66.
[95] Solow, 'Capitalism and Slavery', p. 77. By the first half of the nineteenth century, with higher investment and technical change in England, market widening through exports mattered less than market deepening and slavery no longer had such a starring role.

demand for sugar. The growth of British exports accelerated in tandem and Caribbean-generated demands for domestically produced exports between 1748 and 1776 accounted for almost half of the total. Ninety-five per cent of these exports were manufactured goods, which suggests that Caribbean-based demand accounted for around 12% of English industrial output in these years.[96] Bearing in mind that this demand was concentrated in particular goods and particular industrial sectors, this proportion is highly significant in an analysis of the roots of industrial change. Richardson rightly warns that it is misleading to draw a sharp distinction between external and internal sources of stimulus in the English economy, particularly where New World demand for British manufactures was so closely connected to growing British demand for colonial products. What is clear, however, is that a key exogenous factor was the institution of slavery which, by providing a uniquely cheap and expandable supply of labour, enabled the production of sugar to grow continuously.

Slave ships returned to England with bills of exchange and a mass of additional commercial paper was created by bilateral involvement in the trans-Atlantic economy. As most of these trade remittances came to Liverpool (and to a lesser extent Bristol, and Glasgow), we must enquire to what extent bill circulation and other systems of credit spawned by and multiplied in the Atlantic trade affected the operations and the flexibility of manufacturing and tertiary interests in the industrialising regions.

Anderson's study of the Lancashire bill system suggests that the Liverpool merchant community cleared most of their debts to one another locally (that a major credit market operated at the local and regional level) and sent only their residual obligations to London.[97] Their ability to buy manufactured goods from south Lancashire, Yorkshire, the Midlands and elsewhere on much shorter credit than they in turn were forced to employ in the long-distance trades was a product of the developed nature of the bill market in south Lancashire. This was the key to the mobilisation of mercantile capital in ways vital to the expansion of industry. Few slave-traders' bills were drawn on London but a very large proportion of all their foreign bills were paid there. Bills received in the West Indies for slaves were presented in London where a small number of reputable West India houses accepted final responsibility. Foreign bills from Europe and other trade areas similarly went south for payment. In this manner, and as London succeeded Amsterdam as the premier centre of international finance, the inter-regional and international flow of funds via London from areas of capital surplus to those in need of funds really took off.

96 Richardson, 'Slaves, Sugar and Growth', p.131.
97 This paragraph relies heavily on Anderson, 'Lancashire Bill System'. See also T. S. Ashton, 'The Bill of Exchange and Private Banks in Lancashire 1790–1830, in T. S. Ashton and R. S. Sayers, eds., *Papers in English Monetary History* (Oxford, 1954).

Thus Liverpool's external trade was largely responsible for sucking vital funds northwards into the industrial regions where they underpinned the expansion of trade and of productive capacity.[98]

A final consideration in assessing the role of the slave trade is the way in which it aided the shift into new patterns of international activity and trading after abolition. From the 1780s, in fact, many Liverpool merchants were shifting the balance of their concerns away from the slave trade because competition was putting pressure on profits. Then, as later, they found it relatively easy to shift because of the complex network of exchange in which they were already involved. Bilateral trade with West Africa; direct trade with North America, with South America and with the Far East; assembling mixed cargoes of manufactured exports and dealing with primary product imports; dealing with London finance houses to obtain the necessary credit and cash: all these were within their experience. And because the West Indies became a leading source of raw cotton for a time in the 1780s and 1790s, Liverpool merchants, having handled this, were well placed to expand their role into the cotton trade with the American south in the nineteenth century. Finally, the Liverpool slave trade did much to foster marine insurance, especially from the 1790s.[99] Furthermore, the size, wealth and varied expertise of the Liverpool merchant community did much to promote developments in the industrial heartlands served by the port. The growth of merchant manufacturers in the textile districts during the Napoleonic Wars and their aftermath was greatly facilitated by credit and other marine services available in the port that had accumulated initially around the trade in slaves and its offshoots.[100]

Conclusion

We have seen that domestic demand represented a much larger market for goods and services than did foreign demand throughout the industrial revolution and it is clear that this demand was buoyant and increasingly sophisticated and differentiated. Yet much of this buoyancy came from contemporaneous shifts in the structure of the economy. These bolstered the growth of population but more importantly they promoted wage dependency and the redistribution of income to those increasingly able to buy a wide range of consumer goods, both domestic and imported. This encouraged radical changes

---

[98] Ashton, 'Bill of Exchange', p.59; Chapman, *Merchant Banking*.
[99] J. A. Rawley, *The Trans-Atlantic Slave Trade: A History* (New York, 1981), p.199. On the variety of trades carried on alongside the slave trade in Liverpool, see B. K. Drake, 'Continuity and Flexibility in Liverpool's Trade with Africa and the Caribbean', *Business History* xviii (1976).
[100] Chapman, *Merchant Banking*, p.8.

in consumption patterns and horizons amongst certain groups in the population and the quickening pace of retailing together with innovations in style and fashion must have created an environment from which few in the population could remain entirely immune. However, income levels for the mass of the population minimised their ability to participate in any revolution in consumption and the highly varied nature of products demanded must have restricted the impact of demand upon the technology of mass production.

Foreign demand was smaller but it was felt very strongly by those sectors involved in the mass manufacture of relatively homogeneous goods. For many of the most rapidly developing and technologically innovating sectors of the economy it was their vital underpinning. Furthermore, foreign trade represented much more of an exogenous stimulus than did the home market. The repercussions of surges in external trade during the eighteenth century were widespread and had a particularly strong impact on the internal development of transport and the financial and commercial infrastructure in rapidly industrialising regions, as well as upon the changing technology choices of industrialists. In 1968 Hobsbawm summarised an interpretation of the vital role of external trade in British industrialisation that the current orthodoxy has by no means made redundant and that may be ripe for rehabilitation:

> The export industries did not depend on the modest 'natural' rate of growth of any country's internal demand. They could create the illusion of rapid growth by two means: capturing a series of other countries' export markets, and destroying domestic competition within particular countries, that is by the political or semi-political means of war and colonization. The country which succeeded in concentrating other people's export markets, or even in monopolizing the export markets of a large part of the world in a sufficiently brief time, could expand its export industries at a rate which made industrial revolution not only practicable for its entrepreneurs, but sometimes virtually compulsory. And this is what Britain succeeded in doing in the eighteenth century ... It follows that if one country did this, others would be unlikely to develop the basis for industrial revolution. In other words, under pre-industrial conditions there was probably room for only one pioneer national industrialisation ... but not the simultaneous industrialisation of several 'advanced economies'.[101]

[101] E. J. Hobsbawm, *Industry and Empire* (Harmondsworth, 1969), p.48.

7 CLASS AND GENDER

Earlier chapters have suggested that assessment of the industrial revolution should not be confined to macro-economic indicators, to the magnitude of shifts in industrial technology nor even to economic transformations on a broader front. Socio-cultural and political changes were an integral part of the economic transitions of the time and are vital to our understanding of the radical nature of the period. Much discussion of such changes has concerned the development of social class and of class relations. More recently the construction and reconstruction of notions of gender as well as class in the period has been studied against the backcloth of change in religion, politics, social life and cultural forms such as the role of the family, 'community' and leisure activities. The emergence of a new type of class society has long been central to popular understanding of the industrial revolution but recent literature has played down the extent to which the period was marked by new social identities and power relationships. By contrast, research on the changing economic roles and social status of women has tended to emphasise that the industrial revolution represented a watershed in development. This chapter examines the various claims and suggests that analyses of class and gender have been too separated and too little integrated in the past. Only by combining the insights from both sets of analysis can a fuller understanding of the social and cultural continuities and discontinuities of the period be appreciated.

Class and the industrial revolution

The emergence of new and conflicting class relations features in much early- and mid-nineteenth-century discussion. The Owenite James Hole wrote in 1851 that:

> Class stands opposed to class, and so accustomed have men become to pursue their own isolated interests apart from and regardless of that of others, that it has become an acknowledged maxim, that where a man pursues his own interests alone he is most benefiting society – a maxim . . . which would justify every crime and folly. The principle of supply and demand has been extended from commodities to men. These have obtained thereby more liberty, but less bread. They find that in parting

with the thraldom of Feudalism they have taken on that of Capital; that slavery has ceased in name but survived in fact.[1]

Increasing use of the term 'class' in a new way from the 1830s to describe mutually antagonistic social strata adds further support to the idea that a shift was occuring in the relationships between different social groups.[2]

In most writing on class a distinction is made between class as an objective or descriptive category and class as embodying an antagonistic social consciousness. Marx argued that in so far as millions of families live under economic conditions which separate their way of life, their interests and their education from those of other classes, they constitute a class 'in itself'. Classes in this sense exist in all societies although social and economic change will alter economic and social differences and rearrange the boundaries between classes over time. The acceleration of proletarianisation, urbanisation, technological and organisational change in both agriculture and industry may well have enhanced the formation of class in this sense during the industrial revolution. Marx emphasised the increasing polarisation of experience between those who owned the means of production and the lot of the property-less wage-earning workers whose numbers multiplied in the eighteenth century and who were dependent on the sale of their labour. However, the issue around which most historical debate takes place is whether there was a heightening of class consciousness in the period. Did the working class increasingly exhibit a common consciousness: a recognition that its interests were incompatible with those of employers and landowners and that it was necessary to take collective action to defend class interests? In Marx's terminology (and that of Lenin) we are here talking of the development of class 'for itself'.[3]

In the 1960s and 1970s the growth of class consciousness during the industrial revolution was a dominant theme in the literature, emphasised in the work of Perkin and Thompson in particular.[4] According to Perkin,

---

[1] J. Hole, *Lectures on Social Science and the Organisation of Labour* (London, 1851), quoted in A. Briggs, *Victorian Cities* (Harmondsworth, 1968), p.141. For many similar examples see A. Briggs, 'The Language of Class in Early Nineteenth-Century England', in A. Briggs and J. Saville, eds., *Essays in Labour History* (London, 1967).
[2] Briggs, 'Language of Class'. Systems of social classification in the eighteenth century appear increasingly to have involved active terms of acquisition, production and display rather than inheritance, formal title and ancient lineage: P. Corfield, 'Class by Name and Number in Eighteenth-Century Britain', *History* 72 (1987).
[3] For discussion of these concepts and approaches see R. J. Morris, *Class and Class Consciousness in the Industrial Revolution 1780–1850* (London, 1979).
[4] H. Perkin, *The Origins of Modern English Society 1780–1880* (London, 1969); E. P. Thompson, *The Making of the English Working Class* (London, 1963).

A class society is characterised by class feeling, that is by the existence of vertical antagonism between a small number of horizontal interest groups, each based on a common source of income. Such vertical antagonism and the horizontal solidarity of each class transcend the common source of income which supports them.[5]

In Perkins's view the industrial revolution saw the birth of class in this sense. He argues that, in the eighteenth century and earlier, interest groups were articulated around social pyramids representing an economic sector or sub-sector: the landed interest, various trade interests, the City interest, Bristol sugar, Liverpool slavers, Leeds woollen merchants, Norwich textiles and so forth. Within each sector, bonds of patronage and dependency, paternalism and deference held together the interest of those at the apex with those dependent on the sector for employment. Although class was latent and examples of vertical antagonism in society can be found, Perkin argues that before the early nineteenth century conflict in society occurred between social pyramids more than within them.

But the industrial revolution saw the emergence of three broad and mutually antagonistic classes: the landed aristocracy whose income derived primarily from rents, the bourgeoisie whose income came from profits and the mass of the working population who were wage dependent. These three sources of income were potentially in conflict because each could raise its share only at the expense of the others. Furthermore, the moral consensus which had underpinned income shares and the social structure of the old society was being undermined as the paternalism of the governing élite was increasingly abrogated in favour of market relationships. The landed class became more aloof and withdrew from sympathetic contact with the masses. And there occurred a systematic dismantling of the regulatory protection of the lower orders which was a hallmark of the old society and a justification for its inequalities. In its place was the invigoration of the competitive market and the bourgeois 'entrepreneurial ideal' of self-help and self-aggrandisement. Changes in the structure and organisation of industry and agriculture precipitated a multitude of new opportunities for, and sources of, antagonism which resulted in the emergence of non-local forms of resistance and of manifestations of class feeling. Perkin suggests that struggles over income were never a sufficient motive for class antagonism. Organised antagonism with a nationwide appeal to all members of one broad social stratum depended on the catalyst of opposing ideals: in particular, the profit-seeking, free-market entrepreneurial ideal against an ideal of co-operation between productive independent workers.[6]

5 Perkin, *Origins*, p.176.
6 Perkin, *Origins*, esp. chs.6 and 7.

Thompson similarly argued that the period from the 1790s to the 1830s saw the making of the English working class. He documented a growing identity of interests between diverse groups of the working population – distinct from the interests of other classes – that manifested itself in the emergence of strongly based and self-conscious working-class institutions and movements: friendly societies, trade unions, educational and religious movements, co-operatives, working-class periodicals and Chartism. The main thrust came from specific groups – stockingers, handloom weavers, cotton spinners, artisans, shoemakers, small masters, tradesmen, publicans, book sellers and professional men. These groups came together on the basis of their shared political and industrial organisation through Hampden clubs, constitutional societies, trade unions and friendly societies. Unlike Perkin, and some Marxist historians, Thompson places less emphasis on the objective determinants of class position and class feeling (derived from source of income or relationship to the means of production) and more upon class as lived or perceived experience. He places as much weight on the role of agency as on economic structures in the creation of class:

Classes do not exist as separate entities, look around, find an enemy class and then start to struggle. On the contrary, people find themselves in a society structured in determined ways (crucially but not exclusively in productive relations), they experience exploitation (or the need to maintain power over those whom they exploit), they identify points of antagonistic interest, they commence to struggle around these issues, and in the process of struggle they discover themselves as classes.[7]

[7] E. P. Thompson, 'Eighteenth-Century English Society: Class Struggle without Class', *Social History* 3 (1978), p.149. Thompson's more frequently quoted theorisations of class appear in the early pages of *Making of the English Working Class*: 'class experience is largely determined by the productive relations into which men [sic] are born – or enter involuntarily. Class consciousness is the way in which these experiences are handled in cultural terms: embodied in traditions, value systems, ideas and institutional forms. If the experience appears as determined, class consciousness does not'. Class 'happens when some men, as a result of common experiences (inherited or shared), feel and articulate the identity of their interests as between themselves, and as against other men whose interests are different from (and usually opposed to) theirs'. 'Class is defined by men as they live their own history, and, in the end, this is the only definition.' There was considerable debate amongst Marxists in the 1970s about Thompson's 'humanist' notion of class and more 'orthodox' Marxist interpretations. See for example, E. P. Thompson, 'The Poverty of Theory', in Thompson, *The Poverty of Theory and Other Essays* (London, 1978); Richard Johnson, 'Edward Thompson, Eugene Genovese and Socialist–Humanist History', *History Workshop Journal* 6 (1978); contributions by Stuart Hall, Richard Johnson and Thompson himself to 'Culturalism: Debates around the Poverty of Theory' in R. Samuel, ed., *People's History and Socialist Theory* (London, 1981). For the most even-handed and recent discussion of Thompson's contribution see essays in H. J. Kaye and K. McClelland, ed., *E. P. Thompson: Critical Perspectives* (London, 1990).

Thompson argues that the eighteenth century saw ephemeral episodes of 'class struggle without class'. These occurred before the working class had assumed a common consciousness separate from the ethos of other social groups and before the capitalist class had become unified. Popular protest in the form of crowd action and rioting flourished in the eighteenth century for a number of reasons. It was a century in which more people were becoming freer from discipline in their daily lives and therefore less subordinated. Perquisites (provision of board, payment in kind, hunting and fishing rights) favoured paternal control and their decline in favour of monetary payments contributed to this new freedom. Proletarianisation, urbanisation and migration together enlarged the sector of the economy that was independent of direct relationship with the gentry and resulted in the decline of gentry control over settlement, pauperism, bastardy, courtship and social behaviour. In addition, the proliferation of proto-industrial and other by-employments together with petty land tenures gave people independence from any single source of employment or authority. And the declining spiritual force of the Church, the secularisation of social life and of the social calendar added to crowd licence by promoting a vigorous and independent plebeian culture. Thompson argues that this plebeian culture was increasingly distinct from polite culture from the seventeenth century on, with its own rituals, symbolism and increasingly literate conduits. This plebeian culture was important in making protest more unified and legitimate in the participants' eyes, as well as lending form and structure to crowd action.[8]

Riot and protest in the eighteenth century contained a unifying appeal to lost paternalistic structures and to a moral economy which was seen to be disappearing in face of the innovating market regime. The notion of defending traditional ways of life, in which the role of the market was tempered by regulation in the interests of social justice, was important in the formation of consciousness and of oppositional culture. The idea of an economic price for corn for example (the dissociation between an economic value on the one hand and social and moral obligations on the other) was seen as an outrage. Violence in grain and food riots fell upon middle-men, forestallers, millers and bailiffs who were using the market for their own ends. But what set eighteenth-century protest apart from the oppositional politics of the early nineteenth century was the way in which the power of the gentry and their paternal role was not challenged but endorsed by the articulation of crowd action. The objects of attack from enclosure rioters, grain rioters, and machine wreckers were innovating capitalists and middlemen who were seen to be disrupting the social order in the interests of profits. Landowners and the governing élite who

[8] E. P. Thompson, 'Patrician Society, Plebeian Culture', *Journal of Social History* vii (1974); Thompson, 'Class Struggle without Class'.

exercised their power and pursued their interests from a greater social or geographic distance were less the objects of criticism and in fact they were the authority to which rioters in the first instance appealed for help in maintaining traditional paternalistic structures:

> Food rioters appealed back to the Book of Orders and legislation against forestallers, artisans appealed to apprenticeship regulations and the Tudor regulatory labour code. ... Hence we can read eighteenth-century social history as a succession of confrontations between an innovative market economy and the customary moral economy of the plebs.[9]

The rebellious culture of the eighteenth century was a rebelliousness in defence of customary rights. It was often only when petitions to King and Parliament to activate regulatory legislation had failed that the crowd turned to direct action. In Thompson's view so long as the gentry continued at least to mouth the necessary commitment to regulation, met certain conditions and performed certain (largely theatrical and gestural) roles, the continuation of reciprocity and *noblesse oblige* fundamental to the stability of gentry/plebeian relations was demonstrated and political instability avoided. But the industrial revolution destroyed this eighteenth-century balance of forces.

Crime and the dangerous classes

Endorsing the stress placed by historians such as Perkin and Thompson on the formation of the English working class, other literature of the 1970s and 1980s argued that the eighteenth and early nineteenth centuries were marked by a number of developments in the definition of crime, the operation of the criminal justice system and of punishment that are indicative of radically changing class-specific attitudes to private property and of shifts in social relations more generally.[10]

It is notoriously difficult to interpret crime statistics because they are affected as much by changing definitions of crime, overlapping jurisdictions of different courts, moral panics, and changes in the willingness to bring prosecutions (rather than settle outside court) as

[9] Thompson, 'English Society', and also 'The Moral Economy of the English Crowd in the Eighteenth Century', *Past and Present* 50 (1971). For further analysis of theatre and counter-theatre in maintaining political stability see J. Brewer, *Party, Ideology and Popular Politics at the Accession of George III* (Cambridge, 1976).

[10] See, for example, E. P. Thompson *Whigs and Hunters: The Origin of the Black Act* (London, 1975); D. Hay, P. Linebaugh, J. Rule, E.P. Thompson and C. Winslow, eds., *Albion's Fatal Tree: Crime and Society in Eighteenth-Century England* (London, 1975), esp. ch.1 by Hay: 'Property, Authority and the Criminal Law'; P. Munsche, *Gentlemen and Poachers: The English Game Laws 1671–1831* (Cambridge, 1981); M. Ignatieff, *A Just Measure of Pain: The Penitentiary in the Industrial Revolution 1750–1850* (New York, 1978).

they are a reflection of 'crime' itself. However, it does appear that although the eighteenth century saw a relative decline in criminal prosecutions, the early decades of the nineteenth century were marked by a great upsurge, with prosecutions rising four and a half times in relation to population growth between 1800 and the 1840s. The eighteenth century witnessed major short-term fluctuations in crime, with peaks associated with poor harvests and the termination of wars. Certain crimes such as fraud and forgery appear more prominently than in the seventeenth century but there was little change in the basic nature of offences. Of serious crimes, for example, property offences accounted for between two thirds and three quarters of felonies, with homicides accounting for most of the rest. However, in the early nineteenth century crime tended to be conflated in the eyes of the authorities with political conflict and social unrest and it was increasingly feared. Particularly discussed was the lawlessness and threat to order created by rapidly growing towns and cities and by the dangerous classes within them. It is thus not surprising that the eighteenth century did see an increase in petty regulatory offences reaching the courts and that the mushrooming of prosecutions in the early nineteenth century was particularly felt in this area of offence.[11]

Demographic increase, proletarianisation and urbanisation resulted in the poor coming to be regarded, even more than in the past, as a threat to order and stability. And this perception was strengthened by the social and health problems of growing towns and by differentials in disease and death rates that made the poor seem a race apart. At the same time the power of localised and informal sorts of social control associated with village communities and vestry officials was on the decline. Increasingly therefore it was the lower social orders who filled the courts and the prisons: the period witnessed a marked acceleration in the criminalisation of the poor.[12]

[11] Perhaps not surprisingly prosecution rates for both property offences and for violent crime rose earliest and most markedly in London. J. M. Beattie, *Crime and the Courts in England 1660–1800* (Oxford, 1986), pp. 14–15, chs. 3 and 4. For a range of discussion on eighteenth-century crime, the interpretation of statistics, the effect of war, and the creation of moral panics see J. M. Beattie, 'The Pattern of Crime in England 1660–1800', *Past and Present* 62 (1974); J. S. Cockburn, ed., *Crime in England 1550–1800* (Princeton, 1977); J. A. Sharpe, *Crime in Early Modern England* (London, 1984), esp. chs. 3 and 8; D. Hay, 'War Dearth and Theft in the Eighteenth Century: The Record of the English Courts', *Past and Present* 95 (1982); J. Brewer and J. Styles, eds., *An Ungovernable People: The English and their Law in the Seventeenth and Eighteenth Centuries* (London, 1980); P. King 'Newspaper Reporting, Prosecution Practice and Perceptions of Urban Crime: The Colchester Crime Wave of 1765', *Continuity and Change* 2 (1987).

[12] On the dangerous classes of the city and the importance of differential disease and mortality rates in creating perceptions of class difference see L. Chevalier, *Labouring Classes and Dangerous Classes in Paris During the First Half of the Nineteenth Century* (London, 1973; first published Paris, 1953). On crime, vagrancy and policing in Victorian Manchester and London, see D. V. Jones, *Crime, Protest, Community and Police in Nineteenth-Century Britain* (London, 1982).

Hay has suggested that the number of specific offences against property increased dramatically during the eighteenth century and that many such offences were redefined to carry the death penalty or transportation. This harsh criminal code coupled with the powdered wigs and red robes of the assize courts provided an awesome theatre of power in which hanging was in fact used sparingly (and effectively) as a deterrent to curb poaching, smuggling, embezzlement, forgery and other property offences. Thus in Hay's view mass opposition to the government and to economic change in the eighteenth century was tempered in a subtle manner by changes in criminal law and its mode of practice.[13] Furthermore, many offences were redefined to become offences against things rather than people. This allowed the law to wear a mask of impartiality despite its bias in favour of the propertied.[14]

Interesting though the Hay thesis is, it has been heavily criticised for suggesting that the eighteenth-century criminal-justice system was almost a ruling-class conspiracy. Most of the legal changes were merely codifications of existing practices; and it is difficult to sustain the notion that the discretion of the courts and of juries was subject to the control of a small ruling class seeking to sustain their authority over the common people and to protect their own interests. Many property offence cases were brought by the middle classes, who were also important in exercising their independent discretion as jurors. Discretion was also practised outside the courts (and away from the influence of the élite) in decisions to bring prosecutions by magistrates and constables.[15] Innes and Styles have concluded that 'the law was not the absolute property of Patricians but a limited multiple-use right available to most Englishmen'.[16]

Despite these criticisms of Hay, the shift in prosecutions towards the lower social groups and particularly the proletarianised poor, the growing notion of the dangerous classes, and a court system that favoured defendants who were established members of communities and who could obtain local character references, helps to sustain the idea that crime and justice bore a close relationship to economic and social change and the exercise of power in society more generally. This

---

13 Hay, 'Property, Authority'.
14 Thompson, *Whigs and Hunters*, ch.10.
15 See P. King, 'Decision-makers and Decision-making in the English Criminal Law 1750–1800', *The Historical Journal* 27 (1984); P. Langbein, 'Albion's Fatal Flaws', *Past and Present* 98 (1983); J. Innes and J. Styles, ' "The Crime Wave": Recent Writing on Crime and Criminal Justice in Eighteenth-Century England', *Journal of British Studies* 25 (1986). Hay's exclusive use of Quarter Sessions records may well be unrepresentative as a source for analysing the power of dominant property-owning interests. For a defence of Hay *et al.* and of a wide conceptualisation of the law as ideology see P. Linebaugh, '(Marxist) Social History and (Conservative) Legal History: A Reply to Professor Langbein', *New York University Law Review* 60 (1985).
16 Innes and Styles, ' "Crime Wave" '.

is endorsed by research conducted by historians looking at crime 'from below' and employing the notion of social crime. It is argued that a proportion of criminal activity of the later eighteenth and early nineteenth century gained widespread communal support, was not regarded as criminal by the perpetrators and was even carried out overtly as a form of social protest against innovations that adversely affected the way of life of the mass of the population.[17] However, it is difficult to interpret the motivations of 'criminals' from the sparse records of court cases and from what the accused said in their defence. Far from objecting to enclosures or to the rise of new market imperatives, it has been shown, for example, that sheep rustlers were often commercially orientated gangs, included traders and butchers, and made significant profits from inter-regional sales of meat.[18] But historians of poaching, trespass, body snatching, embezzlement, grain rioting, the taking of shipwrecked goods, rural incendiarism, animal maiming, and machine wrecking have argued convincingly that a significant proportion of certain crimes can be best understood as acts of open defiance and protest which expressed alternative notions of rights and justice.[19]

Evidence thus suggests that the industrial revolutions saw some shifts in criminal activity and a heightened perception of the criminal classes. The period also witnessed a marked change in the nature of punishments, which can again be seen as a response both to changes in the economy and in attitudes to individual rights. Despite the increase in formal statutes which carried the death penalty, the eighteenth century witnessed a decline in the numbers executed in favour of transportation and, later, imprisonment. This was not just the use of leniency as a tool of social control, as Hay suggests, but it corresponds with a decline in the old 'shaming' punishments such as the stocks or ducking stool, used to inflict humiliation on offenders. These had been more appropriate in face-to-face village communities, where people had personal knowledge of offenders, than they came to be in growing towns and cities. The idea of retributive punishment designed to fit the

[17] Hay *et al.*, *Albion's Fatal Tree*; Thompson, 'Patrician Society, Plebian Culture'; the notion of social crime is closely linked to Thompson's moral economy and to the communal support which Thompson and Hobsbawm identified in adding legitimacy to Luddism, arming and drilling: Thompson, 'Moral Economy'; E. J. Hobsbawm 'The Machine Breakers' in Hobsbawm, ed., *Labouring Men* (London, 1964).
[18] For discussion of the problems and pitfalls of applying the notion of social crime see Sharpe, *Crime in Early Modern England*, ch.6; J. G. Rule, 'Social Crime in the Rural South in the Eighteenth and Nineteenth Centuries', *Social History* 1 (1979); R. A. E. Wells, 'Sheep Rustling in Yorkshire in the Age of the Industrial and Agricultural Revolutions', *Northern History* xx (1984); G. Rudé, *Criminal and Victim: Crime and Society in Early-Nineteenth-Century England* (Oxford, 1985), esp. ch.5.
[19] Hay *et al.*, *Albion's Fatal Tree*; Thompson, 'Moral Economy'; Hobsbawm, 'Machine Breakers'; J. P. Dunbabin, *Rural Discontent in Nineteenth-Century Britain* (New York, 1974), esp. chs. 1–4; D. V. Jones, 'Thomas Campbell Foster and the Rural Labourer: Incendiarism in East Anglia in the 1840s', *Social History* (1976).

precise offence and to reflect its seriousness also declined. In their place, as Ignatieff in particular has argued, came the idea of reform through labour discipline: punishment of the body came to be replaced by reform of the mind. The force of evangelical notions of individual reform and redemption was significant in this change and was reflected in the emphasis placed on ·solitary confinement within the prison institution.[20] McGowan has argued that the decline of bodily punishments in the eighteenth century was a response to changing attitudes to the individual whereby the body became a locus of rights and autonomy, reflecting a new individualism. Furthermore, society came to see repair and correction of the person as its role rather than the infliction of pain or hanging because it was clear that the crowd learned nothing about interdependence or duty from witnessing torture or execution.[21]

Although the prison and debates about the relative merits of retribution and reform were not new to the eighteenth century, it was the late eighteenth and first half of the nineteenth century that saw major innovation in this area of punishment with the design and initial construction of a network of prisons and a marked shift in sentencing practices. Some social scientists suggest that there is a close connection between the rise of the prison and the industrial revolution: that prisons were geared to the inculcation of appropriate industrious habits and vocational training. Rusche and Kirchheimer argue that 'every system of production tends to discover punishments which correspond to its productive relationships', whilst others have highlighted the 'intimate link' between the coercive prison and the coercive labour economy and between the total institution of the factory or factory village, the workhouse and the prison.[22]

These interpretations are gross simplifications of a much more complex set of interrelationships between crime, punishment and the development of industrial capitalism. Prison reformers were never a unified group with a unified set of aims. However, offenders did become identified as individuals with disease-like afflictions which threatened society as a whole, not just their victims. And the creation of a law-and-order bureaucracy was the result: a 'policeman state' which reduced individual liberty in the interests of 'order'.[23] It does

[20] Ignatieff, *Just Measure of Pain;* Sharpe, *Crime in Early Modern England,* chs. 3, 4 and 8; M. Foucault, *Discipline and Punish: The Birth of the Prison* (London, 1977).
[21] R. McGowan, 'A Powerful Sympathy: Terror, the Prison, and Humanitarian Reform in Early-Nineteenth-Century Britain', *Journal of British Studies* 25 (1986); McGowan, 'The Body and Punishment in Eighteenth-Century England', *Journal of Modern History* 59 (1987).
[22] G. Rusche and O. Kircheimer, *Punishment and Social Structure* (New York, 1939), pp.5, 40; Ignatieff, *Just Measure of Pain;* Melossi and Paverini, *The Prison and the Factory: Origins of the Penitentiary System* (London, 1981).
[23] V. A. C. Gattrell, 'Crime, Authority and the Policeman State', in F. M. L. Thompson, ed., *Cambridge Social History of Britain 1750–1950* III (Cambridge, 1990).

appear, then, that changing aspects of crime and its perception, and of justice, were integrally related to demographic increase, urbanisation, proletarianisation, poverty and an ideology which placed stress on the need for disciplined and industrious workers. At the same time the notion of the dangerous classes and of the rough, intemperate, improvident, subversive and easily-led nature of the urban masses reflected and endorsed new class identities and divisions.

Factors in the formation of the working class

In addition to the notion of the dangerous classes, much of the literature of the last two decades has emphasised other factors which may have contributed to a widening gulf between different social classes in the period of the industrial revolution. Proletarianisation, landlessness, the relative decline of working-class living standards, the high prices, the deprivations and the legal restrictions of the war years all contributed to heightened tensions. And the urban experience of overcrowding, the concentration of cyclical unemployment in towns, the social segration of housing and the social differentials in disease and death rates all added to the ways in which working people could perceive their experiences and those of their fellow workers in class terms. The spread of working-class Methodism provided a pattern of local organisation, finance, oratory, and self-education which spilled over and gave strength to working-class protest movements in many industrial regions. And improvements in transport and communications promoted the possibility of nationally-organised associations and movements with greater political purchase.

The centralisation of work into larger units, whilst opening the door to greater exploitation and regimentation of labour, promoted the ability of workers to perceive their common interests and to organise against employers and others in their own defence. Technological change which dispensed with traditional skill hierarchies often created a greater homogeneity of interests and experience, as did unemployment caused by the obsolescence of skills. The further decline of paternalistic and regulatory legislation, particularly during the Napoleonic War years, was an overt source of contention in popular protest, as was the burden of taxation, and these were prominent in galvanising resistance to change and in giving resistance a legitimacy in the eyes of its participants.[24]

In the light of these powerful influences it is perhaps surprising that political and social instability in the period was relatively limited in scope and impact. Although there were insurrectionary movements of

---

[24] Most of these factors are those emphasised in Perkin, *Origins* and Thompson, *Making of the English Working Class*. See also E. J. Hobsbawm, 'Methodism and the Threat of Revolution in Britain', in *Labouring Men;* E. P. Thompson, 'Time, Work-discipline and Industrial Capitalism', *Past and Present* 38 (1967). For a text which highlights many of these homogenising influences see J. Rule, *The Labouring Classes in Early Industrial England 1750–1850* (London, 1986).

considerable size in certain localities during the war period Britain did not come close to revolution because many aspects of economic development served to fragment working-class identity and consciousness. Not least of these was the lack of homogeneity of experience of the working class regarding living standards, income-earning opportunities and work conditions. The specialisation of regions in either agriculture or particular industrial or service employments contributed to geographical variations in class identity and class consciousness and meant that the location of most radical parties was far removed geographically from the seat of state power in London. In addition, some skills were increasingly in demand whilst others became redundant, factory workers differed from outworkers, male workers faced wholly different circumstances to female workers, immigrants fared differently to indigenous workers and rural experiences constrasted with urban. Recent economic history has rightly emphasised the complexity of combined and uneven development: putting-out, workshops and sweating existed alongside and were complementary with a diverse factory sector and it is no longer possible to speak of a unilinear process of de-skilling and loss of workplace control.[25] Old hierarchies of labour were destroyed but new ones were erected. The diversity of organisational forms of industry, of work experience according to gender and ethnicity, the importance of composite and irregular incomes and of shifts of employment over the life cycle and through the seasons, meant that workers' perceptions of work and of an employing class were varied and contradictory. Nor can one speak of a homogenous group of industrial employers. There was a huge difference between the attitude and outlook of small workshop masters and factory employers. Even within these groups there were variations of response to competitive conditions ranging from exploitation to paternalism with many mixtures of the two and workers and employers often met on what has been termed a 'terrain of compromise'. There was, furthermore, a wide range of intermediaries from agents down to foremen and leaders of family work groups to deflect opposition and tension in the workplace.[26]

[25] See discussions and references in chs.1, 2, 4 and 5; R. Price, *Masters, Unions and Men: Work Control in Building and the Rise of Labour 1830–1914* (Cambridge, 1980); R. Samuel, 'The Workshop of the World: Steam Power and Hand Technology in Mid Victorian Britain', *History Workshop Journal* 3 (1977); C. Sabel and J. Zeitlin, 'Historical Alternatives to Mass Production', *Past and Present* 108 (1985). W. Lazonick, 'Industrial Relations and Technical Change: The Case of the Self-Acting Mule', *Cambridge Journal of Economics* 3 (1979). For a useful discussion of a range of literature on this and other issues concerning the history of work see P. Joyce, 'Work', in F. M. L. Thompson, ed., *The Cambridge Social History of Britain 1750–1950* ii.
[26] B. Elbaum, W. Lazonick, W. Wilkinson, J. Zeitlin, 'Labour Process, Market Structure and Marxist Theory', *Cambridge Journal of Economics* 3 (1979), p.229. See also P. Joyce, 'Labour, Capital and Compromise: A Response to Richard Price', *Social*

Class and Gender   213

Religious and ethnic differences also fragmented potential working-class solidarity. Methodism had its fatalistic and loyalist aspects. Thompson argues that religious evangelicalism was the 'chiliasm of despair' which deflected working-class energies away from political opposition to change.[27] Religion also created political divisions within social classes: conflict occurred between Catholic and Church of England, between old and new dissent, between observance and irreligion. And religious difference was given a cutting edge where Anglo-Irish antagonism was concerned, as Marx noted in the 1860s:

Every industrial and commercial centre in England now possesses a working class divided into two hostile camps, the English proletarians and the Irish proletarians. The ordinary English worker hates the Irish worker as a competitor who lowers his standards of life. In relation to the Irish worker he feels himself a member of the ruling nation and so turns himself into a tool of the aristocrats and capitalists of his country against Ireland, thus strengthening their domination over himself. He cherishes religious, social and national prejudices against the Irish worker. ... The Irishman pays him back with interest in his own money. He sees the English worker at once the accomplice and the stupid tool of the English domination of Ireland.[28]

Ideological differences also abounded regardless of religious persuasions and ethnic difference. Some justified opposition to change in terms of a past golden age of the free-born Englishman. Other leaders

---

History 9 (1984); Joyce, 'Languages of Reciprocity, and Conflict: A Further Response to Richard Price', *Social History* 9 (1984); M. Burawoy, *The Politics of Production: Factory Regimes under Capitalism and Socialism* (London, 1985); R. Harrison and J. Zeitlin, eds., *Divisions of Labour: Skilled Workers and Technological Change in Nineteenth-Century England* (Brighton, 1985). See also A. Briggs, ed., *Chartist Studies* (London, 1959) and cf. C. Behagg, 'Myths of Cohesion: Capital and Compromise in the Histography of Nineteenth-Century Birmingham', *Social History* 11 (1986); P. Joyce, 'Work' *passim*.
[27] Thompson, *Making of the English Working Class*, ch.11.
[28] K. Marx to S. Meyer and A. Vogt, 9 April 1870, quoted in D. Caute, ed., *Essential Writings of Karl Marx* (New York, 1967), p.199. See Foster, *Class Struggle*, ch.7; A. D. Gilbert, *Religion and Society in Industrial England: Church, Chapel and Social Change 1740-1914* (London, 1976); H. McLeod, *Religion and the Working Class in Nineteenth-Century Britain* (Cambridge, 1980); J. Stevenson, *Popular Disturbances in England 1700-1870* (London, 1979); E. H. Hunt, *British Labour History 1815-1914* (London, 1981); D. Thompson, 'Ireland and the Irish in English Radicalism before 1850', in J. Epstein and D. Thompson, eds., *The Chartist Experience* (London, 1982); S. Gilley, 'English Attitudes to the Irish in England 1780-1900', in Colin Holmes, ed., *Immigrants and Minorities in British Society* (London, 1978).

and movements were working out new ideas about the origins of conflict in society and about the need for a co-operative or communistic future. There was also a strong strain of working-class loyalism and royalism throughout the period which reached a peak in the 1790s in some of the most violent riots of the eighteenth century. Improvements in communications and the spread of literacy did not just promote political radicalism and opposition: they also facilitated popular receptivity to State propaganda and nationalistic consciousness. Expansion overseas, empire-building, the power of the English fleet and national reaction to the American and the French Revolutions were important factors in galvanising nationalism, promoted by the State's use of ceremony and spectacle to focus royalist and nationalist sentiment.[29]

Legislation and policing were also effective in stemming mass opposition to economic and social change. The suspension of Habeas Corpus, the Combination Acts and the Six Acts during the War years restricted overt radical activity, whilst government spies and *agents provocateurs* infiltrated most working-class movements instigating activities which isolated leaders and led to their arrest. Although trade unions were illegal during the War years many continued to operate: some because employers preferred to deal with a unified body of workers, others because the unions went underground and flourished in alliance with political radicalism. Friendly societies multiplied and, although their function was one of self-help and mutual insurance, their membership often overlapped with illegal union and political bodies. But the activities of insurrectionary armies, of machine-wreckers, and of illegal trade unionists were closely circumscribed by the operations of local and regional militia, by the stationing of central government troops in the industrial areas and, later, by the activities of the new police force. The atmosphere of these times was symbolised in the use of crenellated and defensive architecture in factory building.[30]

Arguably more important than overt forms of control were more subtle manifestations of social control, such as the use of housing tied to employment, the promotion of temperance, religious observance and education, the founding of Sunday schools and the teaching of the 'laws of economics' and of the need for political passivity coupled with self-help. For a time in the 1970s stress was placed on these forms of social control imposed by the middle class on the mass of the

[29] L. Colley, 'The Apotheosis of George III: Loyalty, Royalty and the English Crowd', *Past and Present* 102 (1984); Colley, 'Whose Nation? Class and National Consciousness in Britain 1750–1830', *Past and Present* 113 (1986).

[30] Thompson, *Making of the English Working Class;* Stevenson, *Popular Disturbances;* Jones, *Crime, Protest, Community;* C. Elmsley, *British Society and the French Wars 1793–1815* (Totowa, N.J., 1979); F. C. Mather, *Public Order in the Age of the Chartists* (Manchester, 1959); R. D. Storch, 'The Plague of Blue Locusts: Police Reform and Popular Disturbance in Northern England 1840–1867', *International Review of Social History* xx (1975).

population in explaining the relative political stability of the mid nineteenth century in particular. The idea that a more skilled, better-paid and more regularly employed labour aristocracy played a crucial role in the spread and acceptance of bourgeois ideology became fashionable. However, this 'labour aristocracy thesis' seriously under-plays the very incomplete and selective take up of bourgeois ideals on the part of both the labour aristocracy and the masses and the independent growth of self-help and self-improvement initiatives within the working classes themselves. The notion of social control is of only limited use in understanding the extent of popular oppositional politics and the growth of working-class reformism in the nineteenth century. And of course it is an explanation dependent on the supposition that there was a natural tendency for the working class to unite against the innovations of industrial capitalism rather than to be fragmented by them.[31]

The industrial revolution without class?

Despite the fragmentation of working-class experience, legal restric-tions and social control, the consensus of the literature until very recently was that the industrial revolution involved political radicalism on a new scale and with a new class emphasis. Mass movements of the working class protested vigorously about the corruption and vices of the old political order and about innovations in technology and in the organisation of production and distribution that undermined long-established social and communal relationships and an older moral

[31] A. Reid has argued that the latter was the case, thus the containment of the working class does not require special explanations: 'Politics and Economics in the Formation of the British Working Class: A Response to H. F. Moorehouse', *Social History* 3 (1978). For discussion of the contributions of Reid, Moorehouse and others to this debate see Joyce, 'Work'. On social control see the essays in A. P. Donazgrodski, ed., *Social Control in Nineteenth-Century Britain* (London, 1979). For critiques of the social control thesis see F. M. L. Thompson, 'Social Control in Victorian England', *Economic History Review* xxxiv (1981); G. Stedman Jones, 'Class Expression versus Social Control? A Critique of Recent Trends in the Social History of Leisure', *History Workshop Journal* 4 (1977). For a useful discussion of leisure and the control of leisure see H. Cunningham, 'Leisure and Culture', in Thompson, ed., *People and Environment;* P. Bailey, *Leisure and Class in Victorian England: Rational Recreation and the Contest for Control* (London, 1978). On labour aristocracy theories see E. J. Hobsbawm, 'The Labour Aristocracy in Nineteenth-Century Britain' in *Labouring Men* (stressing economic distinctions); Foster, *Class Struggle* (stressing the role of labour aristocrats in positions of authority at work); R. Q. Gray, *The Aristocracy of Labour in Nineteenth-Century Britain c.1850–1900* (London, 1981) and G. Crossick, *An Artisan Elite in Victorian Society: Kentish London 1840–80* (London, 1980), who both stress the role of the labour aristocracy in creating and maintaining ideological hegemony. See also, H. F. Moorehouse, 'The Marxist Theory of the Labour Aristocracy', *Social History* 3 (1978). For a text on mid-Victorian respectability and stability see F. M. L. Thompson, *The Rise of Respectable Society* (London, 1988). On independence and self-respect from within the working class see T. Tholfsen, *Working-Class Radicalism in Mid-Victorian England* (New York, 1976). For a survey of many of these debates see N. Kirk, *The Growth of Working-Class Reformism* (London, 1985).

order. But recent work has played down the extent to which popular politics of the period mark the emergence of new sorts of class formations, allegiances and ideals.[32] Thompson's work has been rightly questioned for its concentration upon male artisans and their institutions and its neglect of the rather different ideologies and reactions of the unskilled, the poor and of women. Other work has provided a necessary and important antidote to the earlier romanticised views of heroic and unified working-class opposition to economic change. The motives of grain rioters, particularly in proto-industrial areas dependent on the inter-regional grain trade, has, for example, been the subject of intense debate.[33] Traditional communities of both craft and locality have been suggested as more vital social foundations of popular radicalism during the industrial revolution than was class.[34] A complete shift in perspective is in train, to a point where class development and class consciousness during the industrial revolution is ceasing to be recognised.

This shift is partly a reflection of unquestioning acceptance of the new gradualist view of the economic history of the period which, I have argued, severely underplays the extent of radical economic change and of developments in the economy affecting the mass of the population in similar ways. In addition, recent work in a post-Marxian mould is much more sceptical than writing of the 1960s and 1970s about any suggestion of a deterministic relationship between socio-economic position and political consciousness. In the reaction against historical materialism the need to relate social and political development directly or even indirectly to shifts in the structure and functioning of the economy is no longer a dominant concern. In fact it has been succeeded by such a fear of economic reductionism that it is seldom now countenanced. Post-structuralist work on language and discourse has further added to the ways in which historians now view the roots of

[32] Joyce 'Work' is the best recent analysis of this shifting emphasis. See in particular, G. Stedman Jones, 'The Language of Chartism' in Epstein and Thompson, *The Experience of Chartism;* P. Joyce, *Work, Society and Politics: The Culture of the Factory in Later Victorian England* (Brighton, 1980); C. Calhoun, *The Question of Class Struggle: Social Foundations of Popular Radicalism During the Industrial Revolution* (Chicago, 1982); R. Glen, *Urban Workers in the Early Industrial Revolution* (London, 1983); W. M. Reddy, *Money and Liberty in Early Modern Europe: A Critique of Historical Understanding* (Cambridge, 1987).

[33] D. E. Williams, 'Morals, Markets and the English Crowd in 1766', *Past and Present* 104 (1985); A. Charlesworth and A. J. Randall, 'Comment', *Past and Present* 114 (1987). For constructive but searching criticisms of Thompson see Kaye and McClelland, eds., *E. P. Thompson: Critical Perspectives*. See also, J. W. Scott, 'Women in the Making of the English Working Class', in Scott, ed., *Gender and the Politics of History* (New York, 1988).

[34] Calhoun, *Question of Class Struggle;* J. Bohstedt, *Riots and Community Politics in England and Wales 1790–1810* (Cambridge, Mass., 1983). For earlier work on the force of communal cultures, practices and loyalties see I. Prothero, *Artisans and Politics in Early-Nineteenth-Century London* (Folkestone, 1979) and B. Bushaway, *By Rite: Custom, Ceremony and Community in England 1700–1880* (London, 1982).

social consciousness, recognising the limits set by long-enduring linguistic structures and the knowledge systems associated with them.[35]

Despite the significance of these new approaches they should not be allowed to edge out all idea that the industrial revolution witnessed radical shifts in social relations and in social consciousness. Balanced analyses of the combined and uneven nature of development within industrial capitalism and of the complex interplay between customary and market relationships (rather than any simple notion of the latter replacing the former), should not obscure the fact that the industrial world of the 1830s and 1840s was vastly different for most workers than it had been in the 1760s. There were more large workplaces, more powered machines and along with these there was more direct managerial involvement in the organisation and planning of work. A stronger notion of the separation of work and non-work time was evolving, partly out of the decline of family work units and of production in the home. Proletarianisation had accelerated and the life chances of a much larger proportion of the population were determined by the market and aggravated by urban mortality and disease. Economic insecurity led to conflicts and to new accommodations between workers and employers based both on coercion and necessity. Long-maintained traditional skills were made redundant and with their passing went long-established communal identities embedded in the cultures of work. Capitalist wage labour and the working class may have developed irregularly and incompletely but they did so with greater speed than in earlier centuries. And regional concentration of similarities of experience of work and of the trade cycle helped to produce social protest and conflict on an unprecedented scale.[36]

Furthermore, popular radicalism did embody different sorts of anti-capitalist critiques in a way not seen before the later eighteenth century. The 'machinery question' was important in crowd action in manufacturing areas before and during the Luddite period, and the notion of legitimacy of opposition based on an alternative moral economy is central to a large spectrum of riot action.[37] In addition,

[35] Joyce, 'Work'. For post-structuralist approaches see Stedman Jones, 'Language of Chartism'; Scott, *Gender and the Politics of History*. For the extreme reaction against Marxist scholarship on this period see J. C. D. Clark, *English Society 1688–1832: Ideology, Social Structure and Political Practice During the Ancien Regime* (Cambridge, 1985); Clark, *Revolution and Rebellion: State and Society in England in the Seventeenth and Eighteenth Centuries* (Cambridge, 1986).

[36] See earlier chapters, esp. 2, 4, 5.

[37] A. J. Randall, *Before the Luddites: Custom, Community and Machinery in the English Woollen Industry* (Cambridge, 1991); Randall, 'The Philosophy of Luddism: The Case of the West of England Woollen Workers', *Technology and Culture* 27 (1983); Thompson, 'Moral Economy'; Hay *et al.*, *Albion's Fatal Tree*; D. J. V. Jones, *Before Rebecca: Popular Protests in Wales 1793–1835* (London, 1973); G. Rudé, *The Crowd in History: A Study of Popular Disturbances in France and England 1730–1848* (New York, 1964).

Stedman Jones's recent and influential view of Chartism as fundamentally a constitutional and not a class movement is undermined by examination of writing and oratory, particularly in the textile districts. Stedman Jones suggests that popular opposition was not directed at the economic system as such but at its abuses which had their origins in a political system that gave too much power to unproductive landowners.[38] But a wider reading of Chartist literature suggests that antagonism over new and changing productive relationships was a fundamental pillar of the movement. In the eyes of Chartists, the growth of industrial capitalism signified 'not freedom, independence and equality in the market place, so beloved of orthodox political economy, but "wage-slavery", dependence, structured inequality between worker and employer, and general misery.'[39]

Finally, whilst the factory never dominated production or employment nationally it did so sufficiently in certain regions to create widespread identities of interest and political cohesion. And where it did not exist it exercised enormous influence not only in spawning dispersed production, sub-contracting and sweating, but also as a major feature of the imagery of the age. The factory and the machine as hallmarks of the period may have been myth but they were symbolic of so many other changes attendant on the emergence of a more competitive market environment and the greater disciplining and alienation of labour. Household and workshop production, wholesaling, retailing, external trade and agricultural activities were all affected by radical change in values, practices and expectations. The factory as a symbol of these changes provided a focus of protest and was a powerful element in the formation of social consciousness and social class.

Capitalist class or classes?

Just as the growth of working-class consciousness has long been integral to popular understanding of what was new in the industrial revolution so also has the idea that the period can be identified with the rise to economic power and political and cultural hegemony of the industrial bourgeoisie. However, recently there has been renewed debate about the nature of the capitalist class and of dominant interests in Britain since the early nineteenth century. A new orthodoxy is emerging around the idea that the industrial revolution was incomplete because the industrial middle class failed to gain the

[38] Stedman Jones, 'Language of Chartism'.
[39] N. Kirk, 'In Defence of Class: A Critique of Recent Revisionist Writing upon the Nineteenth-Century English Working Class', *International Review of Social History* XXXII (1987), p. 20. For other critiques of Stedman Jones on Chartism see R. Gray, 'The Deconstructing of the English Working Class', *Social History* XI (1986); J. Foster, 'The Declassing of Language', *New Left Review* 150 (1985); P. A. Pickering, 'Class without Words: Symbolic Communications in the Chartist Movement', *Past and Present* 112 (1986).

ascendancy economically, politically, and culturally and it thus never came to determine state policy in ways favourable to industrial capitalism. The higher status attached to non-industrial forms of wealth, together with common cultural interests and geographical concentration in the south and east, combined to make the landed and financial élite the decisive and self-serving influence over government and policy-making. Gentlemanly capitalism prevailed, causing long-term problems for British manufacturing industry and a bias in the economy and in state policy in favour of *rentier* interests.[40]

The origins of the gentlemanly capitalism thesis can be found in the 1960s in debates on the Left, primarily between Anderson and Thompson, with each trying to explain the peculiarities of English development and the origins of twentieth-century economic problems. Anderson argued that the 'premature' seventeenth-century revolution and the compromises of 1688 and 1832 left political power in the hands of a landed élite which had an anti-bourgeois culture. This not only explained the relatively poor performance of British industry from the later nineteenth century but also inhibited the development of working-class antagonism to capitalist productive relations: these relations were more difficult to perceive in a society where the industrialist class had failed to gain power.[41] Thompson also placed emphasis on the power of the landed aristocracy and the gentry in understanding English history but argued that there was a convergence between the commercially-minded landed aristocracy and the larger capitalist manufacturers and merchants. Through the merging of their capitals, through intermarriage, through drawing together in face of the threat to property posed by the French Revolutionary and Napoleonic Wars, and through enfranchisement these two classes became one: the dominant capitalist class. The Reform Bill of 1832 was the great betrayal of what had been seen as a common struggle by the unenfranchised middle class and the working classes alike. The Whig measures that followed – Irish coercion, rejection of the Ten Hours Bill, attacks on trade unions, the Municipal Corporations Act and the New Poor Law – were seen as the treachery of the middle class. This left the working class isolated in pursuit of its interests and

---

[40] P. Anderson, 'Figures of Descent', *New Left Review* 161 (1987); M. J. Weiner, *English Culture and the Decline of the Industrial Spirit* (Cambridge, 1981); G. Ingham, *Capitalism Divided: The City and Industry in British Social Development* (Basingstoke, 1984). For useful reviews and critiques of the literature on this subject see M. J. Daunton, ' "Gentlemanly Capitalism" and British Industry 1820–1914', *Past and Present* 122 (1989) and C. Barker and D. Nicholls, *The Development of British Capitalist Society* (Manchester, 1989).

[41] P. Anderson, 'Origins of the Present Crisis', *New Left Review* 23 (1964); E. P. Thompson, 'The Peculiarities of the English', *The Socialist Register* (1965), reprinted in Thompson, ed., *Poverty of Theory*. See also T. Nairn, 'The British Political Elite', *New Left Review* 23 (1964).

220   The Industrial Revolution

conscious that these interests required united opposition to the governing élite.[42]

Much of the difference of opinion between Thompson and Anderson hinged on the question of whether the landed aristocracy and industrial capitalists were different interest groups within the same broad capitalist class or whether they were distinct social classes. Whereas Anderson suggested that aristocratic culture was profoundly antithetical to bourgeois values and aspirations, Thompson stressed the development of the landed aristocracy as a highly successful capitalist class by the late eighteenth century. The landed interest, he argued, gave rise to the market ideal:

> Laissez-faire emerged not as the ideology of some manufacturing lobby, not as an intellectual yarn turned out by the cotton mills but in the great agricultural corn belt … and it was this ideology which formed the bridge during the Napoleonic Wars [between] the interests of cotton and land; the first administrations imbued with … laissez-faire were not post-1832 but those of Pitt, Perceval and Lord Liverpool.[43]

Thompson objected to Anderson's view that the courage of the industrial bourgeoisie had somehow gone after 1832 when the bulk were left unincorporated and unenfranchised:

> what need did … they have to take up arms against primogeniture when, with increasing rapidity, land was becoming only one interest beside cotton, railways, iron and steel, coal, shipping and finance?[44]

After 1790 manufacturers took their place on the bench; coal and class brought them together with the landed interest as did commissions in the volunteers, common service against Luddism, common resentment against income tax. In local government, especially in towns under the influence of the 1835 Municipal Corporations Act, aristocratic influence was largely displaced. Boards of Guardians, the magistracy and the police came under the control of the industrial middle class.[45] At national level, the evidence of middle-class power is more ambiguous as aristocratic influence was apparent in the City and in Oxbridge, though not in London or provincial universities, in the armed forces but not in the press or the media. Thompson argues that

42 Thompson, 'Peculiarities'; Thompson, *Making of the English Working Class*.
43 Thompson, 'Peculiarities', p.44.
44 Thompson, 'Peculiarities', p.51.
45 J. Saville, 'Some Notes on Perry Anderson's "Figures of Descent"', in Barker and Nicholls, *British Capitalist Society;* A. Briggs, *Victorian Cities;* R. Trainor, 'Urban Elites in Victorian Britain', *Urban History Yearbook* (1985); D. Cannadine, ed., *Patricians, Power and Politics in Nineteenth-Century Towns* (Leicester, 1982).

aristocratic power did remain strong but the politicians who are remembered most are Peel, Bright, Gladstone, Disraeli, the Chamberlains, Lloyd George, and Baldwin not Lord Derby, Lord Salisbury or Lord Palmerston. In support of his position Thompson quotes Walter Bagehot's analysis of late-nineteenth-century government in England (published in 1867) which identified the monarchy and aristocratic institutions as the 'dignified' part of the constitution, which deflected attention from the real operation of power in the 'efficient' part (which was where middle-class influence held sway). The theatrical show of the dignified part held the masses in awe and was a major factor in political stability.[46]

Weiner has more recently popularised Anderson's ideas by arguing that industrial entrepreneurship in Britain from the later nineteenth century was dogged by 'entrenched pre-modern elements'.[47] Businessmen sent their sons to public schools, prepared them for the professions and a gentlemanly lifestyle rather than running industry, and themselves aspired to the more socially acceptable life of a landowner. Rubinstein and the Stones added further weight to the notion of the enduring power of the landed interests by suggesting that the aristocracy formed a caste which, although aspired to, was very difficult to enter.[48] Rubinstein's work on probate inventories suggested that only a minority of new men of wealth in the nineteenth century became landowners and only the fortunes left by the commercial and financial classes of the City came near to rivalling the estates of landed families. Thus the success of the aristocracy in maintaining cultural and political hegemony was, at least up to 1880, he argues, based upon its stability and economic power rather than its capacity to absorb new wealth. Neither was there a delegation of political power to the aristocracy by the bourgeoisie. The latter remained junior partners, their strength sapped by the marked divisions of interest and wealth-holding between London merchants and bankers on the one hand and the very varied class of provincial industrialists on the other.[49]

By the late 1980s the notion of 'gentlemanly capitalism' was widely accepted as a means of understanding several centuries of English development, as well as the fate of industry in the twentieth century. Analyses of shifts in external trade policy and in imperial development (discussed in chapter 6), together with work on the influence over government of the City, the Treasury and the Bank of England, added

---

[46] Thompson, 'Peculiarities', pp.53–4.
[47] Weiner, *English Culture.*
[48] W. D. Rubinstein, *Elites and the Wealthy in Modern British History: Essays in Social and Economic History* (Brighton, 1987), esp. essay on 'New Men of Wealth and the Purchase of Land in Nineteenth-Century England', first published in *Past and Present* 92 (1981); L. & J. F. C. Stone, *An Open Elite? England 1540–1880* (Oxford, 1984).
[49] Rubinstein, *ibid.*

new dimensions to the thesis.[50] Anderson, influenced by the findings of these later studies, revised his earlier interpretation by suggesting that the landed aristocracy was not moribund but a thrusting capitalist class. However, he argued, after 1880 'when agrarian property lost its weight, it was not industry but finance which became the hegemonic form of capital'. Landed incomes started to fall in the face of food imports and landowners increasingly turned to City investments to cushion their fortunes. Thus landed magnates and financiers came together in an 'increasingly integrated plutocracy' from which industrialists were excluded. Aspirations to gentility were perfectly compatible with finance and commerce: they involved contact only with one's own social class, did not involve the control of a large workforce, and · were carried on in fashionable areas of the metropolitan south and east.[51]

Gentlemanly capitalism and the industrial revolution

The notion of gentlemanly capitalism as variously espoused by Anderson, Weiner and others adds weight to the idea of the industrial revolution being much less of a watershed in historical development than earlier historians (and contemporaries) thought. Not only was it not accompanied by a significant change in the nature of the dominant economic and political élite but even overseas expansion in the nineteenth century, it is argued, can no longer be seen primarily as a reflection of industrial capitalism's search for raw materials and markets.[52] Is this new orthodoxy of a dominant gentlemanly capitalism and a subordinated industrial capitalism really justified? Much criticism has been levelled at the empirical work of both Rubinstein and of the Stones, whose evidence has been used to underpin certain aspects of the thesis. Rubinstein's study of wealth distribution based on probate inventories is likely to have seriously underestimated the status of industrialists, partly because real property (including investment in fixed plant) was not included in the inventories. His use of evidence of landownership is also likely to have underplayed the openness of the landed class at its lower end (because he deals only

50 P. J. Cain and A. G. Hopkins, 'Gentlemanly Capitalism and British Overseas Expansion: i) The Old Colonial System', *Economic History Review* XXXIX (1986) and ii) 'New Imperialism 1850–1945' XL (1987); Ingham, *Capitalism Divided;* C. Leys, 'The Formation of British Capital', *New Left Review* 160, (1986); E. H. H. Green, 'The Political Economy of the Bimetallic Controversy', *English Historical Review* CIII (1988); Y. Cassis, 'Bankers and English Society in the Late Nineteenth Century', *Economic History Review* XXXVIII (1985); C. Jones, *International Business in the Nineteenth Century: The Rise and Fall of a Cosmopolitan Bourgeoisie* (Brighton, 1987).
51 Anderson, 'Figures'. Also from the 1880s there is some evidence that the landed élite became more open to entry from City financiers and merchant bankers: Rubenstein, 'New Men of Wealth'.
52 Cain and Hopkins, 'Gentlemanly Capitalism'. For a critique of this see M. Barratt Brown, 'Away With All The Great Arches: Anderson's History of British Capitalism', *New Left Review* 167 (1988).

with large estates of a minimum 2,000 acres) and the Stone's notion of a closed landed élite has been seriously questioned by recent empirical work.[53]

More importantly, as Daunton and Nicholls have recently stressed, wealth in itself is no key to identifying the hegemonic fraction of the ruling class.[54] Assimilation was not a one-way process: the culture and outlook of the aristocracy may have changed as much if not more than that of the middle class. Recent work by Mandler and Jupp illustrates the importance of adaptation in the philosophy and the policies of the aristocratic élite with respect to both local and national politics and in line with their varied economic interests. Furthermore, in the capitalist class of the nineteenth century the interests as well as the fortunes of landed, commercial, financial, and industrial groups appear to have been inextricably mixed and all were concerned with what Ruskin identified as 'the first of all the English games ... making money'.[55] Also, much overseas investment was direct active investment in productive enterprise and in securing raw-material supplies, not passive *rentier* 'coupon-clipping'. Thus the motivation and nature of *rentier* investment cannot so easily be separated from industrial investment. 'The needs of northern industrialists for materials and markets was part of the City not something alien',[56] and overseas loans were intimately connected with the export of capital goods. Nicholls has argued that banking and commercial capital were dependent on productive capital and that the dominant power block was made up of shifting fractional alliances of City and industrial interests.[57] Certainly, City interests were not homogenous or cohesive. Constant shifts in commodity trade and in the location of overseas investment activity made for disparate interests, a high rate of entry and exit, and the absence of a united 'City view' on many issues of government policy in the late nineteenth century. Neither was this on the whole a gentlemanly or leisured élite. In fact, many metropolitan merchants and financiers were wedded to hard work and repudiated 'aristocratic values'.[58]

[53] Daunton, 'Gentlemanly Capitalism', pp.128-30.
[54] Daunton, 'Gentlemanly Capitalism', p.131, quoting D. Nicholls, 'Fractions of Capital: The Aristocracy, the City and Industry in the Development of Modern British Capitalism', *Social History* XIII (1988), p.72.
[55] Ruskin, 'Work', 1865, quoted by Cain and Hopkins, 'Gentlemanly Capitalism', p.501; P. Mandler, 'The Making of the New Poor Law *Redivivus*', *Past and Present* 127 (1990); P. J. Jupp, 'The Landed Élite and Political Authority in Britain c. 1760–1850', *Journal of British Studies* 29 (1990).
[56] Daunton, 'Gentlemanly Capitalism', p.138.
[57] Daunton, 'Gentlemanly Capitalism', pp.133–42; Nicholls, 'Fractions of Capital'; Barratt Brown, 'Away With All the Great Arches'.
[58] Daunton, 'Gentlemanly Capitalism', p.147; S. D. Chapman, 'Aristocracy and Meritocracy in Merchant Banking', *British Journal of Sociology* XXXVII (1986).

In addition, it has been argued that the notion of the gentleman changed in the nineteenth century along with a shift in the idea of character and of the state. The politics of Gladstone can be interpreted as a rejection of the ethics of politeness and sociability in favour of the advancement of character and the nation by hard work and voluntarism: 'the value system was remade between 1832 and 1867, and the outcome was much closer to the views of the business élite than to the traditional standards of the aristocracy.'[59] Emphasis on the self-regulatory privatised state was as marked in the City as it was in the provincial industrial regions.

The gentlemanly capitalism thesis has provided some insights into the nature of British capitalism and has created a valuable debate where socio-economic and political change are seen as integrated developments. However, the notion of an early leader's handicap probably explains more about the inflexibility of the manufacturing base and the financial and trading preferences of the early-twentieth-century economy than does the notion of gentlemanly capitalism.[60] After all, 'the century of the Great Exhibition, of Smiles's heroic engineers, of Dickens's faith in progress, ... of Arnold's visions of the future, produced abundant images and arguments sympathetic to industrial expansion'.[61] And the industrial provinces of the nineteenth century were everywhere dominated by the industrial and commercial middle class in government, philanthropy, patronage of the arts, and in social and cultural life more generally.[62] English industrial capitalism may have had some peculiarities but anti-industrial it was not. It is in fact impossible to sustain the idea that there is a 'normal' route or pattern in industrialisation against which England or Britain can be judged:

> Just as while there may be any number of permutations of breeds of dogs and of mongrel cross breeds, all dogs are doggy (they smell, bark, fawn on humans), so all capitalisms remain capitalist

[59] Daunton, 'Gentlemanly Capitalism', p.132; S. Collini, 'The Idea of Character in Victorian Political Thought', *Transactions of the Royal Historical Society* xxxv (1985).
[60] See B. Elbaum and W. Lazonick, eds., *The Decline of the British Economy* (Oxford, 1986). The persistence of landed and aristocratic power and cultural prestige (albeit in rather different forms) are much too general phenomena throughout Europe before 1914 to provide a full explanation of British economic performance: A. J. Mayer, *The Persistence of the Old Regime: Europe to the Great War* (London, 1981).
[61] J. Raven, 'British History and the Enterprise Culture', *Past and Present* 123 (1989).
[62] J. Wolff and J. Seed, eds., *The Culture of Capital: Art, Power and the Nineteenth-Century Middle Class* (Manchester, 1988), esp. S. Gunn, 'The Failure of the Victorian middle-class, a critique'; R. J. Morris, 'The Middle Class and British Towns and Cities of the Industrial Revolution', in D. Fraser and A. Sutcliffe, eds., *The Pursuit of Urban History* (London, 1983); A. J. Kidd and K. W. Roberts, eds., *City, Class and Culture* (Manchester, 1985).

(foster acquisitive values, must by their nature leech the proletariat) etc. The transformation from one species to another is
what we mean by revolution.[63]

If the notion of transformation to an industrial capitalist order is
sufficiently flexible to include overseas expansion and the development of *rentier* interests alongside and intimately tied to a revolutionising manufacturing and service economy, the idea of the industrial
revolution as a major historical discontinuity, in which the culture of
all social classes was changed, can be appreciated.

Within social classes women's lives were changing and the relationships between men and women were also experiencing renegotiation,
a fact missing entirely from much class analysis but of central
importance to our understanding of cultural norms and ideals and of
class allegiances, identities and actions.

Women and the industrial revolution

It has been argued that first proto-industry and then the industrial
revolution itself, by expanding the opportunities for female employment and income earning, helped to transform the relationship
between men and women within the family and in wider society. Both
the status and the independence of women increased, marriage
became a partnership based on affective individualism and the force of
patriarchy declined particularly with the breakdown of the family work
unit and with the greater involvement of women in waged work outside
the home. The expansion of female employment is argued to have
brought greater parity between partners in emotional and sexual life as
well as in decision-making regarding housework, production in the
household and consumption.[64] Shorter, for example, argues that the
individualism of the market place became transferred to community
obligations and behaviour and to family power structures and sex roles
with liberating effects on women.[65] And Pinchbeck, though carefully
documenting the low wages, long hours and changing employment
options of women during the industrial revolution, argues that women
benefited in the longer term because industrialisation led to the
assumption that men's wages should be paid on a family basis and
prepared the way for 'the modern conception that in the rearing of

63 Thompson, 'Peculiarities', pp.81–2.
64 For key examples of this optimistic interpretation see Shorter, *Making of the Modern
Family passim;* L. Stone, *The Family, Sex and Marriage in Britain* (Harmondsworth,
1979); M. Young and P. Wilmott, *The Symmetrical Family* (London, 1973). On the
effects of proto-industry and proletarianisation see Medick, 'Proto-industrial Family
Economy'; John Gillis, 'Peasant, Plebeian and Proletarian Marriage in Britain 1600–
1900', in D. Levine, ed., *Proletarianisation and Family History* (Orlando, Fla., 1984).
65 Shorter, *Making of the Modern Family*, p.253.

children and in home-making, the married woman makes an adequate contribution'.[66]

These optimistic views of the impact of the industrial revolution on women's lives contrast sharply with that of Alice Clark who wrote of the adverse effect on women of the decline of the family as a unit of production from the seventeenth century onwards. The decline of family and domestic industry shattered the interdependent relationship between husband and wife. The substitution of an individual for a family wage, the withdrawal of wage-earners from home life and the increase in wealth which permitted women of the upper classes to withdraw from involvement in business were all stressed by Clark as features of the seventeenth century that disadvantaged women. More recent research on proto-industry and its decline and on middle-class business has identified the industrial revolution period as witnessing a greater acceleration in these trends.[67]

A different sort of pessimistic perspective is expressed in Marxist feminist ideas, in which the oppression of women is seen as functionally necessary for the operation of industrial capitalism. It is argued that the free labour of women in the household provides capital with greater profit: male wages can be low because the services provided by women (such as cooking, cleaning, laundry and sex) do not have to be bought in the market. In addition, women, being partly supported by the wage of the male breadwinner, provide a cheap and flexible supply of labour which can be utilised in times of boom or technological restructuring and then dropped again as the economy resettles. Finally, it is argued that women have become the major force in consumption decisions within the household and form the pillar of demand upon which capitalism depends. Thus advancing capitalism utilised and gained strength from the pre-existing subordination of women and this subordination then became a necessary element in the continued operation of the mode of production.[68]

Women and the industrial revolution: an assessment

To what extent and in what ways did changes in the economy affect perceptions of gender and the social relations between men and

---

[66] Pinchbeck, *Women Workers*, p.313.

[67] Clark, *Working Life*, p.296; L. Davidoff and C. Hall, *Family Fortunes: Men and Women of the English Middle Classes* (London, 1987). The separation of home and of family life from work was of course protracted and partial even in the nineteenth century and beyond: Berg, 'Women's Work, Mechanisation and the Early Phase of Industrialisation in England', in P. Joyce, ed., *The Historical Meanings of Work (Cambridge, 1987)*; P. Hudson and W. R. Lee, eds., *Women's Work and the Family Economy in Historical Perspective* (Manchester, 1990), chs. 1, 2, 4, 7, 11.

[68] See for example M. Barrett, *Women's Oppression Today* (London, 1980). For discussion of this and other perspectives on the changing status of women with the development of capitalism see J. Thomas, 'Women and Capitalism: Oppression or Emancipation? A Review Article', *Comparative Studies in Society and History* 30 (1988), pp.534–49.

women? And to what extent were pre-existing gender divisions important in structuring the nature of economic change? If we consider the impact of proto-industry in the eighteenth and early nineteenth centuries one can see weaknesses in the notion of any wholesale change in the status or perception of women occurring alongside economic transition. Although there is some evidence of young women marching into pubs, demanding their pints and smoking their pipes like men, we must match this against what we know of the poverty and economic insecurity of many women workers and the continuous childbearing alongside arduous domestic manufacturing.[69] The view that proto-industrial employment had a liberating effect on women suggests that they were accorded a lower status in rural agricultural households and in urban crafts than in proto-industry but this is very doubtful. It also ignores the fact that there was a sexual hierarchy of labour within most proto-industrial trades, processes and households which may have endorsed female subordination rather than emancipation. The view that proto-industry had an emancipating effect on women also supposes that a woman's earnings were regarded as her own to dispose of and were high enough to bestow some independence.[70]

There is in fact little evidence that women's commercial employment in household manufacture enhanced their job status or prestige. They often worked as part of a family group and were neither paid separately nor saw their earnings as individual rather than familial. Their indispensible role in household-based activities was akin to the place in the peasant household or urban domestic workshop. This gave them power and status within the general framework of the patriarchal unit.[71] Nor did proto-industry result in high earnings levels for women. The highest-paid female workers in eighteenth-century England were probably those girls and unmarried women who worked outside of the home in workshops and early factories. Proto-industry soaked up cheap underemployed and unemployed female and child labour precisely because it was cheap. Furthermore, it remained cheap even when there was great pressure on labour supplies, as in cotton and wool spinning, because women's work was seen as low status and supplemental to household income. The labour market was segmented so that excess demand for female labour did not translate itself into higher female wages. According to Pinchbeck it was during the proto-

[69] Hudson and Lee, *Women's Work*, ch.1; Berg, 'Women's Work'; Pinchbeck, Women Workers, p. 126.
[70] Berg, 'Women's Work,' Pinchbeck, *Women Workers*, *p.126 and passim.*
[71] For fuller discussion of this point see Hudson and Lee, *Women's Work*, ch.1. J. W. Scott and L. A. Tilly, *Women, Work and Family* (New York, 1978); M. Segalen, *Love and Power in the Peasant Family* (Oxford, 1983); G. L. Gullickson, 'Love and Power in the Proto-industrial Family', in M. Berg, ed., *Markets and Manufactures in Early Industrial Europe* (London, 1991).

industrial period that the association of women's industrial work with low wages really became entrenched.[72]

We also have little evidence that women's involvement in domestic manufacturing released them from their traditional domestic priorities even in areas where the demand for female labour outstripped that for men. To the extent that decisions about who should do housework and rear children were partly dependent upon the wage income foregone by staying at home, low female wages endorsed traditional gender roles. Proto-industrial tasks were added onto rather than substituted for women's normal work in the home or in agriculture. Like other forms of domestic and sweatshop work in the nineteenth century, proto-industry added to the drudgery of female existence. Spinning with the distaff (a light hand instrument), for example, continued into the nineteenth century because it could be done by old women and children and by women who were simultaneously engaged in other tasks such as carting potatoes, tending sheep or taking produce to market.[73]

Some historians argue that the high participation rates of women in proto-industry occurred because the work was compatible with family responsibilities, child-rearing and breast-feeding. This argument is also used to explain the proliferation of female labour in the household sweated trades of the nineteenth and twentieth centuries. But as domestic manufacturing became dependent on fluctuating markets bringing periods of intense demand followed by layoffs, it became more difficult to integrate manufacturing with the demands of housework and infant care.[74] The extended role of women in domestic manufacturing had more to do with ideology than with biology: more to do with competition for cheap labour, the association of women with the domestic environment, and large families to support, than with women's choices about what best fitted their domestic schedules.

Neither did technological change radically affect the type of work most women did nor the status of their work. For example, although the identification of weaving as men's work broke down following the removal of spinning from the household, handloom weaving became a lower-status and lower-paid occupation because of the flooding of labour markets by agricultural and Irish workers as well as by former spinners. Furthermore, although male and female piece-rates in cotton-weaving were similar in Lancashire (for weaving the same cloths), women were generally confined to lighter-weight products

[72] Pinchbeck, *Women Workers*, chs. 6, 7, 8 and 10. Berg, *Age of Manufactures*, chs. 6 and 10.
[73] See for example, J. Dyer, *The Fleece* (London, 1757), pp.67–71, quoted by Pinchbeck, *Women Workers*, p.129; Berg, *Age of Manufactures*, pp.142–3.
[74] Shorter, *Making of the Modern Family*, pp.172–3, cf. C. Middleton, 'Women's Labour and the Transition to Preindustrial Capitalism', in L. Charles and L. Duffin, eds., *Women and Work in Preindustrial England* (London, 1985).

defined as requiring less skill and therefore commanding lower piece-rates. Similarly, new sorts of broad and Jacquard looms introduced into silk and other weaving were reserved for men and defined as more highly skilled than the narrow and ribbon looms operated by women. The introduction of the Dutch engine loom in Coventry, for example, separated ribbon weavers into a skilled male division using the new looms and an 'unskilled' female section using single hand looms.[75]

Technological change in most sectors during industrialisation created the practical conditions for the breakdown of a sexual division of labour based on physical strength but it was accompanied by a reworking of gender notions which served to retain the more prestigious and better-paid work for men. For example, in English cotton-spinning the jenny and frame were mainly associated with women but the more efficient mule rapidly became a male enclave. Women could and did work the early mules but they were squeezed out by male workers and their union during the shift from short to 'doubled' hand mules. By the time of the introduction of the self-actor the inter-generational transmission of female craft skills had been lost.[76]

Men retained their ability to define their superior social status through their work whilst women, denied parity of status through work, were as likely as in the past to seek their social definition through their domestic and mothering roles even where they held permanent or casual jobs in the labour market. Assumptions about women's weaker physical capacity and inferior intelligence were used to justify the male monopoly of high-status processes of production.[77] Arguments of that kind also surrounded the growing professionalisation of certain occupations and their restriction to men who had access through education and training. The professionalisation of medicine during the later eighteenth century, for example, saw the decline of surgeonesses, midwives, nurses and wisewomen in favour of trained doctors, surgeons and male apothecaries. In the 1790s in particular there was an evangelical attack on popular culture and vernacular medicine lost authority and status. Undertaking, tailoring, pawnbroking and others

[75] Berg, 'Women's Work', pp.81–2. For similar patterns elsewhere see Levine, *Family Formation*, pp.28–33; B. Collins, 'Proto-industrialisation and Pre-famine Emigration', *Social History* 7 (1982), pp.130, 140.
[76] M. Freifeld, 'Technological Change and the Self-acting Mule: A Study of Skill and the Sexual Division of Labour', *Social History* 1 (1986).
[77] J. Lewis, *Women in England 1870–1950: Sexual Divisions and Social Change* (Brighton, 1984); L. Duffin, 'The Conspicuous Consumptive: Women as Invalid', in S. Delamont and L. Duffin, eds., *The Nineteenth-Century Woman: Her Cultural and Physical World* (London, 1978).

also developed as largely male monopolies.[78] Although more women than ever before were working in commercial production and in the service sector, in their own homes, in the homes of others, in workshops and in factories during the industrial revolution, little of the work bestowed incomes or status comparable with male employment, and at the same time declining opportunities for live-in farm service, for petty market trading, gleaning, commons and wayside grazing, and small-scale dairying made many women more economically vulnerable and more dependent on the earnings of their fathers and husbands.[79] The declining age of marriage and the rising rate of marriage endorsed this dependency and reduced the prevalence of women as independent economic agents. Higher rates of illegitimacy and single parenthood and the constraints placed on female property rights during the eighteenth century added further to female dependency. It could in fact be argued that in the process of proletarianisation, women were often proletarianised first, increasing their vulnerability and their dependence upon men.

It is difficult to assess the impact of the rise in female commercial employment upon intra-family relations. In some regions one would expect this to be significant where male employment was uncertain and where wives and daughters became important income earners. It would, however, be a mistake to adopt a purely materialist perspective on the relationship between changing sex-specific work roles and the status of women both inside and outside the family. Many forces aside from the impact of labour-market participation and paid work combined to structure and restructure the force of patriarchy and female subordination over time. And from the indirect evidence of popular attitudes to female workers in all employments outside the household, particularly in factories (which were seen to conflict with fit and proper female modesty, chastity and domestic roles), it appears unlikely that patriarchal attitudes were significantly modified in this period. However, the expansion of commercial waged work for women on an unprecedented scale opened up the possibility of radical shifts in power relations between the sexes and created the conditions for a backlash against female participation in the formal world of work (on equal terms with men) which came with the growth of the Victorian ideal of domesticity, endorsed by state protective legislation

---

[78] A. L. Wyman, 'The Surgeoness: The Female Practitioner of Surgery 1400–1800', *Medical History* 28 (1984); J. Barry, 'Piety and the Patient', in R. Porter, ed., *Patient and Practitioners* (Cambridge, 1985); Clark, *Working Life*, pp.236–89; Pinchbeck, *Women Workers*, pp.300–6.

[79] For recent surveys of these trends see M. Berg, 'Women's Work and the Industrial Revolution', *Refresh* 12 (1991); J. Rendall, *Women in an Industrialising Society 1750–1880* (Oxford, 1990).

and the campaign for the male breadwinner wage in the mid nineteenth century.[80] The debate about the relationship between industrialisation and the place of women in society is far from resolved. We currently know too little about the position of women and gender ideology in pre-industrial society to be sure whether the industrial revolution represented any sort of watershed in attitudes. Furthermore, both optimistic and pessimistic perspectives tend to be unduly functionalist: seeing women's economic roles, familial relations and female subordination as passive and dependent variables in the process of economic change. They also often underplay the enormous regional, class and life-cycle diversity of experience and fail to explore the subjective as opposed to th.. objective condition of women both before and after the industrial revolution.[81] Finally, many interpretations are concerned to isolate long-term trends in female experience and in social development when the complex interplay of economic and social forces makes it more likely that the social status of women has shifted, waxed and waned in a much less linear fashion both in this period and in others. Much can be gained by turning away from the linear perspective of the optimist/pessimist debate about the impact of the industrial revolution on women. We need instead to look at long cycles of demand for female labour, the economic conditions that create these (for example, the demand for manufactured goods, price competition, technological and organisational innovation and the age structure of the population) and the ways in which individuals, families, institutions and ideas shift to accommodate and in turn to modify the social and cultural impact of such cycles. In this perspective, the industrial revolution can be seen as a distinct period in which the commercial employment of female waged labour increased in an unprecedented fashion. This created the conditions for what Seccombe has termed the destabilisation of patriarchy and involved some reworking and renegotiation of intra-family relationships and of notions of gender in the mid-Victorian period.[82]

[80] E. Jordan, 'The Exclusion of Women from Industry in Nineteenth Century Britain', *Comparative Studies in Society and History* 31 (1989); W. Seccombe, 'Patriarchy Stabilised: The Construction of the Male Breadwinner Wage Norm in Nineteenth Century Britain', *Social History* 11 (1986); S. O. Rose, 'Gender Antagonism and Class Conflict: Exclusionary Strategies of Male Trade Unionists in Nineteenth Century Britain', *Social History* 13 (1988), pp.191–208; Davidoff and Hall, *Family Fortunes;* J. Humphries, 'Protective Legislation, the Capitalist State and Working Class Men. The Case of the 1842 Mines Regulation Act', *Feminist Review* 7 (1981); Humphries, '"The Most Free from Objection"', The Sexual Division of Labour and Women's Work in Nineteenth Century England' *Journal of Economic History* XLVII (1987); A. V. John, ed., *Unequal Opportunities: Women's Employment in England, 1800–1918* (Oxford, 1985).
[81] Hudson and Lee, *Women's Work*, esp. ch.1.
[82] Seccombe, 'Patriarchy Stabilised'.

Gender ideology

Discussions of the nature of womanhood were common in the nineteenth century. Debate about sexuality and morality, prostitution, illegitimacy, the free lifestyles of factory girls and the impropriety of wearing hair ribbons and colourful dresses flourished. Women's moral and spiritual inspiration, the tension between this and their social subordination, and the proper nature of women's work and social activities were all present in political, religious and scientific debates and in art and literature, suggesting that the construction of gender was closely related to the quickening pace of economic and social change.[83]

Within the middle class existing assumptions about sexual difference were endorsed and extended. It was argued that women possessed a character best fulfilled in the domestic setting where their tendency to moral and sexual weakness could be controlled. That idea was strengthened in the middle decades of the nineteenth century by evangelical religion and by biomedical theories of gender difference. Internal political instability of the early nineteenth century was followed by a crusade for national regeneration, which was closely linked to the place of women in the family. Evangelicalism stressed the importance of women in transforming national morality partly through the creation of well-ordered domestic routines. Women would be the keepers of moral order in the home and hence in the nation. They were continuously to revive the piety of their menfolk, damaged by the cares of the outside world, and their charitable and voluntary social work were seen as vital in giving proper instruction to the poor. Some women were able to use the language of moral influence to make new claims for themselves to act independently as women but this was rare, particularly because evangelical beliefs were endorsed by scientific theories of gender difference that stressed different proclivities and mental powers. It was believed that women were mentally unstable and prone to insanity, especially at the times of menarche and menopause. It was also understood that the mental evolution of women had been arrested earlier than men to conserve their energies for childbirth and child-rearing. Doctors thus agreed with scientists that, for the health of the race and thus the future of the empire, the range of women's activities outside of reproduction should be severely curtailed. The impact of these ideas and of the Victorian domestic

[83] J. Rendall, *The Origins of Modern Feminism: Women in Britain, France and the United States 1780–1869* (London, 1985), ch.2; J. K. Walkowitz, 'The Making of an Outcast Group: Prostitutes and Working Women in Nineteenth-Century Plymouth and Southampton', in M. Vicinus, ed., *A Widening Sphere: Changing Roles of Victorian Women* (London, 1977); A. V. John, *By the Sweat of their Brow. Women Workers and Victorian Coalmines* (London, 1980).

ideal was widespread in middle-class society.[84] 'Their political committees excluded women, their churches demarcated male and female spheres, their botanical gardens assumed that men would join on behalf of their families, their philanthropic societies treated men and women differently, their business associations were for men only'.[85]

Middle-class views were also important in the formation of gender ideology in the mass of the population. The role of Sunday schools, charity schools, temperance movements, domestic service and private charity were influential in spreading ideals. But, although middle-class discourse about masculinity, femininity and domestic life did have appeal for some sections of the working classes and related to their experience, the mass of the population did not accept middle-class values wholesale. Notions of 'proper' gender roles are likely to have been rooted firmly in working-class culture itself: in community and family life. And working-class radicalism had its own gender influences. Paine, for example, drew on Locke, whose idea of the individual agent never extended beyond propertied males who naturally took responsibility for their dependents: wives, children and servants. Locke distinguished between the natural world of the family which men rightly dominated and the political world where men consented to laws of the State. The distinction between the family and civil society was important in enlightenment thinking and in associated theories of sexual difference. Cobbett's radicalism placed women firmly in the domestic sphere: reason and God both decreed that wives should obey their husbands. Only domestic skills made women into persons worthy of respect and 'the very nature of their sex [made their exercise of civil rights] incompatible with the harmony and happiness of society'.[86]

Class and gender

Given the strength and nature of gender ideology, particularly in the mid nineteenth century, it is interesting to consider the nature and degree of female involvement in the creation of 'bourgeois culture' and in working-class politics: to consider the intersection of class and

[84] C. Hall, 'The Early Formation of Women's Domestic Ideology', in S. Burman, ed., *Fit Work For Women* (London, 1979); Lewis, *Women in England;* Davidoff and Hall, *Family Fortunes;* P. Branca, *Middle Class Women in the Victorian Home* (London, 1975).
[85] C. Hall, 'The Tale of Samuel and Jemima: Gender and Working Class Culture in Nineteenth Century England', in Kaye and McClelland, eds., *E. P. Thompson: Critical perspectives*, p.95
[86] W. Cobbett, *Cottage Economy* (1822) discussed in Hall, 'The Tale of Samuel and Jemima', pp.92–3. Thompson, *Making of the English Working Class*, pp.84–203; See also E. Fox Genovese, 'Property and Patriarchy in Classical Bourgeois Political Theory', *Radical History Review* 4 (1977); S. Moller Okin, *Women in Western Political Thought* (London, 1980).

gender in the social history of the period. The ideal (if not the reality) of the 'angel in the house' and the public and private activities of middle- and upper-class women did much to endorse the voluntarism and philanthropy advocated by nineteenth-century political economy. At the same time, the creation by middle-class women of a fit and proper domestic environment and feminine image had a wide impact upon consumption patterns, fashion, decor, leisure and hence upon industrial demand and tertiary employments.[87]

Similarly, in the rioting and crowd actions of the eighteenth and early nineteenth centuries women appear to have had a high profile. Crowd actions often took place in the market place where women were actively present as consumers and were regarded as important defenders of communal and customary rights.[88] In Chartism women were very prominent partly because whole families became involved together. Chartist autobiographies are full of descriptions of the radicalising influence of mothers and of maiden aunts and of the importance of family networks and radical tea parties in generating solidarity. But within most radical movements of the industrial revolution period, women had a clearly defined role associated with the perceived nature of their sex. Bamford's account of his radicalism stresses the importance at the end of his day of the warm fire at home and of his wife and children reading the Bible. Female Chartists were prominent in catering, in the temperance movement, in book-keeping, in raising subscriptions, in heckling and in exclusive dealing but they rarely held high office or chaired or spoke at mixed meetings. Chartists were also almost unanimously against the female vote: it was seen as creating trouble within families and it was argued that women were often involved in radicalism only on behalf of their menfolk. It was also of course feared that if women got the vote before the working class, it would lead to an extension of the power of the propertied classes.[89]

Mary Wollstonecraft had raised the issue of sexual difference in the 1790s but the only working-class movement to incorporate the idea that the politics should be as much about gender as about class was Owenite Socialism.[90] Owenite analysis questioned all social relations,

[87] Davidoff and Hall, *Family Fortunes;* Lewis, *Women in England;* Samuel, 'Workshop of the World'.
[88] J. Bohstedt, 'Gender, Household and Community Politics: Women in English Riots 1790–1810', *Past and Present* 120 (1988); D. Thompson, 'Women and Nineteenth-century Radical Politics: a Lost Dimension', in J. Mitchell and Ann Oakley, eds., *The Rights and Wrongs of Women* (Harmondsworth, 1976).
[89] Hall 'Samuel and Jemina'; D. V. Jones, 'Women in Chartism', *History* 68 (1983); M. I. Thomis and J. Grimmet. *Women in Protest 1800–1850* (London, 1982); E. Yeo, 'Some Practices and Problems of Chartist Democracy', in Epstein and Thompson, *Chartist Experience.*
[90] M. Wollstonecraft, *Vindication of the Rights of Women* (Harmondsworth, 1982). B. Taylor, *Eve and the New Jerusalem: Socialism and Feminism in the Nineteenth Century* (London, 1983).

including the institutions of marriage and the family, monogamy and heterosexuality, but these aspects of the movement were not widely influential. Radical working-class culture rested on 'commonsense' assumptions about the relative place of men and women which were not subjected to the same scrutiny as the monarchy, aristocracy and other institutions of 'Old Corruption'. In addition, technological change and new methods and relations of production increased the tensions and antagonism between male and female workers. In defending their place in the world of work and in labour hierarchies men could be as bad as their masters.[91] Trade unions of the first half of the nineteenth century seldom included women workers. In some sectors and regions women formed their own unions and worked for their separate interests but in other areas and industries and for particular periods it is possible to argue that solidarities of class overrode gender divisions. In the Lancashire weaving sector, for example, and in some coal-mining areas, women worked alongside men for state regulation of labour, especially that of women and children. This was compatible with their avowed domestic and family priorities and with the general principles of minimising and regulating exploitation. In most occupations it is, however, more likely that gender divisions undermined industrial solidarity and that employers used this to their advantage. In all sectors it is impossible to understand the impact of changes in the labour process on the formation of new solidarities and divisions without reference both to male and female workers.[92]

Parliamentary reform clubs, self-improvement and debating societies were also central to the formation of working-class consciousness but women were deterred from entering them. They offered a much easier forum for men to operate in than women. Literacy, for example, was important in forming a common culture but, with fewer opportunities of schooling and less free time in the household, women lagged significantly behind men in levels of active literacy. As formal societies with constitutions and officers replaced customary patterns of crowd action women withdrew. Jargon and constitutional procedures, as well as the pub as a central meeting place for both political and social activities, alienated and excluded women. Once protest was removed from the street, the automatic participation of women and children was lost.[93] In addition, as the location of protest shifted from the market place (the point of consumption) to the workplace (the point of

---

[91] Taylor, *Eve and the New Jerusalem*, ch.4; Hall, 'Samuel and Jemima'.
[92] Rose, 'Gender Antagonism'; S. Walby, *Patriarchy at Work* (Oxford, 1986), chs.2–4; J. Humphries, 'Class Struggle and the Persistence of the Working Class Family', *Cambridge Journal of Economics* 1 (1977).
[93] Thompson, 'Women in Radical Politics'; T. Lacquer, 'Literacy and Social Mobility in the Industrial Revolution in England', *Past and Present* 64 (1974); Hall, 'Samuel and Jemima'.

production) and as the radicalism of the mid nineteenth century focused more on conditions of work and wages than on broader political issues, women were less involved as their interests at work were usually radically different from those of men. In the 1830s and 1840s 'working women' became a publicly defined social problem and certain areas of work were gradually closed to them through a combination of the activities of male trade unionists, middle-class philanthropists and the State. This silenced their political voice: while the public role of men was reinforced, women became associated more exclusively with the private sphere of the household.[94]

Conclusion

The solidarities created by communities and the role of language in the construction of social meaning should not be ignored, but analysis of the shifting power relations of the period of the industrial revolution requires an understanding of the role of both class and gender and of significant redefinitions of each. The period itself saw a marked increase in the proportion of women in paid work both inside and outside the home, in workshops, factories, domestic service, as well as in the casual trades of the expanding urban economies. That created the possibilities of greater female status and power. But technological and economic change also fostered antagonism between male and female workers in the labour market and created conditions for a major moral and legal backlash against the expansion of 'improper' forms of work outside the home, especially for married women. The backlash had the effect of making it much more difficult for women to find employment outside domestic service, the casual trades and sweatshops. Although regional, class and life-cycle variations of experience were marked, women's work became more exclusively associated with low status and low pay. Gender ideology, evangelical religion and scientific theories of sexual difference sustained and endorsed this backlash and the influence of strengthening views of gender difference had a major impact on the identity, the culture and the consciousness of both sexes and of all social classes.

[94] Hall, 'Samuel and Jemima'; S. Alexander, 'Women, Class and Sexual Differences in the 1830s and 1840s. Some Reflections on the Writing of Feminist History', *History Workshop Journal* 17 (1984).

EPILOGUE

The physical order of communities, in which the production of the necessaries of subsistence is the first want and chief occupation, has in our case been rapidly inverted, and in lieu of agricultural supremacy, a vast and overtopping superstructure of manufacturing wealth and population has been substituted. It is to this extraordinary revolution, I doubt not, may be traced ... sudden alternations of prosperity and depression – of internal quiet and violent political excitement; extremes of opulance and destitution; the increase of crime; conflicting claims of capital and industry; the spread of an imperfect knowledge, that agitates and unsettles the old without having definitely settled the new foundations; clashing and independent opinions on most public questions with other anomalies peculiar to our existing but changeful social existence.[1]

A great mass of contemporary commentary suggests that the industrial revolution should be seen as, and was, more than 'a piece of economic history in the form of a curve'.[2] So long as analyses of the period rest on the movement of long-run growth indicators, other sorts of economic change will be ignored and the scope for understanding the discontinuities as well as the continuities of industrialisation will be limited. As Coleman argued almost four decades ago, we cannot deduce an industrial revolution simply from observing the existence in the appropriate figures of an increase in the growth rate.[3] In the same way, we cannot conclude that fundamental economic discontinuities are absent where growth rates remain stable. And with the growth figures themselves we must ask: how slow is slow? Growth rates during the industrial revolution were not low compared with earlier centuries and they accelerated sufficiently to increase the pace of per capita income growth thereafter in an unprecedented manner. They are clearly lower than some historians expected to find but looking back from the perspective of the twentieth century, the comparison of growth during the industrial revolution with growth spurts since is misleading. The potentialities and the social and cultural repercussions of waves of innovations in the late nineteenth and twentieth centuries may appear

[1] J. Wade, *History of the Middle and Working Classes* (London, 1842), preface, p.1.
[2] J. A. Schumpeter, *Business Cycles* (2 vols., New York, 1939) I, pp.201–4, quoted in D. C. Coleman, 'Industrial Growth and Industrial Revolutions', *Economica* (1956), p.10.
[3] Schumpeter, *Business Cycles,* p.19.

to make the achievements of the 1760s to 1830s pale into insignificance. But the point to emphasise is that these potentialities (and their social and ecological dangers) are integral to economic growth in the industrialised era. This stems essentially from the nature of the classical industrial revolution.

The chapters in this volume have indicated that the industrial revolution witnessed considerable innovation in the organisation as well as the finance of industry and commerce; in the knacks and work practices of production as well as in technology; in urbanisation and demographic behaviour as well as in the development and disciplining of labour. The role of government at both national and local levels was considerably transformed and the dynamism of the economy shifted firmly from agriculture to industry and trade. Some regions rapidly industrialised, others concentrated on commercial agriculture or stagnated. The industrial revolution radically affected the lives of women and children as much as those of men; it involved changing ideas of gender and ethnicity as well as class; it affected consumption and commerce as much as industry, leisure as much as work, and it involved shifts in motivations, aspirations, ideologies and aesthetics as well as changes in the labour process and in the relations of production.

This volume represents a plea to reintegrate a wider conception of industrial revolution into our analyses of the period. In the process many continuities will inevitably be uncovered but so will those radical changes in economy and society that make the period such an exciting one to study.[4]

---

[4] For a recent study of the compatibility of evolutionary and revolutionary perspectives, see J. Mokyr, *The Lever of Riches: Technological Creativity and Economic Progress* (Oxford, 1990).

INDEX

acceptance houses, 60-1, 104, 198
'affective individualism', 141
agriculture, crops, 68-70; during
Napoleonic Wars, 60; effects on
home market for manufactures,
86-90, 167; in the north-east, 127-8;
in the Weald, 130; innovators in, 69;
organisational structure of, 65,
70-75, 85-6; agricultural prices, 74
84-90 *passim*; output of, 86;
productivity of, 66-8; release of
capital from, 65, 91-6, 127; release
of labour from, 65 78-83, 118-9; role
of in economic growth, 64-6, 78-97
passim, 127; supply of food, 85-6;
supply of industrial raw materials,
84-5
Allen, R. C., 71-3, 80-1, 85-6, 90
Amalgamated Society of Engineers,
105
America, 122, 184-5, 187, 197; credit
in trade with, 61; *see also* United
States; Latin America
American War of Independence, 58
Amsterdam, 189, 198
Anderson, B. L., 196n, 198
Anderson, M., 137n, 138-9
Anderson, P., 35, 219-20, 222
anti-Poor Law movement, 34, 107
apprenticeship, 143, 145
Arkwright, Richard, 93
artisans, 46, 110
Asia, trade with, 184, 185, 187; *see
also* Far East
Ashley, W. J., 13
Ashton, T. S., 16, 21, 26, 29
attorneys, 25, 95

Bagehot, Walter, 221
Bairoch, P., 67
Bamford, Samuel, 234
bankruptcies, 58, 60, 104, 132
banks, 25, 60-1, 94, 104
Beard, Charles, 11
Behagg, C., 124
Bellini, J., 35-6

Berg, M., 114, 123
Beveridge, W., 16
bills of exchange, 121, 198-9; *see also*
credit
Birmingham, 45, 57, 92, 107, 121-6
passim, 143, 151, 182
Birmingham Political Union, 123, 124
Black, R. A., 58
bondage system, 128
bourgeoisie, 35, 218; *see also*
gentlemanly capitalism
breast feeding, 141-2
Bradford, 119
Brenner, R., 21, 70-1
Briggs, A., 10n, 123
Bristol, 57, 151, 193, 195
Buckinghamshire, 112
building industry, during eighteenth
century wars, 57
business history, 21-2

Cain, P. J., 190-2
Campbell, C., 177
canals, 90, 102, 122, 189; landed
finance in construction of, 92
Cannadine, D., 9n, 36
capital markets, 25-6, 40, 57, 94-6,
104; *see also* attorneys, banks,
crowding out; crowding in; loans;
London; mortgages of land
Carlyle, Thomas, 10
Carus-Wilson, E. M., 15
census, 133, 134
Chambers, J. D., 71, 73, 78-9
Chapman, J., 74
Chartism, 31, 33, 106, 110, 119, 218;
and women, 234
Chartres, J., 77
child labour, 28, 43, 124-5, 143-4,
161-4
Civil Registration, 133
Clapham, J. H., 14, 27, 29
Clark, Alice, 226
Clark, J. C. D., 217n
Clark, P., 157

239